THE AUSTEN GIRLS

About the Author

After leaving university with a Bachelor's degree in English literature and history, Helen Amy worked for a number of years in the Court Service before becoming a full-time mother of three. Her interest in the life and works of Jane Austen developed from the research she did for her MA dissertation which was about the lives of women in late Georgian England.

Other Works by Helen Amy

Jane Austen
Jane Austen's England
The Jane Austen Marriage Manual
The Jane Austen Files
Jane Austen's Men

THE AUSTEN GIRLS

THE STORY OF JANE AND CASSANDRA AUSTEN THE CLOSEST OF SISTERS

HELEN AMY

AMBERLEY

The author would like to thank the following:

Jane Austen House Museum, Chawton, for permission to reproduce the portrait of Henry Austen.

The staff of the Kent History and Library Centre for their assistance and for permission to publish extracts from *Fanny Knight's Diary*.

This edition published 2026

Amberley Publishing
The Hill, Stroud
Gloucestershire, GL5 4EP

www.amberley-books.com

ISBN 978 1 3981 3347 1 (paperback)
ISBN 978 1 4456 7587 9 (ebook)

British Library Cataloguing in Publication Data.
A catalogue record for this book is available from the British Library.

Typesetting and Origination by Amberley Publishing.
Printed in the UK.

Appointed GPSR EU Representative: Easy Access System Europe Oü, 16879218
Address: Mustamäe tee 50, 10621, Tallinn, Estonia
Contact Details: gpsr.requests@easproject.com, +358 40 500 3575

CONTENTS

LIST OF ILLUSTRATIONS

20. Covent Garden, London. Henry Austen lived in Henrietta Street near Covent Garden from 1813 to 1816. (Yale Center for British Art, Paul Mellon Collection)
21. Carlton House, London, home of the Prince Regent, which Jane visited in 1815. (Yale Center for British Art, Paul Mellon Collection)
22. Abbey Church, Bath, where the Austen family are believed to have worshipped.
23. Pulteney Bridge, Bath. Cassandra and Jane crossed this elegant bridge regularly in their walks around Bath.
24. The Holbourne Museum (originally the Sydney Hotel) in Sydney Gardens, Bath. Cassandra and Jane lived near here from 1801 to 1804.
25. Royal Crescent, Bath, the grandest of all the residential streets in Bath.
26. Queen Square, Bath, where Jane stayed in 1799.
27. Pump Room, Bath, which Jane often visited with her uncle when he drank the waters there.
28. Pump Room, Bath, interior view.
29. 25, Gay Street, Bath, home of Cassandra and Jane from 1805 to 1806.
30. The Roman Baths, Bath.
31. Dawlish, Devon which Cassandra and Jane visited in 1802.
32. Stoneleigh Abbey, the ancestral home of Mrs Austen's family, the Leighs.
33. Southampton, home of Cassandra and Jane from 1806 to 1809.
34. *Village Scene* by Thomas Rowlandson. All of Jane's novels are set in country villages such as this one.
35. Chawton Cottage, home of Cassandra and Jane from 1809.
36. The parlour in Chawton Cottage, where Jane wrote her last three novels.
37. Plaque on Chawton Cottage.
38. Chawton House, Hampshire, unchanged since it was inherited by Edward Austen in 1797.
39. Cottages in the village of Chawton.
40. 8, College Street, Winchester, where Jane died in July 1817.
41. Winchester Cathedral, where Jane is buried.
42. Jane's grave.

All illustrations are the author's own, except where otherwise stated.

INTRODUCTION

Cassandra and Jane Austen were the daughters of the Reverend George Austen, rector of Steventon in Hampshire, and his wife Cassandra. They were born and brought up in rural north Hampshire at the end of the eighteenth century. The Austen sisters belonged to a happy, loving family, whose members were clever, intellectual, talented and cultured. Cassandra and Jane had an extremely close bond and were described as leading their own separate life within the life of the family.

The Austen family were well-connected, highly respected, patriotic and conservative-minded members of the gentry. The society into which Cassandra and Jane Austen were born was a hierarchical one, in which everyone knew their place. It was also a patriarchal society in which women were very much dependent second-class citizens. Women of that class were expected to devote their lives to being good wives, mothers and housekeepers. There were very few opportunities for women to earn money or achieve anything outside the private domestic sphere. One of these opportunities was writing novels for the ever-growing reading public – an opportunity of which Jane Austen took advantage.

The Austen sisters lived during a period when England was undergoing a great upheaval. Society was rapidly changing. The stable old order was being challenged in a number of ways. England was turning from an agricultural to an industrial nation, new money was replacing old wealth, a new meritocratic system was replacing the old patriarchy and Anglicanism was being challenged by Methodism. There were stirrings of political discontent, inspired by the French Revolution, as well as serious social and industrial unrest. In art and literature, the formal Augustan era was making way for the gentler Romantic era. Cassandra and Jane were not directly affected by many of these changes, as life in peaceful, rural north Hampshire continued in much the same way as it had done for centuries. This changing order is important, however, as it formed the backdrop to their lives and to Jane's novels.

This joint biography of Cassandra and Jane Austen explores their extremely close relationship. It also seeks to show how Cassandra, who has always seemed a rather shadowy figure in the background of her famous sister's life, was central to her success and achievement as a novelist. Without Cassandra's support and encouragement, Jane, who did not rate her own abilities highly, may never have written her novels.

Not surprisingly, there is far more material to draw on about Jane's life than her sister's. Cassandra is rather elusive, and information about her has to be searched for – but it does exist. The main sources for this book are the surviving letters written by Jane to Cassandra, other family letters and papers, family memoirs of Jane and a diary kept by their niece, Fanny Knight.

Note: James Edward, Cassandra's and Jane's nephew, who played an important part in their story, was known to his family as Edward. He is referred to in this book by his full name of James Edward, to avoid confusion with other family members of the same name.

Incorrect spellings and unconventional use of capital letters in quotations have not been changed or indicated.

I

STEVENTON

1773–1775

Cassandra Elizabeth Austen, the fifth child and first daughter of the Reverend George Austen, rector of the parish of Steventon in Hampshire, and his wife Cassandra, was born on 9 January 1773. The baby was privately baptised on the day of her birth and her public baptism took place on 25 January. Mrs Austen took part in a churching ceremony on the same day. This was a Christian custom in which the new mother was given a blessing following her recovery from childbirth, which included thanksgiving for her survival.

Nearly three years later Mrs Austen gave birth to her second daughter, and seventh child, who was named Jane. She was privately baptised on 17 December 1775, the day after she was born. Her public baptism was not held until 5 April 1776. Cassandra and Jane became the most devoted of sisters and Jane, with the support and encouragement of her sister, became one of the most famous and best-loved of English novelists.

George Austen's ancestors came from Kent. One branch of his family made a large fortune in the clothing trade and, by the end of the sixteenth century, owned two manor houses at Grovehurst and Broadford, near Horsmonden. George, however, was descended from a less affluent branch of the family. He was born in 1731 to William Austen and his wife Rebecca, who already had a son from her previous marriage to William Walter. George had two older sisters – Hampson, who died at the age of two, and Philadelphia, as well as a younger sister, Leonora. William Austen was a surgeon, which was a relatively lowly profession in the eighteenth century.

Rebecca died soon after the birth of Leonora and it was not long before William married again. His second wife was Susannah Kelp of Tonbridge, but this marriage was not destined to last long, as William died just eighteen months later, in December 1737. His widow, who was reputedly not well-disposed towards her step-children, did not undertake to care for them. Relatives of their parents stepped in to look after the three siblings and their half-brother William. George, who was six years old when his father died, went to live with his aunt, Ann Hooper, and attended Tonbridge School. His school fees were paid by his uncle, Francis Austen, a successful lawyer, who recognised the intelligent boy's exceptional potential. Francis helped him partly out of a sense of duty, but also because he was very fond of his amiable nephew.

George was nine when he went to Tonbridge School. His cousin Henry Austen was already a pupil there and the boys became close companions. George received the standard classical education provided in the eighteenth century for the sons of the aristocracy and gentry. He did very well at school and won a scholarship to St John's College, Oxford, and subsequently the Fellowship assigned to a pupil of Tonbridge School. George attended Oxford University at a time when the two universities in the country had a reputation for idleness and dissipation. Unlike many of his fellow students, however, George had to make his own way in the world. He was a diligent student who was determined to do well, and he took full advantage of the opportunities offered to him.

George was awarded a Bachelor of Arts degree in 1751 and a Master of Arts degree three years later. In 1753 he was awarded a Smyth Exhibition, which had been instituted to enable poor former pupils of Tonbridge School to study at Oxford with a view to taking Holy Orders. He went on to be ordained a deacon and a priest. His first appointment was as perpetual curate of Shipbourne in Kent, which he combined with the post of Second Master, or Usher, at his old school. George then returned to St John's College where he was appointed chaplain and Junior Proctor for the year 1759–60. The latter position included responsibility for enforcing university regulations and, because of his good looks, particularly his bright hazel eyes and wavy hair, George became known as the 'handsome Proctor'.

In 1760 George added to his qualifications by obtaining a Bachelor of Divinity degree. The following year he was presented with the living of Steventon in Hampshire by his wealthy distant cousin Thomas Knight, who owned extensive property and land in that county and in Kent. George did not immediately take up his post but left his new parish in the hands of the curate, another cousin named Thomas Bathurst. It was around this time that he met Cassandra Leigh.

Cassandra, who was born in 1739, was from a higher social class than George Austen. One of her illustrious ancestors was Thomas Leigh, who, as Lord Mayor of London, played an important part in the coronation of Queen Elizabeth I. He was later knighted by the queen. Cassandra was a member of the Leigh family of Adlestrop in Gloucestershire, of which the aristocratic Leighs of Stoneleigh Abbey in Warwickshire were a younger branch. She was very proud to be related to the owners of Stoneleigh Abbey and also proud of her aquiline aristocratic nose, a feature which several of her children inherited.

Cassandra's grandparents were Theophilus and Mary Leigh, née Brydges, who was the sister of the 1st Duke of Chandos. Cassandra was one of the four surviving children of the Reverend Thomas Leigh and his wife Jane. Her siblings were James, Jane and Thomas. The Leigh family had connections with Oxford University. Cassandra's father was a graduate and Fellow of All Souls College, who was known as 'Chick' Leigh, because of the very young age at which he was awarded his Fellowship. He was the rector of Harpsden, near Henley-on-Thames, in Oxfordshire, which was a college living, and he had the reputation of being an excellent parish priest. Thomas' brother Theophilus, who was renowned for his wit, was Master of Balliol College for fifty years.

In the early 1760s Thomas Leigh retired to Bath with his wife and two daughters. Bath was then at the height of its popularity as a health resort and a place of pleasure. Since the beginning of the eighteenth century Bath had grown from an insignificant watering place into a vibrant capital of fashion. The old medieval city, with its poorly constructed, badly ventilated houses had been transformed with the erection of substantial Palladian-style houses arranged in streets, crescents and circuses. New public buildings, entertainment venues and elegant shopping streets were part of the transformation. Bath had acquired a reputation for being a good place to find a husband and this may have added to its attraction for Thomas and Mary Leigh, whose daughters were well past the optimum age for marriage.

It may have been in Bath that George Austen first met Cassandra Leigh or, alternatively, at the home of her uncle Theophilus in Oxford, where she often stayed. George and Cassandra's relationship developed and they decided to marry. A marriage settlement was drawn up in March 1764. George's contribution to the marriage was some land in Tonbridge, Kent, and a third share of some property in the same town, which he was due to inherit on the death of his stepmother. Cassandra contributed some leasehold property in Oxfordshire and £1,000, which she would inherit on the death of her mother. When George and Cassandra later came into their inheritance the money was used to buy some South Sea Company annuities.

George Austen and Cassandra Leigh were married on 26 April 1764 at St Swithin's Church, an old medieval building in Walcot Street, Bath. The parish register contains the following entry:

> Geo. Austen Bachelor of the parish of Steventon, cty. of Hampshire to Cassandra Leigh, Spinster. Married by licence this 26 April by me – Thos. Powys Minister in the presence of James Leigh Perrot and Jane Leigh.

Thomas Powys, the officiating minister, was a friend of the Leigh family and Cassandra's brother and sister were witnesses. After the ceremony the couple left for their new home in Hampshire, stopping overnight at Andover on the way. Mrs Austen wore a fashionable red riding costume on the journey, a costume which did her good service for many years.[1]

Unlike her good-looking husband, Cassandra, as she said herself, 'was never a beauty'; she had a pleasant face with well-cut features and large grey eyes, but a dull complexion. The Austens were a well-suited couple; the sensible, clever, witty and lively Cassandra was an ideal wife for the placid, scholarly, gentle and amiable George, who also possessed a good sense of humour. Cassandra was the intellectual equal of her husband but, as a woman, she was not as well-educated. As the daughter of a country clergyman, she was well prepared for the role of a rector's wife in rural Hampshire.

A few months after the Austens' marriage Cassandra's elder brother James, of whom she was very fond, married Jane Cholmeley, who belonged to an old Lincolnshire family. James was a wealthy man, having been fortunate enough to inherit a large estate from his uncle Thomas Perrot, on the condition that he added the name of Perrot to his own. The Leigh-Perrots lived in a large house, which had been built for them, in Wargrave near Maidenhead in Berkshire. They also had a home in Bath, where they lived for part of the year so that James, who suffered from gout, could benefit from the medical facilities and treatments available there. The Leigh-Perrots were to play an important part in the lives of Cassandra and Jane Austen.

When George and Cassandra Austen moved into their first marital home they were joined by Mrs Austen's mother, who had recently been widowed, and a seven-year-old boy named George Hastings. The son of Warren Hastings, later the Governor-General of Bengal, George had been sent home from India to be educated. It is not entirely clear how the Austens came to be caring for the child, but the arrangement was probably made through George Austen's sister Philadelphia, who lived in India and was a friend of Warren Hastings.[2] The Austens were happy to take little George into their home and look after him. They also had to make arrangements for Cassandra's younger brother Thomas, who was mentally disabled. He was placed in the care of a local family.[3]

Sadly, George Hastings died of diphtheria in the autumn of 1764, to the great distress of the Austens[4] who had become attached to him and felt his loss as if he had been their own child. Warren Hastings did not learn of his son's death until he returned from India the following year,[5] but he did not hold it against the Austens, who had done their best for George. Hastings became a good friend of the Austen family.

Warren Hastings was accompanied to England on board the *Medway* by George Austen's sister Philadelphia, her husband, her child and two Indian servants.[6] Philadelphia, who had been brought up by her maternal aunt Catherine and her husband John Cope Freeman,[7] had gone to India in 1752 in search of a husband among the European community there.[8] With a family of their own, the Freemans were not able to provide for Philadelphia when she reached adulthood. She was briefly apprenticed to a milliner[9] before she decided her best option was to find a husband. Philadelphia's lack of a dowry was a serious disadvantage in England, but in India, where unmarried white women were in short supply, her chances were far better. Philadelphia must have been a courageous and determined woman to embark on the long and perilous journey to India. Within six months of her arrival there, Philadelphia had met and married Tysoe Saul Hancock, a friend of Warren Hastings. Hancock was nearly twenty years her senior and worked as a surgeon for the East India Company. The couple had a daughter Elizabeth, known as Betsy during her childhood, who was born in 1761. On arrival in England in 1765 the Hancocks moved into a house in Norfolk Street, London.[10]

George Austen had to relinquish his Fellowship at St John's College on marriage. He now took up his duties as rector of Steventon but the Austens did not move into the rectory straight away, as it was in a bad state of repair and not fit to live in. Instead they moved into the empty rectory in the nearby village of Deane, while improvements were carried out at Steventon. The living of Deane belonged to Francis Austen, who had bought it together with the neighbouring living of Ashe, with the intention of presenting the first to become vacant to his nephew George. Deane rectory was empty because the rector had chosen to live elsewhere.

Cassandra Austen was disappointed when she first saw the surroundings of her new home. The countryside of north Hampshire was pretty and covered with woodland, hedgerows and wild flowers. To Cassandra, however, it appeared unattractive compared with the more dramatic scenery around her childhood home in Henley-on-Thames, with its wide river, hills and fertile valleys.[11]

George Austen became a clergyman during a period of laxity and indifference in the Church of England. This was a reaction to the Puritanism and religious strife of the previous century, as well as a response to scientific discoveries and a more questioning culture. Many clergymen did not have a real vocation and regarded the Church as merely a way to make a living. Pluralism and absenteeism among clergymen were rife at this period. The majority of Church livings were in the gift of wealthy landowners and were given to men, like George Austen, who had the right connections. In the words of the poet William Cowper, 'The parson knows enough who knows a Duke.' George, despite his lucky connections, was a dedicated and diligent clergyman with a true vocation. He lived among his parishioners, took an interest in their lives and served them faithfully. After taking up his position as rector of Steventon it was not long before he earned the respect and affection of his flock, on account of his conscientiousness and learning.

The Austens were respected and liked by all the people of Steventon, including the gentry. Although not as well off as other members of that class, they were accepted on equal terms with them. This was partly because George was an educated professional, with an important position in the community, but also because he was a relative of the landowner. They enjoyed the consideration and respect normally given to the squire.[12] Cassandra's aristocratic and academic connections also helped to make the couple acceptable in gentry circles.

George soon acquired more responsibilities. In February 1765 the Austens' first child, James, was born at Deane Rectory. He was joined in August of the following year by George, and, in October 1767, by Edward. Mrs Austen breast-fed her babies for a few months and then, following a practice not uncommon at that time among women of her class, she placed them in the care of a dry nurse for a year or more. It is thought that the Austen babies were cared for by Elizabeth, the wife of John Littleworth, a local farmworker.[13] This practice was described by Mrs Austen's grandson, James Edward Austen-Leigh, the son of James and author of the first biography of Jane Austen.

> Her [Jane's] mother followed a custom, not unusual in those days, though it seems strange to us, of putting out her babies to be nursed in a cottage in the village. The infant was daily visited by one or both of its parents, and frequently brought to them at the parsonage, but the cottage was its home, and must have remained so till it was old enough to run about and talk: for I know that one of them, [presumably James] in after-life, used to speak of his foster mother as 'Movie', the name by which he had called her in his infancy...It would certainly seem from the results that it was a wholesome and invigorating system.[14]

The Austen children certainly thrived, as they were all physically strong and survived childhood at a time of high infant mortality.

In the summer of 1768 the renovation of Steventon Rectory was complete and the Austens were able to move in. The lane between Deane and Steventon was then a rough cart track, made impassable for a carriage by deep ruts. Mrs Austen, who was in poor health, travelled to her new home on a feather bed balanced on some soft items of furniture, in the waggon containing their household goods.[15]

The rectory was situated in a shallow valley at one end of the village of Steventon. A new Georgian façade had been placed on the seventeenth-century brick building and a carriage drive added in front. The front door, with its latticed porch, opened into one of two reception rooms; there were also seven bedrooms, three attic rooms, a study and kitchens. Behind the house were a bakery, dairy, brewhouse, well and water-pump. According to George and Cassandra's granddaughter Anna, the rectory

> ... had been of the most miserable description, but in the possession of my grandfather it became a tolerably roomy and convenient habitation; he added and improved, walled in a good kitchen garden, and planted out the east wind, enlarging the house until it came to be considered a very comfortable family residence.
>
> On the sunny side was a shrubbery and flower garden, with a terrace walk of turf which communicated by a small gate with what was termed the 'wood-walk'; a path winding through clumps of underwood and overhung by tall elm trees, skirting the upper side of the home meadows.[16]

A path known as the 'church walk' led up through the rectory grounds to the church.[17] Attached to the rectory were three acres of glebe land for the rector's use and a tithe barn across the lane. As George Austen's living was worth only £100 a year, he also rented Cheesedown Farm in Steventon from Thomas Knight.[18]

Steventon was, and still is, a tranquil village with winding country lanes and plenty of trees. Like other villages in England at that time, it was an isolated and largely self-sufficient community.

Although roads and transport were improving, many country dwellers, especially the poorer ones, did not travel further than their nearest town, which for the inhabitants of Steventon was Alton. Due to its remoteness it took time for news from the outside world to reach Steventon, which added to its isolation. Life in the village revolved around events in the farming calendar, such as ploughing, haymaking and harvest.

The village consisted of the church, the rectory, the manor house, a number of brick and flint cottages and farmland. St Nicholas Church was in a lonely position away from the rest of the village and a short walk from the rectory. This rather plain building, with its narrow windows, was built in the twelfth century. The churchyard was sheltered by elm trees, old hawthorns and an ancient yew tree. An abundance of purple and white violets grew under the south wall. When Mrs Austen's mother, Jane Leigh, died in 1768 she was buried here, in the churchyard of her son-in-law's church.

A wicket gate in the churchyard wall led to the grounds of a sixteenth-century manor house with a stone porch, tall chimneys covered with ivy and mullioned windows.[19] In front of the house was a wide lawn overshadowed by trees. The manor house and its 900-acre farm had been rented for many decades by the Digweed family. When the Austens lived at the rectory the tenants were Hugh Digweed, his wife Ruth and their four sons. They occupied the squire's pew in the church and the young Digweeds later became friends of the Austen boys.

The cottages in the village bordered both sides of a long lane, which was little more than a rough track. The male cottage dwellers worked as farm labourers, or in other occupations connected with the land. Their wives were either employed as domestic servants or stayed at home to work in cottage industries, such as spinning and weaving, and to look after their children, animals and poultry. These women also supplemented their family's income by doing occasional domestic work for the local gentry, or casual farm work at busy times in the farming year. The cottagers' children also worked on the land, scaring birds and picking up stones.

The overcrowded houses of the poor inhabitants of Steventon were basic dwellings with earth floors and rough walls. They grew vegetables and fruit in their gardens, which helped them to eke out a living. As living standards were lower in the eighteenth century than during the medieval period, life for these and other members of the rural lower classes was a relentless struggle to survive.

As well as performing his clerical and pastoral duties, George Austen looked after his garden and orchard, worked on his glebe lands and ran Cheesedown Farm.[20] Although he was assisted by two farm bailiffs, George was in charge of the wheat and hay, and also looked after his pigs himself. His income came from his stipend, from the tithes due to him as rector, and the sale of the farm produce that was surplus to his family's needs. His wife, meanwhile, ran the home, and cared for her children, poultry and animals. Mrs Austen, who was a good manager and efficient housekeeper, was very contented with country life and her growing family.

The Austens kept in contact with their wider family by letter and visits. Philadelphia Hancock and her daughter Betsy lived in London from 1768, so that Betsy could be taught by the best masters available. They visited their relatives at Steventon whenever they could. Tysoe Hancock returned to India that year to make more money, as the funds they had brought to England were running out.[21] Philadelphia and her daughter lived in a variety of rented houses in London, and also rented a cottage in Byfleet, Surrey[22] to give them a change from city life. Some of Philadelphia's visits were timed to coincide with the expected arrival of her sister-in-law's babies, so that she could help during the confinements. George Austen seems to have lost contact with his younger sister Leonora, as there is no further reference to her in family records.

The Austens travelled to Wargrave in Berkshire and Bath to see the Leigh-Perrots. They also visited Mrs Austen's sister Jane, to whom she was close. Jane was married to the Reverend Edward Cooper, vicar of Sonning near Reading and rector of Whaddon near Bath. In the spring of 1770 Mrs Austen left her own family to assist her sister following the birth of her first child, Edward.[23]

George Austen's half-brother, William Hampson Walter, and his wife Susannah were also part of their wider family. The Walters, who had six children, lived in Kent. George kept in touch with William, who was eight years his senior, and they maintained an affectionate interest in each other and their respective families. A series of letters, written between 1770 and 1775, by George and Cassandra Austen to Susannah Walter provide a glimpse of everyday life in their household. They also reveal the Austens' growing concern about their son George, who had started to suffer from seizures at a young age. In a letter dated 2 July 1770 George Austen wrote,

> God knows only how far it [George's improvement] will come to pass, but from the best judgment I can form at present, we must not be too sanguine on this Head; be it as it may, we have this comfort, he cannot be a bad or a wicked child.[24]

A few months later Mrs Austen wrote,

> My poor little George is come to see me today, he seems pretty well, tho' he had a fit lately: it was near a Twelvemonth since he had one before, so was in hopes they had left him, but must not flatter myself so now.[25]

When she wrote this letter Mrs Austen was expecting another baby and six months later, in June 1771, Henry Thomas was born. During the next year or so little George's health became so bad that he was placed in the care of a family in the nearby village of Monk Sherborne. As well as suffering from epilepsy, George had learning disabilities and was probably deaf as well. Like his uncle, Thomas Leigh, George was cared for away from his family. It was common practice in the eighteenth century for people with mental disabilities to be removed from polite society. Although the Austens visited George regularly, he was no longer really a part of their lives.

Cassandra's next letter was written in November 1772, when Henry was walking, and she was expecting her fifth baby. Her affection for, and pride in, her growing family is evident.

> My little boy is come home from Nurse, and a fine stout [strong] little fellow he is, and can run anywhere, so now I have all four at home, and some time in January I expect a fifth, so you see it will not be in my power to take any journeys for one while ... Thank God we are all well in health; I begin to be very heavy & bundling as usual, I believe my Sister

> Hancock will be so good as to come and nurse me again, for which I am sure I will be much obliged to her, as it will be a bad time of the year for her to take so long a journey.[26]

The fifth child, who arrived at the expected time, was Cassandra Elizabeth. She was named after her mother and her grandmother, Elizabeth Leigh of Adlestrop in Gloucestershire.

Soon after Cassandra's birth George Austen became rector of Deane, as well as Steventon, on the death of the incumbent Mr Hillman. As Steventon and Deane were so close, with a combined population of only 300, George was allowed by the Archbishop of Canterbury to be rector of both.[27] The additional income from this new living helped the Austens but, with a growing family, George soon needed more money. To supplement his income he began to teach a few sons of the local aristocracy, gentry and clergy, who boarded at the rectory. With his calm and patient temperament and extensive learning, George was particularly suited to teaching. It was common for clergymen at that time to take in paying pupils. George's earliest pupils included the young Lord Lymington and William Vanderstegen, the son of a family friend.[28] The arrival of these young pupils added to Cassandra Austen's workload, as she became responsible for their care.

A letter written by Mrs Austen to Susannah Walter, a few months after her daughter's birth, contained more family news and shows how important their wider family were to the Austens.

> We will not give up the hopes of seeing you both (and as many of your young people as you can conveniently bring) at Steventon before the summer is over. Mr Austen wants to show his brother his Lands and his Cattle & many other matters; and I want to shew you my Henry and my Cassy, who are both reckoned fine Children. I suckled my little Girl thro' the first quarter; she has been wean'd and settled at a good Woman's at Dean just Eight weeks; she is very healthy and lively, and puts on her short petticoats today … Jemmy and Neddy are very happy in a new play-fellow, Lord Lymington, whom Mr Austen has lately taken the charge of; he is between five and six years old, very backward of his age, but good tempered and orderly: He is the eldest son of

Lord Portsmouth who lives about ten miles from hence ... My sister Cooper has made us a visit this spring, she seems well in health, but is grown vastly thin – her boy and girl are well, the youngest almost two years old, and she has not been breeding since, so perhaps she has done. We expect my brother and sister Perrot to-morrow for a fortnight, we have not seen them near a twelvemonth. I have got a nice dairy fitted up, and am now worth a bull and six cows, and you would laugh to see them; for they are not much bigger than Jack-asses and here I have got Jackies and Ducks and Chicken for Phylly's [Susannah's daughter] amusement. In short you must come, and, like Hezekiah, I will shew you all my Riches.[29]

Six months later Cassandra reported to her sister-in-law that they were all well and that her little daughter was 'almost ready to run away'.[30] The Austen family continued to increase rapidly. In April 1774 another son, Francis William [always known as Frank] was born. He is referred to in Cassandra's next letter to Susannah Walter, written in August 1775, when she was expecting yet another baby.

We are all, I thank God, in good health, and I am more nimble and active than I was last time, expect to be confined some time in November. My last boy is very stout, and has run alone these two Months, and he is not yet Sixteen Months old. My little girl talks all day long, and in my opinion is a very entertaining Companion. Henry has been in Breeches some months and thinks himself near as good a man as his Bror. Neddy. Indeed no one would judge by their looks that there was above three years and a half difference in their ages, one is so little and the other so great.[31]

The baby due in November 1775 was Jane, who arrived later than expected on 16 December. George Austen wrote to his sister-in-law the following day to announce her safe arrival.

Dear Sister,
You have doubtless been for some time in expectation of hearing from Hampshire, and perhaps wondered a little we

> were in our old age grown such bad reckoners, but so it was, for Cassy certainly expected to have been brought to bed a month ago; however, last night the time came, and without a great deal of warning, everything was soon happily over. We have now another girl, a present plaything for her sister Cassy, and a future companion. She is to be Jenny and seems to me as if she would be as like Henry as Cassy is to Neddy. Your sister, I thank God is pure well after it, and sends her love to you and my brother, not forgetting James and Phylly.[32]

Jane was named after her godmother, her great-uncle Francis Austen's second wife and her two aunts Mrs Cooper and Mrs Leigh-Perrot. Jane's christening service did not take place until the following April. The winter of 1775–6 was a particularly severe one. It seems that Jane was kept indoors until the weather improved and the country lanes were clear of snow.[33] George Austen recorded her birth and christening in the family Bible:

> Jane Austen. Born 16 Decr 1775. Privately baptised 17 Decr 1775. Rec$^{'d}$ into the Church 5 Apl 1776. Sponsors Rev^{d}. Mr Cooke Rector of Bookham, Surry. Mrs Jane Austen of Sevenoaks, Kent, Father's Uncle's Wife. Mrs Musgrave of Chinnor, Oxon.[34]

Mrs Musgrave was the wife of a cousin of Mrs Austen. The name Jenny was only used during Jane's childhood, as there is no further reference to her by this name. Her father's comment to Susannah about Cassandra's resemblance to Edward and Jane's to Henry is interesting, as these were the brothers they became especially close to in later life. Not only did Jane look like Henry, but it soon became clear that she resembled him temperamentally as well. They both enjoyed a cheerful, positive and optimistic outlook on life – an outlook they shared with their father.

The Austen family was completed in June 1779 with the birth of Charles John. Cassandra and Jane became very protective of the youngest member of the family and later referred to him affectionately as 'our own particular little brother', a misquotation from the novel *Camilla* by Fanny Burney.[35]

2

STEVENTON, OXFORD, SOUTHAMPTON AND READING

1776–1786

George Austen's expectation that Jane would be a companion for her sister was more than fulfilled – they became the most devoted of sisters. Their closeness and deep affection for each other was evident very early on. It was natural that they would be close, as the only girls in a household of brothers and boy pupils but, in the words of their niece Anna: 'Their affection for each other was extreme; it passed the common love of sisters; and it had been so from childhood.'[1]

Jane was a shy child and this was, no doubt, one reason why she attached herself so firmly to her sister. Cassandra mothered and protected her adoring little sister. Being nearly three years older she was the leader in the relationship and Jane looked up to Cassandra throughout her life, always regarding her as 'wiser and better'[2] than herself. Jane's adoration was so great that she hated being separated from her sister. Nevertheless, they were occasionally separated when Cassandra stayed on her own with the Cooper family in Bath. During one of these periods of separation Jane missed Cassandra so much that she could not wait for her to return with their father, who had gone as far as Andover to collect her. As the time of their expected return drew near, Jane, who was six years old at the time, set off with her little brother Charles in tow, to meet them. The two children walked some way along the route, to a place called New Down, before they saw the hack chaise carrying their father and sister approaching. Jane and Charles had the pleasure of returning home in the carriage with them.[3]

Cassandra and Jane received their earliest education from their mother, as their elder brothers had done. It was a mother's responsibility at that time to provide her children, of both sexes, with basic literacy skills, religious instruction and moral guidance. The Austen children learned to read using primers. Mrs Austen read them fairy tales and nursery stories, such as 'The Hare and Many Frienda',[4] a popular poetic fable by John Gay which was published in 1727. Jane is known to have owned a copy of *The History of Little Goody Two Shoes*,[5] one of the earliest nursery stories, which was published in 1765. Children's literature of the eighteenth century combined moral lessons with entertainment. Books of verses for children, such as those written by John Gay, were also popular. The siblings listened to Bible stories at their mother's knee. Their strong Christian faith, which was to play such an important part in the adult lives of the Austen sisters, grew from this early religious instruction.

Having received their initial education from their mother the Austen boys were taught by their father, alongside his pupils. Boys from the gentry and the younger sons of the aristocracy were educated for leadership roles in national and local government, for business and for professional careers in the Church, the law, the army and navy. George Austen provided his sons with a typical male education based on the classics. According to his sons, George was an excellent teacher. As an old man Frank Austen recorded in his memoirs that his father 'was admirably calculated to the instruction of youth as he joined to an unusual extent of classical learning and a highly cultivated taste for literature in general, a remarkable suavity of temper and gentleness of manners.'[6]

In July 1779 James Austen, at the precociously early age of fourteen, left home to study at St John's College, Oxford, his father's old college. James was awarded a Founder's Kin Scholarship as a descendant, on his mother's side of the family, of the college founder. When he arrived at the college James was invited to supper by his great-uncle Theophilus Leigh, who was Master of Balliol College. Being new to university life and not quite sure how to behave, James took off his college gown before sitting down to eat. His great-uncle, who was renowned for his wit and sense of humour, was reported to have said, 'Young man, you need not strip, we are not going to fight.'[7]

James, who was of a serious and sometimes melancholy disposition, was the scholar in the family. His passions were reading and the English countryside. James was a close friend of Fulwar Craven Fowle, the son of the Reverend Thomas Fowle, vicar of Kintbury in Berkshire, who was one of his father's pupils. The two friends enjoyed walking and spending time together in the countryside of Hampshire and Berkshire. James, who had a talent for writing, expressed his love of nature in pastoral poetry.[8]

After James left for university, George Austen's remaining pupils were his sons Henry and Edward as well as George Nibbs, the son of a family friend, Fulwar Craven Fowle and his brother Tom. Mrs Austen played a considerable part in running her husband's school, which added significantly to her workload. She was responsible for catering for the pupils and for their day-to-day care; tasks she undertook with diligence and humour. There is evidence of the latter in an amusing poem which Mrs Austen wrote when two pupils complained about the 'scooping sound' made by the weathercock, which was perched on the top of a maypole in the rectory grounds. When the pupils asked her to draw this nuisance to her husband's attention she wrote the following verse;

The Humble Petition of R. Buller and William Goodenough:
Dear Sir, We beseech and entreat and request
You'd remove a sad nuisance that breaks our night's rest.
That creaking old weathercock o'er our heads
Will scarcely permit us to sleep in our beds.
It whines and it groans and it makes such a noise
That it greatly disturbs two unfortunate boys
Who hope you will not be displeased when they say
If they don't sleep by night, they can't study by day.
But if you will kindly grant their petition
And they sleep all night long without intermission
They promise to study hard every day
And moreover as bounden in duty will pray.[9]

In the same summer of 1779, when Cassandra was six and Jane was nearly four, Thomas Knight II, the son of George Austen's wealthy kinsman and benefactor, visited the Austens with his new wife Catherine. Mrs Knight, who came from an old Kentish family, was the daughter of the Reverend Dr Wadham Knatchbull, Prebendary of Durham, and vicar of Chilham and Molash in Kent. The Knights were on their wedding tour when they stopped in Hampshire, so that Catherine could meet her new relatives.

During their stay the Knights took a liking to twelve-year-old Edward Austen, who was an easy-going, good-natured and likeable boy. He made such a favourable impression on the Knights that they asked him to accompany them on the remainder of their tour. The couple became so fond of Edward that the following year they wrote to his father requesting that he spend the summer with them at Godmersham House, which Thomas had recently inherited on the death of his father. George Austen, who was concerned at the impact this would have on his son's education, was initially reluctant to allow him to go. His practical and sensible wife, however, knowing that Edward was not as academic as his brothers and realising the potential benefits of agreeing to the request, persuaded her husband by saying, 'I think, my dear, you had better oblige your cousins and let the child go.' Edward was accompanied to Godmersham by Thomas Knight's coachman, who had been sent to collect him. He rode all the way from Hampshire to Kent on the pony which the coachman had brought for him, with the coachman beside him on horseback. At the end of the summer Edward returned to the rectory to resume his education.[10]

While George Austen educated his sons, his wife prepared their daughters for their expected future roles in the private domestic sphere as wives, mothers and housekeepers. The sisters learned by accompanying their mother as she supervised the servants who cooked, baked, brewed and washed for the household, and by helping her to look after the animals and poultry of which she was so proud. Mrs Austen was a competent and efficient housekeeper who taught her daughters well. Cassandra and Jane were also taught the principles of what was termed 'prudent economy', or how to manage a household budget and to keep proper accounts of expenditure. Mrs Austen also passed on the important knowledge and skills necessary to treat and care for sick family members. This was another responsibility which fell to women of their class and Mrs Austen, with a large household to look after, had plenty of experience in this field.

Cassandra and Jane were taught how to sew by their mother. They learned how to make clothes, to make and mend household items, and to do embroidery and fancy needlework, which was always referred to as 'work'. Sewing was not only an essential practical skill, but could also be an enjoyable pastime for ladies. The Austen sisters both became very proficient with the needle and Jane was proud of her neat stitching. It was quite acceptable for ladies to do decorative sewing in the presence of visitors, but Mrs Austen had a disconcerting habit, which embarrassed her daughters, of continuing with her darning and mending when visitors arrived.

As well as making clothes for herself and her family Mrs Austen, and later Cassandra and Jane, made items for her husband's poor parishioners. The girls may well have accompanied their mother when she called on the poor villagers of Steventon and Deane and thus learnt early in life the importance of observing the commandment to 'Love thy neighbour'.

Cassandra and Jane spent most of their time together, and began to develop a secret life of their own. Their characters and temperaments complemented each other. Cassandra felt things deeply, was reserved and kept her emotions in check; Jane was a far more lively and outgoing child, although she could also be shy. Both sisters were affectionate and even-tempered. They enjoyed quiet, feminine pastimes such as reading, drawing, sewing and indoor games. Jane was particularly good at games requiring manual dexterity; her two favourite games were Spillikins and Bilbocatch, also known as Cup and Ball.

The sisters probably played outdoor games in the rectory garden with Frank and Charles. Jane's description in *Northanger Abbey* of Catherine Morland playing cricket with her brothers and rolling down grassy slopes may have been based on her own childhood memories. The Austen children were not just siblings, they were also the best of friends. As previously mentioned, Cassandra and Jane each had a favourite brother. Cassandra's favourite brother was Edward, or Neddy as he was affectionately called, who was a kind, thoughtful and sweet-natured boy. Jane's favourite was Henry, or Harry, who was a cheerful, talkative child and whose 'eagerness in everything' Jane recalled many years later. Edward and Henry were the brothers whom the sisters most resembled physically, as their father noted at the time of Jane's birth. The closeness of the Austen siblings could be summed up with the words Jane used in *Mansfield Park* to describe the relationship between Fanny and William Price:

> Children of the same family, with the same associations and habits have means of communication which no subsequent communication can supply.

The Austen children all enjoyed being outdoors. The boys participated in a variety of outdoor activities and spent a lot of time with the four Digweed boys, who lived at the Manor House. They particularly liked following the hunt, and, as relatives of Thomas Knight, who owned all the land around Steventon, the Austens were allowed to hunt freely. They hunted upon any animal they could get hold of and, in the absence of an animal, they hunted on foot.[11] Frank, at the age of seven, presumably with his father's permission and assistance, bought a chestnut coloured pony[12] which he named Squirrel, but which his brothers nicknamed Scug to tease him. He rode his pony when hunting, dressed in a suit which his mother made for him from the scarlet riding-habit she wore to travel in after her wedding and in the early years of her married life.[13] The curly haired Frank, who was a bold and courageous boy, must have cut quite a figure on the hunting field. Jane later described him as 'fearless of danger'[14] and recalled that the only thing that ever intimidated him was the bray of a donkey.[15] The enterprising Frank sold Squirrel a year after buying him, making a handsome profit of £1.1s.[16]

George and Cassandra Austen were a loving couple who created a happy home for their family. Their grandson's description of Jane's childhood home in his *Memoir* of her applies equally to her siblings:

> It cannot be doubted that her early years were bright and happy, living, as she did, with indulgent parents, in a cheerful home, not without agreeable variety of society.[17]

George was a gentle, kind and affectionate father who always had time for his children. His quiet but busy life centred on his family, his parishioners, his pupils and his farm. As a cultivated scholar with a fine taste in literature, George owned a large well-stocked library to which his children were allowed full access.

Cassandra was an excellent mother and a supportive wife, with plenty of energy, despite not always being in the best of health. Some of her fine character traits were passed on to her daughters. Cassandra inherited her mother's common sense and practical abilities, while Jane inherited her ironic sense of humour and her writing talent. Jane also inherited what her mother referred to as her 'sprack wit', which was an old English term meaning a lively perception of the character and foibles of other people. Mrs Austen's wit and sparkle were evident in her conversation and her lively letters.

The Austen children were firmly and fairly disciplined by their parents, who set them a good example in their own behaviour and their relationship with each other. The children were taught to live according to the tenets of the Christian faith and also to respect learning and culture. Much contentment was derived from being part of a highly literate, cultivated and talented family who were also close and loving. Their happy and harmonious family life gave Cassandra and Jane the best possible start in life. The children were encouraged to develop their own interests, which for Cassandra was drawing and for Jane were playing the piano and, later, writing. There was much laughter, gaiety and high-spiritedness in the Austen household. The sense of humour which Jane was to display in her novels and letters was shared, to a greater or lesser extent, by the rest of the family, including the serious-minded James. The family were so united by temperament and affection that there were hardly ever any harsh words or arguments in their home. According to James Edward Austen-Leigh:

> The family talk had abundance of spirit and vivacity, and was never troubled by disagreements even in little matters, for it was not their habit to dispute or argue with each other: above all, there was strong family affection and firm union, never to be broken but by death.[18]

The family members were also united by their enjoyment of doing things together. One shared pastime was the performance of amateur theatricals. The arts, including drama, flourished during the Georgian and Regency periods. So great was the interest in the theatre that many families put on private theatrical performances in their own home. The first performance by the Austens, which was put on over Christmas 1782, was the tragedy *Matilda* by Thomas Francklin.[19] James wrote a prologue and epilogue which were read by his brother Edward and his father's pupil Tom Fowle.[20] Cassandra, who was nearly nine, may have played a small part, but it is unlikely that Jane, at the age of seven, was old enough to join in. An audience of family and friends watched the play, which was performed in the rectory dining room. This was the first of a number of productions performed by the family.

The Austens' financial situation at this time was comfortable in comparison with that of most clergy families, but their money had to be managed carefully and George Austen had, on occasion, to borrow money from his wealthy brother-in-law James Leigh-Perrot. When they lived at Steventon the family could afford to run a carriage, using the horses that worked on the farm. This carriage, which was mainly for the use of Mrs Austen and her daughters, enabled them to travel to the nearby towns of Basingstoke and Winchester to shop, and to visit friends locally. For longer journeys there were the public stage-coaches, which picked up and dropped off passengers twice daily at nearby Deane Gate and Popham Lane. The Austens occasionally travelled by post-chaise.

The Austen family were well-liked and respected members of their local community. George was looked up to as a gentleman and a scholar. He stood out among the rather boorish local country squires who lacked his education, culture and refinement. His grandson recorded, as an example of the deference paid to him, that a neighbouring squire who owned many acres of land, once asked George to settle a dispute he was having with his wife as to whether France was in Paris, or Paris was in France. The same squire was renowned for his coarse language and habit of uttering oaths;[21] whether he tempered his language in the presence of the refined rector and his wife is not known.

George also got on well with the local farmers, with whom he came into regular contact. He enjoyed activities connected with farming, such as ploughing matches and harvest celebrations. George was friendly with Lord Bolton of Hackwood Park, through their shared interest in pigs. He was also friendly with his neighbour Hugh Digweed, with whom he pooled his money to buy sheep at the local livestock auctions. When they returned to Steventon the first half of the flock that ran out of the pen were considered as belonging to the rector.[22]

The Austens also mixed with cultured and genteel society, including the Lefroy family. In 1783 the Reverend I. P. G. (George) Lefroy became rector of the neighbouring parish of Ashe, on the death of the long-term incumbent. George and his charming wife Anne, who became known locally as Madam Lefroy, soon became leaders in the local community. Anne Lefroy involved herself in good works among the poor and needy, such as teaching children to read and write.[23] The Lefroys rebuilt Ashe Rectory and held many social gatherings there, to which the local gentry including the Austens, were invited.

The Austen family did not spend all their time in north Hampshire. When Cassandra and Jane were children they often paid visits to their relatives. Travel was easier than earlier in the century, due to improvements in roads and transport. The Austen sisters went to Bath with their parents to visit the Coopers, who lived at 14, Bennett Street, opposite the Upper Assembly Rooms, and the Leigh-Perrots who lived nearby at 1, The Paragon, for part of the year. During these childhood visits Jane began to build up her knowledge of the topography of Bath, which she later used when writing *Northanger Abbey* and *Persuasion*. She also became familiar with the unique atmosphere of the city, which she was to evoke so effectively in these novels. It was while staying in Bath that a portrait, believed to be of Jane as a child, was probably painted. There is some question as to whether this portrait, by the German artist Johann Zoffany, is of Jane or a distant cousin of the same name. It certainly looks as if it could be Jane, when compared with the only authenticated portrait of her as an adult. Doubters question how the Austens could have afforded to pay for such a portrait, although Jane's wealthy uncle could have commissioned and paid for it.

Relatives, including the Coopers and Leigh-Perrots, visited the Austens at Steventon. Mrs Austen's cousin, the Reverend Thomas Leigh of Adlestrop in Gloucestershire, stopped at the rectory when travelling to London. He usually gave his great-nephews and nieces a small gift of money.[24]

There had been no visits from Philadelphia Hancock and her daughter Betsy since Jane was born, but they had kept in touch. Philadelphia lost her husband in 1775. Two years later she took Betsy, now known by the more grown-up name of Eliza, to the Continent to finish her education. By the time this was completed Eliza was an exceptionally accomplished young lady. In 1779 they were living in Paris, from where Eliza sent her uncle a miniature portrait of herself wearing a white dress trimmed with blue and with blue ribbons in her powdered hair. In the letter accompanying the portrait she wrote that she was sending 'my picture in miniature done here to my Uncle G. Austen... It is reckoned here like what I am at present. The dress is quite the present fashion & what I usually wear.'[25] Eliza managed to secure introductions to members of Parisian society and embarked on a busy social life. She even obtained entry to Versailles, where she saw the queen. The fun-loving Eliza greatly enjoyed her time in Paris.

In 1780 she met Jean-Francois Capot de Feuillide, who claimed to be a count, but it later transpired that this was a false claim.[26] He was a Captain of Dragoons in the Queen's Regiment and owned estates in south-west France. The couple soon became engaged and were married in 1781. It appears that this was not a love match for Eliza and that she was attracted largely by what she described as 'an easy fortune with the prospect of a very ample one',[27] and the advantages of rank and title. Eliza was to play an important part in the lives of Cassandra and Jane, particularly the latter.

Two significant events occurred in the year 1783. Early that year George and Cassandra Austen received another letter from Thomas and Catherine Knight, which was to have a lasting impact on their family. By this time it was becoming apparent that the Knights, who had been married for nearly four years, were unlikely to have a child of their own. Naturally, being the owners of valuable and extensive land and property in Kent and Hampshire, including the whole of the village of Steventon, they were anxious to find someone to whom they could pass on their estates and wealth, and they had chosen the young Edward Austen. They asked his parents for permission to adopt him, to which the Austens assented, but not without some hesitation on his father's part. The formal adoption of the sixteen-year-old Edward was recorded in a silhouette picture by the famous London artist William Wellings, which shows George handing over his son to Catherine Knight, with Thomas Knight and another lady watching.[28] The Knights also commissioned a portrait of Edward wearing a blue jacket and a white shirt, with a serious expression, to commemorate the occasion. Edward agreed to adopt the name of Knight when he came into his inheritance. Cassandra and Jane were ten and seven at the time of their brother's adoption and subsequent move to Kent. Cassandra must have felt the separation from her favourite brother deeply when the time came for him to leave. This event was to become very significant to both sisters as they grew older. Despite moving away from his family, Edward maintained a close and affectionate relationship with them.

Cassandra and Jane did not have much time to dwell on Edward's absence, as shortly after he moved to Kent they were sent away to Oxford with their cousin Jane Cooper to be tutored by Mrs Ann Cawley. Mrs Cawley was Jane Cooper's aunt, being the sister of her father Edward Cooper. It was not originally planned that Jane, due to her tender age, would go with her sister and cousin, but she was included because being separated from Cassandra would have devastated her. Mrs Austen was more in favour of sending the girls away to be educated than their father was. It must have eased her heavy workload and made life more comfortable in the overcrowded rectory.

Very little is known about Mrs Cawley, who was the widow of the Principal of Brasenose College, except that she was a severe, formal and 'stiff-mannered' person. It is believed that James Austen, now a Fellow of St John's College after gaining his Bachelor of Arts degree in 1783, showed his sisters and cousin around the city. Not long after their arrival Mrs Cawley and the three girls moved to Southampton, a move which nearly cost Jane her life. An epidemic of 'putrid fever', probably typhoid fever or diphtheria, broke out in Southampton. The town was heaving with soldiers and sailors, and it is thought that some troops who had recently arrived from Gibraltar brought the fever with them. Both Cassandra and Jane became ill, but probably not realising how seriously ill they were Mrs Cawley did not inform their parents. Luckily, Jane Cooper took it upon herself to write and alert her aunt. Mrs Austen and her sister hastened to Southampton and took their daughters home. Due to her cousin's timely action Jane, who nearly died of the fever, was saved. Mrs Austen treated her daughters with a herbal remedy and they eventually recovered but, sadly, Mrs Cooper contracted the infection and died soon after her return to Bath.[29] Not surprisingly the three girls did not return to Southampton and Mrs Cawley. Christmas at Steventon was a sombre affair that year and there were no family theatricals.

A few months later Edward Cooper, who was heartbroken at the loss of his wife, left Bath with all its memories of her and returned with his children to his home town of Sonning in Berkshire. He gave each of his nieces a small memento of their aunt; Cassandra received one of her rings and Jane received a headband, which she wore years later at balls and dances.[30]

After leaving Southampton, the Austen sisters were educated at home for a while. We know that this education included learning the basics of French grammar as a French primer, containing Jane's name and the date 15 December 1783, is still in the possession of the Austen family.[31] Cassandra and Jane also helped their mother in the house, and joined in with family activities which included, in the summer of 1784, another theatrical production. This time the Austens performed *The Rivals*, a popular play with twelve characters by Richard Sheridan. Once again James wrote a prologue and epilogue.[32] Cassandra and Jane probably played small parts and the artistically talented Cassandra may have helped to make the scenery. This performance, as it took place in the summer, was held in George Austen's tithe barn across the lane from the rectory.

In early 1785, at the ages of twelve and nine, the Austen sisters left home again to go to boarding school with their cousin Jane Cooper. As before, young Jane was included because of her attachment to Cassandra. The Austens' main concern was the happiness of their children so, despite the additional expense, Jane went away to school too. Many years later James Austen's daughter Anna wrote about this decision:

> My Grandmother talking to me once of by gone times; & of that particular time when my Aunts were placed at the Reading Abbey School, said that Jane was too young to make her going to school at all necessary, but it was her own doing, she **would** go with Cassandra; 'if Cassandra's head had been going to be cut off Jane would have her's cut off too.'[33]

It was a common practice at this time for members of the better-off classes to send their daughters to boarding schools. The education provided by these establishments placed much emphasis on the acquisition of ornamental accomplishments such as singing, playing a musical instrument, dancing and drawing. These skills enabled women to entertain at social functions and to occupy their leisure time, which could be considerable in the case of young unmarried women. This was the type of education offered at Mrs Goddard's school in Jane's novel *Emma,* where 'a reasonable quantity of accomplishments were sold at a reasonable price' and where girls could 'scramble themselves into a little education, without any danger of coming back prodigies'.

Girls were also taught good manners and deportment to help them attract a husband; their education reinforced the feminine qualities admired by men such as compliance, gratitude, devotion and obedience. Academic learning was discouraged in girls for most of the eighteenth century, as it was deemed unwomanly. There was also a belief that females were intellectually incapable of serious study. Towards the end of the century changes were being made in the education of girls and limited intellectual study was introduced.

The Abbey School in Reading, to which the Austen girls were sent, was a famous private school for the daughters of the clergy and minor gentry. This well-run and comfortable establishment was kept by a Mrs Latournelle, whose real name was Sarah Hackitt. It is not known whether she was married to a French man or whether her French name was adopted for educational purposes. George Austen paid £35 per year for each of his daughters to attend the school, which was housed partly in the ancient gateway of Reading Abbey and partly in an adjacent building. The school uniform was a dark dress, a pinafore and a plain cap. Lessons were taught by Mrs Latournelle's assistant, Miss Pitts, and a few other female teachers. Instruction in spelling, French, needlework and drawing were held in the mornings only, allowing the pupils plenty of free time. The older pupils were tutored in more academic subjects by masters from the nearby grammar school for boys, which was run by a Dr Valpy.[34]

The school's regime appears not to have been too strict, as the Austen sisters and their cousin were allowed out occasionally to dine with their brothers at a local inn.[35] The girls were also visited, in October 1785, by their great-uncle Thomas Leigh, who was on his way to London. The kindly clergyman gave his great-nieces half a guinea each.[36] Pupils were permitted to borrow books from a local circulating library, and it is likely that Cassandra and Jane borrowed the works of contemporary novelists, such as Fanny Burney and Maria Edgeworth, which are frequently referred to in the letters that Jane wrote to her sister when they were adults.

Neither of the sisters left a description of their experiences at the Abbey School, but there is no reason to doubt that they enjoyed their time there, not least because it was a shared experience and they had the support and companionship of their older cousin. Many years after she left, Jane commented in a letter to her sister 'I could die of laughter, as they used to say at school.'[37] This suggests that their memories of school were pleasant ones.

Some idea of life at the Abbey School can be found in the memoirs of a pupil who was there a few years after the Austen sisters. Mary Butt, later the children's author Mrs Sherwood, wrote

> ... there was a beautiful old-fashioned garden, where the young ladies were allowed to wander under tall trees in hot summer evenings. The liberty which the first class had was so great that if we attended our tutor in his study for an hour or two every morning, no human being ever took the trouble to enquire where else we spent the rest of the day between our meals. Thus, whether we gossiped in one turret or another, whether we laughed about in the garden, or out of the window above the gateway, no one so much as said 'Where have you been Mademoiselle?'[38]

She remembered the headmistress as

> ... a person of the old school – a stout person hardly under seventy, but very active, although she had a cork leg ... She had never been seen or known to have changed the fashion of her dress. Her white muslin handkerchief was always pinned with the same number of pins, her muslin apron always hung in the same form; she always wore the same short sleeves, cuffs, and ruffles, with a breast bow to answer the bow in her cap, both being flat with notched ends ... She was only fit for giving out clothes for the wash and mending them, making tea, ordering dinner, and in fact doing the work of a housekeeper.[39]

Mrs Sherwood also remembered first arriving at the school and being received by Mrs Latournelle in a 'wainscoted parlour, the wainscot a little tarnished, while the room was hung round with chenille pieces representing tombs and weeping willows. A screen in clothwork stood in a corner, and there were several miniatures over the lofty mantelpiece.'[40]

The Austen sisters left the Abbey School at the end of 1786, when they were aged thirteen and eleven, having been there for less than two years. It was unusual for girls to finish their formal education so young but George Austen was probably struggling to pay the fees, as he had fewer pupils by this time and, therefore, a smaller income.

When Cassandra and Jane returned to Steventon Rectory only two of their brothers remained at home – Henry and seven-year-old Charles. The former was still being prepared for university with a view to him entering the Church. Frank had left home a few months earlier, at the age of twelve, to enter the Royal Naval Academy at Portsmouth. It had been his own decision to join the Navy and his parents fully supported him in his choice of profession.[41] This was the beginning of a long and illustrious naval career for the 'self-contained and steadfast' boy. The rectory must have been a quieter place without the boisterous Frank, who was nicknamed 'Fly' by his family because of his boundless energy. James Austen was absent from the family home too, as he was travelling on the Continent. He visited France, where he stayed with his cousin Eliza's husband, the Count de Feuillide, and went on to Spain and Holland.

Edward Austen was also travelling on the Continent at this time. Instead of sending him to university his adoptive parents sent Edward on a Grand Tour of Europe. He was not academic and a university education was not necessary for his future role as an English country gentleman and landowner. A Grand Tour of the classical sights of Europe, particularly the ancient statues and the Renaissance paintings in Italy, was a fashionable way for the sons of the English aristocracy to finish off their education. Some young men who embarked on the Grand Tour did not use the opportunity wisely, but Edward was not among them. His tour lasted for two years, and included a visit to Dresden, where he was received at the Saxon court. It concluded in Rome, where a full-length portrait was painted of Edward.[42] The portrait depicts a tall, rosy-faced, handsome young man with powdered hair and dressed in expensive fashionable clothes. To show that Edward had actually seen the classical sights, the artist included part of a marble frieze and a Corinthian capital in the portrait. Edward had much to tell his family at Steventon when he returned to England. He then settled down to learn the skills necessary to manage the Knight properties and estates that he would one day inherit. Many years later Edward was to use the knowledge of classical architecture, which he had acquired in Europe, when he carried out improvements to his country houses.

There was a family gathering at Steventon Rectory over Christmas 1786 that included Philadelphia Hancock, Eliza, and Eliza's son Hastings, named after her godfather, who was born in London in June of that year. Also present were Edward and Jane Cooper. Mrs Austen wrote a letter to Philadelphia Walter on 31 December containing a vivid depiction of life in her household over the festive period.

> We are now happy in the company of our Sister Hancock, Madame de Feuillide & the little Boy; they came to us last Thursday Sennet [seven-night or one week] & will stay with us till the end of next Month. They all look & seem to be remarkably well, the little Boy grows very fat, he is very fair & very pretty; I don't think your Aunt at all altered in any respect. Madame is grown quite lively, when a child we

used to think her too grave. We have borrowed a Piano-Forte, and she plays to us every day; on Tuesday we are to have a very snug little dance in our parlour; just our own children, nephew & nieces (for the two little Coopers come tomorrow) quite a family party. I wish my **third niece** could be here also; but indeed, I begin to suspect your Mother never intends to gratify that wish. You might as well be in Jamaica keeping your Brother's House, for anything that we see of you or are like to see. Five of my children are now at home. Henry, Frank, Charles & my two Girls, who have now quite left school; Frank returns to Portsmouth in a few days, he has but short holidays at Christmas. Edward is well & happy in Switzerland. James set out for La Guienne, on a visit to the Count de Feuillide, near Eight weeks ago, I hope he is got there by this time and am impatient for a Letter; he was wind-bound some weeks in the little island of Jersey or he would have got to the end of his long Journey by the beginning of this Month – Every one of our Fireside join in Love, & Duty as due and in wishing a happy 87 to our dear Friends at Seal.[43]

Jane's Aunt Philadelphia and cousin Eliza gave her a present for her eleventh birthday, just before Christmas. It was a set of Arnaud Berquin's *L'ami des enfans;* interestingly, 'real-life' stories, not fairy tales, exemplifying happy familial relationshiops between parents and offspring.[44] During their stay Jane grew fond of her beautiful, sophisticated and charming cousin, and listened enthralled to her descriptions of life in fashionable Paris. A firm and affectionate friendship developed between Jane and Eliza, which lasted until the end of the latter's life.

3

STEVENTON

1787–1789

When the Austen sisters returned home from school their real education began. The Austens were enlightened parents who wanted their daughters to receive a better education than the limited one prescribed for girls at the end of the eighteenth century. George Austen, with fewer pupils to teach, now had time to devote to the academic education of his intelligent daughters. The daughters of clergymen, who were brought up in a more cultured environment than many girls of the gentry, often received a superior education. They were either taught by their fathers, like the Austen sisters, or shared their brothers' tutors.

An important element of the education provided by George Austen, especially for Jane, was an early introduction to the classics of English literature. Henry Austen, in the first biographical information about Jane's life, described his father as a 'profound scholar' who possessed 'a most exquisite taste in every species of literature'.[1] He added that it was not, therefore, surprising 'that his daughter Jane should, at a very early age, have become sensible to the charms of style, and enthusiastic in the cultivation of her own language'.[2] As Cassandra was taught with Jane she too benefited from her father's knowledge and love of English literature. George Austen allowed his daughters full access to his extensive library, which contained many volumes of literature of all genres, including novels. The Austens were not ashamed of enjoying novels, even though they were looked down on as a form of literature by many, despite the fact that the invention of the novel was the greatest literary achievement of the eighteenth century.

After returning home from the Continent in the autumn of 1787 James Austen, an avid reader with a considerable knowledge of English literature, helped to direct his sisters' reading and form their taste in literature. Over the next few years Cassandra and Jane supplemented the education provided by their father by reading widely. There is no detailed record of Cassandra's reading, but there is plenty of information about Jane's. Her reading included the works of Shakespeare, Samuel Johnson, the racy novels of Smollett, Richardson and Fielding, the poetry of Crabbe and Cowper, and the essays published in *The Spectator* and other periodicals. Henry Austen wrote that it was 'difficult to say at what age she was not intimately acquainted with the merits and defects of the best essays and novels in the English language'.[3] From the references to literature in the letters Jane wrote to her sister when they were adults it is clear that Cassandra was familiar with many of the books Jane enjoyed, suggesting that she was just as avid a reader. Cassandra and Jane were intellectually equal and their pleasure in literature was enhanced because they could read and discuss books together. Despite reading so much at this period of her life, Jane later regretted not reading more in her youth.

Cassandra and Jane studied English history as well as English literature. Their father used *The History of England from the Earliest Times to the Death of George II,* by Oliver Goldsmith, in his history lessons.[4] In the margin of this book Jane showed her sympathy for the Stuarts by writing 'a family who were always ill-used, betrayed or neglected, whose virtues are seldom allowed, while their errors are never forgotten.'[5] In another note she showed her sympathy for the poor with the comment 'How much the poor are to be pitied and the Rich to be Blamed.'[6] Jane also read the recently published *Mary Queen of Scots Vindicated* by John Whitaker. Cassandra and Jane learned a little Italian and some French,[7] possibly with the occasional help of their cousin Eliza.

Mental training formed an important element of the education the sisters received at home. Being part of a clever, cultured and highly literate family helped them to develop enquiring minds and to think for themselves. Such mental training was not normally encouraged in women at that time because it was not necessary for the subservient position they were allotted in a patriarchal society, and may have led to them questioning their lot in life.

Jane valued her academic education highly and there is no reason to suppose that Cassandra was not of the same mind. They knew how disadvantaged women were by the limited conventional female education. Women's education and its influence on their behaviour, decisions, choices and happiness were to be important themes in Jane's novels. The moral and religious instruction, which began in Cassandra's and Jane's early childhood, also continued. In her book *Personal Aspects of Jane Austen,* their great-niece Mary Augusta Austen-Leigh described how the Austen children were taught to do their 'duty to God and duty to Man' and that their lives revolved 'round these twin poles'.[8]

The ornamental accomplishments the sisters learned at school were not neglected when they returned home. William Charde, the assistant organist at Winchester Cathedral, was engaged to teach Jane to play the piano.[9] She played for her own amusement rather than to entertain others, which was one reason why girls learned to play a musical instrument. Jane, who was the most musical member of the family, also had a good singing voice. Both sisters may also have received instruction in drawing, as their father's bank account shows a payment to a Claude Nattes – probably the artist John Claude Nattes,[10] who worked as an art tutor and later produced some of the earliest watercolour paintings in Britain. Cassandra was a talented artist and, according to Henry Austen, Jane also 'evinced great power of hand in the management of the pencil'.[11] It may have been around this time that Jane developed an interest in landscape painting. According to Henry:

> She was a warm and judicious admirer of landscape, both in nature and on canvas. At a very early age she was enamoured of Gilpin on the Picturesque; and she seldom changed her opinions either on books or men.[12]

A small sitting room was set aside in the rectory for Cassandra and Jane, to provide them with a private space. Their niece Anna described this room,

> ... a sitting-room was made upstairs, 'the dressing-room', as they were pleased to call it, perhaps because it opened into a smaller chamber in which my two aunts slept. I remember the common-looking carpet with its chocolate ground, and the painted press with shelves above for books, and Jane's piano, and an oval glass that hung between the windows; but the charm of the room, with its scanty furniture and cheaply-papered walls, must have been, for those old enough to understand it, the flow of native household wit, with all the fun and nonsense of a large and clever family.[13]

In their sitting room Cassandra and Jane created a private world of their own. Here they led their own secret lives. The sisters completely understood and trusted each other; they knew that whatever confidences they shared would never be repeated, even to other family members. It was in their private room that the sisters pursued their own occupations, away from the activities of the rest of the household. They read a large number of books, both to themselves and aloud to each other, and practised their sewing skills. They made clothes for the family, as well as small items for their father's parishioners, such as baby layettes. Both Cassandra and Jane enjoyed doing fancy needlework and made decorative items for the home as well as for presents. Their sewing skills were very useful to them later when, as adults, they had to refashion old clothes and make some of their own clothes and accessories because, unlike most women of their class, they had a very limited clothing allowance. They also pursued their separate interests; while Cassandra drew and painted watercolour pictures, Jane made her first attempts at writing. The sisters shared a bedroom in the rectory; they would sleep in the same room in all the houses to which they later moved.

As previously stated, there was already a tradition of writing in the Austen family. This was started with Mrs Austen's clever epigrammatic verses – she even reputedly wrote recipes in verse – and she was also an excellent letter writer. The tradition was continued by James in his religious and pastoral poetry. Jane's earliest attempts at writing, described by her nephew as her 'childish effusions',[14] and now referred to as her *Juvenilia*, were copied into three manuscript notebooks which she called *Volume the First, Volume the Second* and *Volume the Third*. These early works reveal the extent of Jane's reading by her early teens, as well as her knowledge of contemporary literature, which she parodied in them. They included a short play entitled *The Mystery. An Unfinished Comedy,* which was dedicated to her father, with mock solemnity, in the style of the day. *The Beautifull* [sic] *Cassandra* was another early work, which was dedicated to her sister in the flowery language used by contemporary authors. This work, written in fewer than thirty sentences, parodies the popular sentimental and melodramatic novel. It tells the story of the daughter of a London milliner who sets off in the world to make her fortune, but ends up back where she started from. This early piece shows that Cassandra was privy to Jane's imaginary world from the beginning and, no doubt, offered her opinion on the works as they were being written. Two other works which were probably also written in 1787 or 1788 were *Sir William Mountague* and *The Memoirs of Mr. Clifford* which were dedicated to Jane's brother Charles. The humour, wit and comedy in these early pieces anticipate the talent so evident in her mature works. Jane's early works were greatly enjoyed by her family, who all loved nonsense and shared the same sense of humour.

When they were not in their private sitting room, Cassandra and Jane were most likely to be found walking in the country lanes around Steventon. Their nephew James Edward believed that the Hampshire countryside inspired Jane to write. According to him:

> This was the cradle of her genius. These were the first objects which inspired her young heart with a sense of the beauties of nature. In strolls along those wood-walks, thick-coming fancies rose in her mind, and gradually assumed the forms in which they came forth to the world.[15]

There was another family gathering at Steventon Rectory over the Christmas and New Year period of 1787–8. James was back from his travels abroad and Philadelphia Hancock, Eliza and her son Hastings were there. The Austens and their guests performed two plays over the festive period. The vivacious and outgoing Eliza was involved in organising these performances and took leading roles in them. A theatre was created in the tithe barn and all the young people were encouraged to take part. Eliza wrote to her cousin Philadelphia Walter, with whom she and her mother had spent some weeks during the summer, to persuade her to join them at the rectory and participate in the fun. She informed her cousin that she was

> …particularly commissioned by My Aunt Austen & her whole Family to make the earliest application possible, & assure you how very happy you will make them as well as myself if you could be prevailed on to undertake these parts & give us all your company … I assure you we shall have a most brilliant party & a great deal of amusement, the House full of Company & frequent Balls. You cannot possibly resist so many temptations, especially when I tell you your old Friend James is returned from France & is to be of the acting party.[16]

Philadelphia replied that she would not mind being a spectator but that she did not want to act. This, however, did not appear to be an option as Eliza informed her that 'My Aunt Austen declares "she has not room for any idle young people."'[17] This was enough to put Philadelphia off visiting Steventon and she made various excuses not to go.

The first play to be performed was *The Wonder: A Woman Keeps a Secret,* a popular comedy written by Susanna Centlivre in 1714, for which James wrote a prologue and epilogue.[18] The second play, which was performed a few days later, was *The Chances,* a sixteenth-century play by John Fletcher, which had recently been adapted for modern audiences by the famous actor David Garrick.[19] It is not recorded whether Cassandra and Jane joined in with these theatricals but it is very likely that they did. Jane would, no doubt, have been delighted to oblige her charming cousin Eliza, whom she admired very much, by taking part. At the age of twelve she was old enough to join in and, although prone to shyness, she would not have felt uncomfortable among family and friends. If Cassandra took part Jane would have been anxious to do likewise. Perhaps Cassandra helped to design the theatre and make costumes.

The enthusiasm for theatricals continued into 1788, after Eliza's return to London. James organised the performance of the farce *The Tragedy, or, The Life and Death of Tom Thumb the Great,* written by Henry Fielding. This was acted to a small circle of friends in March. A private *Theatrical Exhibition* was also put on later that year. These performances made a lasting impression on the young Jane, who was inspired to try her own hand at writing dramatic sketches. She wrote two, one of which – *The Visit, A Comedy in Two Acts* – she dedicated to her brother James adding that she hoped the sketch would afford him 'some amusement ... which was the end in view when it was first composed by your Humble Servant, the Author.' Jane used her memories of the family theatricals when she wrote *Mansfield Park,* in which much of the action revolves around the amateur performances put on by the young members of the Bertram family and their friends.

Another pastime enjoyed by the family was the writing of charades and conundrums. In *Personal Aspects of Jane Austen* Mary Augusta Austen-Leigh imagined

> ... a family group gathered round the fireside ... to enliven the long evenings of a hundred years ago by merry verses and happy, careless inventions of the moment, such as flowed without difficulty from the lively minds and ready pens of those amongst whom she [Jane] lived.[20]

Cassandra and Jane both composed charades and verses.

The year 1788 continued to be an eventful one for the Austens. In the summer Henry went up to St John's College, Oxford, on a Founders' Kin Scholarship. Eliza de Feuillide met Henry at Oxford soon after he arrived and noted how he had adopted the fashionable habit of powdering his hair in what she described as a 'very tonnish style.' James, who had recently been ordained a deacon and been awarded his M.A. degree, was a Fellow there. In July James was appointed curate of Stoke Charity, a small village in Hampshire, but remained at Oxford instead of taking up residence there.

Soon after Henry left for Oxford, Cassandra and Jane went with their parents on their first known visit to Kent, to see George

Austen's ninety-year-old uncle Francis. A childhood memory of Henry Austen's gives an idea of Francis Austen's appearance.

> All that I remember of him is, that he wore a wig like a Bishop, & a suit of light gray, ditto, coat, vest & hose. In his picture over the chimney [presumably at Steventon Rectory] the coat & vest had a narrow gold lace edging, about half an inch broad, but in my day he had laid aside the gold edging, though he retained a perfect identity of colour, texture & make to his life's end.[21]

While in Kent, Cassandra and Jane met some relatives who were known to them only by name. These included George's half-brother William, his wife Susannah and Philadelphia who lived at Seal. Philadelphia sent a letter to her brother describing the meeting. In this letter, dated 23 July 1788, Philadelphia makes an unfavourable comparison of the twelve-year-old Jane with her fifteen-year-old sister.

> Yesterday I began an acquaintance with my 2 female cousins, Austens. My uncle, aunt, Cassandra & Jane arrived at Mr. F. Austen's the day before. We dined with them there. As it's pure Nature to love ourselves I may be allowed to give the preference to the Eldest who is generally reckoned a most striking resemblance of me in features, complexion & manners... The youngest (Jane) is very like her brother Henry, not at all pretty & very prim, unlike a girl of twelve but it is hasty judgement which you will scold me for. My aunt has lost several fore-teeth which makes her look old: my uncle is quite white-haired, but looks vastly well: all in high spirits & disposed to be pleased with each other.[22]

A little later Philadelphia added these further comments to the letter.

> I continue to admire my amiable likeness the best of the two in every respect: she keeps up conversation in a very sensible & pleasing manner. Yesterday they all spent the day with us, &

> the more I see of Cassandra the more I admire [her]. Jane is whimsical and affected.[23]

While Philadelphia was summing up her cousins, Jane was undoubtedly making her own assessment of her. As a budding author Jane was developing a habit of observing the behaviour, mannerisms, foibles and weaknesses of others. She was curious about the people she met, and was storing up her observations for use as material for her writing.

On their way home from Kent the Austens stopped in London to see Philadelphia Hancock, Eliza and Hastings, who were staying in Orchard Street, Westminster. This was probably the first time Cassandra and Jane visited the capital. Eliza later described the meeting in a letter to Philadelphia Walter, '… he (George) appeared more amiable than ever to me. What an excellent & pleasing man he is; I love him most sincerely as indeed I do all the family.'[24] Soon after the Austens' visit, Philadelphia, her daughter and grandson returned to France.

It was around this time that Jane became close to Anne Lefroy, the wife of the rector of Ashe. They became friends despite the fact that Mrs Lefroy was twenty-five years older than Jane. They had a shared interest in English literature, particularly poetry. According to Mrs Lefroy's brother Samuel Egerton Brydges, a poet and antiquarian bibliographer, who had moved into the rectory at Deane to be near his sister and her family:

> She had an exquisite taste for poetry, and could almost repeat the chief English poets by heart, especially Milton, Pope, Collins, Gray and the poetical passages of Shakespeare.[25]

Anne Lefroy, who wrote poetry herself, encouraged Jane in her writing. Jane became very attached to her older friend and, according to her niece Caroline Austen, regarded her as 'a perfect model of gracefulness and goodness'.[26] In a sign of the maturity of her relationship with Cassandra, Jane's close friendship with Anne Lefroy did not appear to come between her and her sister. Cassandra would have been pleased that Jane had found a friend who shared her interest in literature and also enjoyed writing.

At the end of 1788 Frank Austen completed his training at the Royal Naval Academy at Portsmouth and embarked on his naval career. He had worked hard at the academy and attracted the attention of the Lords of the Admiralty, with the result that he was marked out for early promotion. He left the academy at the age of fourteen and on 23 December he set sail for the East Indies aboard HMS *Perseverance*. He joined this frigate as a Volunteer, the first step on the naval career ladder, to learn the practical skills of seamanship.[27] Before his departure George Austen set out his advice to his son in a *Manuscript for the Use of Mr. F. W Austen*. This made such an impression on the young Frank that he treasured it for the rest of his long life, and it was found among his papers after his death. This memorandum provides an interesting insight into the moral values and duties that George Austen taught his children, and the behaviour he expected of them. The following excerpt gives an idea of George's own character as well as showing him as an affectionate, caring and interested father, who was always there to advise and encourage his children.

> Your behaviour, as a member of society, to the individuals around you may be also of great importance to your future well-doing, and certainly will to your present happiness and comfort. You may either by a contemptuous, unkind and selfish manner create disgust and dislike; or by affability, good humour and compliance, become the object of esteem and affection; which of these very opposite paths 'tis your interest to pursue I need not say.
>
> The little world, of which you are going to become an inhabitant, will occasionally have it in their power to contribute no little share to your pleasure or pain; to conciliate therefore their goodwill, by every honourable method, will be the part of a prudent man. Your commander and officers will be most likely to become your friends by a respectful behaviour to themselves, and by an active and ready obedience to orders. Good humour, an inclination to oblige and the carefully avoiding every appearance of selfishness, will infallibly secure you the regards of your own mess and of all your equals. With your inferiors perhaps you will have but little intercourse, but when it

does occur there is a sort of kindness they have a claim on you for, and which, you may believe me, will not be thrown away on them. Your conduct, as it respects yourself, chiefly comprehends sobriety and prudence. The former you know the importance of to your health, your morals and your fortune. I shall therefore say nothing more to enforce the observance of it. I thank God you have not at present the least disposition to deviate from it. Prudence extends to a variety of objects. Never any action of your life in which it will not be your interest to consider what she directs! She will teach you the proper disposal of your time and the careful management of your money, – two very important trusts for which you are accountable. She will teach you that the best chance of rising in life is to make yourself as useful as possible, by carefully studying everything that relates to your profession, and distinguishing yourself from those of your own rank by a superior proficiency in nautical acquirements.

I have nothing to add but my blessing and best prayers for your health and prosperity, and to beg you would never forget you have not upon earth a more disinterested and warm friend than,

Your truly affectionate father,

Geo. Austen[28]

Less than a year after starting his career Frank was promoted to Midshipman.

George Austen cared just as much about his daughters as his sons. As they were always with him and not out in the world of work, however, they would not have needed his advice in the same way. George was also very close to and supportive of his daughters, and did his best for them.

The Austens were joined for Christmas 1788 by Edward and Jane Cooper. The gathered company put on two theatrical productions. The plays performed were *The Sultan,* a farce by Isaac Bickerstaff, in which the main role was played by Jane Cooper, and *High Life Below Stairs,* another farce by the lesser-known James Townley.[29] These plays marked the end of the Austen family theatricals. This may have been due to the absence of Eliza, who had played such a leading part in managing and acting in them, and the fact that James, the other leading light, now turned his literary talents in another direction. In January 1789 he began to publish a weekly magazine named *The Loiterer* for the students and lecturers of Oxford University, about life there at the end of the eighteenth century. This magazine was in the style of *The Spectator* and *The Rambler,* the satirical papers published by Addison and Steele. Its aim was the same – to reform by ridicule. James edited and wrote most of the articles for the magazine, with contributions from his brother Henry and his cousin Edward Cooper, who was also a student at the university, and other undergraduates. The magazine was published every week until James finally left Oxford a year later. It is believed that Jane made a contribution to the magazine, as a letter signed 'Sophia Sentiment' is written in the same burlesque style she used in some of her early writing.[30]

Jane was still busy writing her *Juvenilia*; two works probably dating from around the turn of the year 1788–9 were *Henry and Eliza*, a playful novel dedicated to Jane Cooper, and *The Visit,* a short two-act play, dedicated to James Austen. Jane's characters were frequently named after family members.

In the spring of 1789 new tenants moved into Deane Rectory, which had been empty since Samuel Egerton Brydges moved out some months previously. George Austen's new tenants were Mrs Martha Craven Lloyd, the widow of the Reverend Noyes (or Nowis) Lloyd, late incumbent of Emborne, in Berkshire, and her two daughters Martha and Mary. A third daughter Eliza had married her cousin Fulwar Craven Fowle, who was George Austen's former pupil. Cassandra and Jane became friends with the Lloyd sisters, and were particularly close to Martha. Both Martha and Mary later married into the Austen family and played an important part in the lives of the Austen sisters.

Jane's literary output continued. Her next pieces were *the Adventures of Mr. Harley,* an extremely brief story, and *Jack and Alice*, a comic novella parodying the conventional polite novel. These were both dedicated to her brother Frank and sent to him on board HMS *Perseverance*. Jane continued to write her works neatly into manuscript notebooks and these two pieces went into the first volume. *Volume the Second* was written in a notebook given to Jane by her father, who supported and encouraged her in her writing from her earliest endeavours.

The first item in the second volume was *Love and Freindship* [sic], a novel in letter form parodying the contemporary romantic novel. Its subtitle was *Deceived in Freindship and Betrayed in Love*. The misspelling of the word 'Friendship' in the title was one of many in this story and in other works by Jane. Spelling was not her strong point and she had particular difficulty in remembering when to put 'i' before 'e'. *Love and Freindship* was dedicated to 'Madame la Comtesse de Feullide', who had returned to England with her mother and her son Hastings, who was in poor health. They may well have visited their relatives at Steventon before Eliza took her son to Margate for the benefit of the sea air and bathing in sea water, which was believed to have healing properties, especially in winter!

These works were written in the private sitting room upstairs in the rectory, and were shared with her sister before being read to the rest of the family. Cassandra's enjoyment and praise of Jane's writing was all the encouragement she needed to continue. Jane's *Juvenilia* provides a foretaste of the themes and style developed in her later work, and was originally written to amuse and entertain herself and her family. Jane's nephew described these early works as 'of a slight and flimsy texture' and generally intended to be 'nonsensical' but, he added, that 'the nonsense has much spirit in it.'[31]

It was probably around this time, in 1790, that Jane filled in the specimen pages in the Steventon parish marriage register. George Austen must have brought the register home from the church and Jane amused herself by inserting, in her beautiful, neat handwriting, some fictitious entries. These included an entry for the publication of banns between Henry Frederic Howard Fitzwilliam of London and Jane Austen of Steventon, and a record of the marriage of Edmund Arthur William Mortimer of Liverpool and Jane Austen of Steventon. Fitzwilliam and Mortimer were probably figments of Jane's imagination rather than real men. This bit of fun shows that the fifteen-year-old Jane's thoughts were turning to romance and the main ambition of all girls of her class – to meet and marry an eligible man. Cassandra had already reached the age when she would be expected to 'come out' into society and enter the highly competitive marriage market.

4

STEVENTON

1790–1793

The following few years were eventful ones for the Austen family. In April 1790 James became curate of Overton, a village 3 miles from Steventon. He was soon part of the local community and began to hunt with the Kempshott pack. It was while living at Overton that James met the young woman who was to become his first wife. Anne Mathew, who was five years older than James, was the daughter of General Edward Mathew and his wife Jane, who lived at the Old Manor House in the nearby village of Laverstoke. General Mathew was a former Governor of Grenada and Commander-in-Chief of the British West Indies as well as equerry to George III from 1762 to 1776. Anne, who was one of three sisters, was later described by Jane as having 'large dark eyes and a good deal of nose'.[1]

James was not the only Austen who met his future spouse around this time. In March 1791 Edward became engaged to Elizabeth Bridges, who was a neighbour and a member of his social circle in Kent. Elizabeth was one of the thirteen children of Sir Brook Bridges, the 3rd baronet, and his wife Fanny, whose home was Goodnestone Park, Wingham, near Canterbury. Sir Brook was one of the many wealthy landowners of Kent. Elizabeth had been educated at a famous boarding school for daughters of the aristocracy and gentry, known as the 'Ladies Eton', which was located in Queen Square, London.[2] A miniature portrait by the artist Richard Cosway reveals that Elizabeth was a beautiful, fair-skinned young lady with striking eyes, a perfect complexion and curly hair. The engagement was a source of much delight to members of both families, including Cassandra and Jane, who were very pleased to hear of their brother's love match. In later years Elizabeth became close to Cassandra. Two of Elizabeth's sisters became engaged at the same time as she did, and their mother wrote to her relative Mrs Fielding, excitedly informing her of the news. The following paragraph is taken from this letter.

> We had for some time observed a great attachment between Mr. Austin [sic] (Mr. Knight's Relation) and our dear Elizth; and Mr. Knight has, in the handsomest manner, declared his entire approbation of it; but as they are both very young he wish'd it not to take place immediately, and as it will not suit him to give up much at present, their Income will be small, and they must be contented to live in the Country, which I think will be no hardship to either party, as they have no high Ideas, and it is a greater satisfaction to us than if she was to be thrown upon the world in a higher sphere, young and inexperienced as she is. He is a very sensible, amiable young man, and I trust and hope there is every prospect of Happiness to all parties in their union.[3]

George Austen's uncle and benefactor Francis died at his home in Sevenoaks in June 1791, at the advanced age of ninety-three. Francis, who had done so much to help his orphaned nephew as a child and presented him with the living of Deane, did not forget him in his will. He was left £500,[4] a considerable sum of money for George who, although well-off compared to many country clergymen, had always struggled to make ends meet.

In July 1791 twelve-year-old Charles Austen, Cassandra's and Jane's 'own particular little brother', left home to enter the Royal Naval Academy at Portsmouth, following in the footsteps of his older brother. Frank had taken notice of his father's thoughtful advice and was making excellent progress in the navy. In November 1791 he was transferred from HMS *Perseverence* to HMS *Minerva,* remaining in the East Indies. Frank sent regular letters to his family. His sisters were always eager to hear his news and were proud of his achievements; they were very fond of their affectionate and warm-hearted brother. Two items of Jane's *Juvenilia, Jack and Alice* and *The Adventures of Mr Harley,* were dedicated to Frank in 1791,[5] indicating her admiration and esteem for him. Jane also made a reference to him in her work *The History of England,* suggesting that he would one day equal the achievements and fame of his namesake Sir Francis Drake.

In 1791 Jane finished writing *The History of England from the reign of Henry 4th to the death of Charles 1st. By a Partial, Prejudiced and Ignorant Historian.* This was a spoof on Goldsmith's *History of England,* which George Austen had used in the teaching of his daughters. Jane's version had a pro-Stuart bias and presented English history as a tragedy, with Mary Queen of Scots as a heroine. As with Jane's earlier writing, Cassandra took an interest in this book from the beginning and Jane asked her to illustrate it. The finished book was dedicated to her.[6]

When the last of their brothers left home to make his way in the world, Cassandra and Jane remained in the large rectory with just their parents for company. The rectory, which had once been home to a large and noisy household of Austens and boy pupils, must have seemed eerily quiet and empty. Like all girls of their social class, the Austen sisters had grown up knowing that their future lay in the private domestic sphere and that finding a husband to support them was their only realistic ambition in life. However well-prepared they were for this future, it could not have been easy for these intelligent young women, whose horizons had been widened by the academic education they had received, to be financially dependent on their father. For this reason they had to live with their parents until such time as suitable husbands came along, which was by no means a certainty at a time when there were not enough eligible young men to go around. Fortunately, Cassandra and Jane had a happy home life with absorbing interests and duties to occupy them, both inside the home and outside, among their father's parishioners.

They could also look forward to hearing about their brothers in their letters and when they returned home on visits. Events in their brothers' lives were to have an impact on Cassandra and Jane, and broaden their interests beyond the narrow confines of Steventon and rural north Hampshire.

The first of these events was the marriage of Edward and Elizabeth on 27 December 1791, at Goodnestone, in Kent. They were married in a double ceremony with Elizabeth's sister Sophia who married William Deedes of Sandling. Edward and Elizabeth moved into a small country house called Rowling, which belonged to the Bridges family, and was not far from Goodnestone Park. Jane commemorated the marriages of the three Bridges sisters who married in 1791 in her story *The Three Sisters,* which she dedicated to Edward.[7] The marriage of Edward and Elizabeth was the beginning of Cassandra's and Jane's association with Kent, which was to give them an insight into the lives of the English aristocracy and would provide Jane with material for her future novels. Cassandra paid her first visit to Rowling in the summer of 1792.

Cassandra's and Jane's friends Mary and Martha Lloyd and their mother moved out of Deane Rectory in January 1792. George Austen needed the rectory for James, who was to become his curate, a post he was to hold in addition to that of vicar of Sherborne St John, to which he had been appointed the previous September. The Lloyds moved to the little village of Ibthorpe in Hampshire. The Austen sisters were sad to see their close friends leave and Jane made a little 'housewife' for Mary as a parting gift. A 'housewife' was the name given to a fabric holdall containing a small sewing kit. In a tiny pocket Jane placed a scrap of paper on which she had written the following rhyme;

This little bag, I hope, will prove
To be not vainly made;
For should you thread and needles want,
It will afford you aid.

And, as we are about to part
'Twill serve another end:
For when you look upon this bag,
You'll recollect your Friend.
Jan[y] 1792 [8]

Cassandra and Jane promised to write to their friends regularly and visit them in their new home whenever they could.

A few months later, on the 23 March, James Austen married Anne Mathew at Laverstoke, in a ceremony conducted by George Austen. The couple moved into Deane Rectory, James's birthplace, and he commenced work as his father's curate. James, like his father, was a diligent clergyman with a genuine vocation for the Church. General Mathew gave his daughter and son-in-law a generous allowance of £100[9] a year which, added to James' income of £200 a year, enabled him to keep a pack of hounds, so that he could continue hunting, and to buy a carriage for his wife.

In the summer of that year Eliza de Feuillide and her son arrived at Steventon Rectory, in need of comfort and support. Eliza had not long lost her mother, after months of nursing her through breast cancer. Mother and daughter had been inseparable and Eliza was devastated at her loss. The Comte de Feuillide, who had been in England to support his wife, had returned to France when revolution broke out. The Comte had been warned that if he did not return to France immediately he would be deemed an émigré and his estates would be confiscated.[10] It was too dangerous for Eliza and Hastings to accompany him, as the Reign of Terror was now established. Eliza sought comfort, therefore, with her relations at Steventon, who were anxious to ease her distress in any way they could. A letter to her cousin Philadelphia Walter provides an up-to-date description of the Austen family.

> Yours found me as You expected quietly settled at Steventon, in regard to which place and its inhabitants I will endeavour to answer all your enquiries as well as I can. In the first place then I have the real pleasure of informing You that our Dear Uncle & Aunt are both in perfect Health. The former looks uncommonly well, and in my opinion his likeness to My beloved Mother is stronger than ever. Often do I sit and trace her Features in his, till my Heart overflows at my Eyes. I always tenderly loved my Uncle, but I think he is now dearer to me than ever, as being the nearest and best beloved Relative of the never to be sufficiently regretted Parent I have lost; Cassandra & Jane are both very much grown (The latter is now taller than myself) and greatly improved as well in Manners as in Person both of which are now much more

> formed than when You saw them. They are I think equally sensible, and both so to a degree seldom met with, but still My Heart gives the preference to Jane, whose partiality to me, indeed requires a return of the same nature.[11]

Not long before Eliza had described her cousins as 'two of the prettiest girls in England'.[12] This suggests that Jane must have blossomed since Philadelphia Walter had described her as 'not at all pretty'.

Another relative arrived at Steventon Rectory that summer who was also in need of comfort. In June Mrs Austen's nephew and niece, Edward and Jane Cooper, had taken their father, who was in poor health, to the Isle of Wight in the hope that a change of air and scenery would be of benefit to him. While on holiday Jane met and became engaged to Captain Thomas Williams of the Royal Navy and an early wedding date was fixed. Unfortunately, the holiday did not lead to an improvement in Dr Cooper's health and in August, soon after their return to Sonning Rectory, he died suddenly. Jane's wedding was postponed and she arrived at Steventon Rectory to be looked after by the Austens.[13] Cassandra and Jane were grieved at the distress of their cousin, with whom they had enjoyed an affectionate relationship since their shared schooldays.

In October of that year the Austen sisters went to Ibthorpe to stay with the Lloyds. While there they met one of their father's former pupils, Thomas Craven Fowle, the younger son of Reverend Thomas Fowle, the vicar of Kintbury, in Berkshire. Tom, as he was called, was the brother of James Austen's close friend Fulwar Craven Fowle, the husband of Martha and Mary's sister Eliza. During their stay the Austen sisters got to know Tom, and he and Cassandra fell in love. Their courtship was brief and culminated in their engagement in December. Tom, who was eight years older than his fiancée, had recently been ordained and was expecting to be given one of a number of valuable livings in the gift of his cousin Lord Craven.[14] The engagement was not made known outside the family. This secrecy was possibly due to the fact that the couple could not marry until Tom had secured a better living or because Cassandra, being a very private person, did not like to draw attention to herself.

Cassandra was lucky to have met and fallen in love with Tom, as her chances of finding a suitable husband were limited because her father could not afford to give her a dowry.

In the same month as he became engaged, Tom Fowle officiated at the postponed wedding of Jane Cooper and Thomas Williams, which was held at Steventon Church. Cassandra and Jane were glad to see their cousin happily married after her recent bereavement. Edward Cooper, Cassandra and Jane were witnesses at the marriage ceremony. The newly married couple set up home in Ryde on the Isle of Wight.[15]

Despite her lack of a dowry it is not surprising that Cassandra, being an attractive young lady with a pleasing personality, found herself a suitable husband so quickly. Jane was also physically attractive with an engaging, but different, personality and temperament to her sister. A silhouette of Cassandra as a young woman is the only surviving evidence of her appearance and there is just one authenticated portrait of Jane as an adult, which was painted by her sister, but was said not to be a good likeness of her. There are, however, several descriptions of them. Both sisters were tall and slender and, as previously mentioned, both were said to be 'pretty' as young women. Cassandra had dark eyes and the same aquiline aristocratic nose as her mother. Jane had a round face with rather full cheeks, brown curly hair, a quite small but well-shaped nose and expressive hazel eyes. She had clear brown skin and was inclined to blush easily.

The sisters' different characters and temperaments complemented each other. Cassandra was calm, measured and kept her deeply felt feelings well hidden. The saying 'still waters run deep' could be used to describe her. Cassandra was also shrewd and sensible, and possessed good judgement. Although reserved, she had an easy manner and was easy to talk to. Jane, on the other hand, was spontaneous, demonstrative and less restrained than her sister. Her cheerfulness, liveliness and high spirits meant that she attracted more notice than Cassandra. Jane was also even-tempered. There was a saying in the Austen family that 'Cassandra had the merit of having her temper always under command, but that Jane had the happiness of a temper that never required to be commanded.'[16] Both sisters shared the family's sense of humour.

On 27 January 1793 Cassandra and Jane became aunts when Fanny Catherine was born at Rowling, to Edward and Elizabeth. Fanny was to be the first of a large family. Nearly three months later, on 15 April, Jane Anna Elizabeth (known as Anna) was born to James Austen's wife Anne, following a difficult pregnancy. Mrs Austen got out of bed in the middle of the night and walked along the lane to Deane Rectory to attend her daughter-in-law during her confinement.[17] Both Fanny and Anna were to become close to their aunts, who took their roles seriously and excelled in them. Many years later Jane wrote a letter to another niece, who had just become an aunt. The words she used on this occasion sum up how both she and Cassandra felt about being aunts:

> Now that you are become an Aunt, you are a person of some consequence & must excite great Interest whatever You do. I have always maintained the importance of Aunts as much as possible, & I am sure of your doing the same now.[18]

Jane wrote some humorous verses to her new nieces to mark their births. She wrote *Opinions and Admonitions on the Conduct of Young Women* for Fanny and *Miscellanious* [sic] *Morsels* for Anna.[19] In dedicating her verses for Anna, Jane wrote '...if you seriously attend to them. You will derive from them very important Instructions with regard to your Conduct in Life.'[20] Cassandra's and Jane's many nephews and nieces would become a source of great delight and interest to them.

Events in the Austens' wider family at this time included the marriage of Mrs Austen's nephew Edward Cooper to Caroline Lybbe Powys. Edward became curate of Harpsden in Oxfordshire, the living once held by his grandfather Thomas Leigh. Cassandra and Jane were never as close to Edward as they were to his sister and, in later life, Jane found him rather irritating. They always took an interest in him and his family, however, and remained in touch with him.

In the spring of 1793 Henry Austen, who had graduated the year before and stayed on at St John's College as a Fellow, became a Lieutenant in the Oxfordshire Militia. Henry had originally planned to follow his father and brother James into the Church, but he was not yet old enough to be ordained. He decided instead to join the militia and help in the defence of his country.[21] It was a time of national danger, as France had recently declared war on Great Britain, and many young men were joining up to fight the enemy. The militia regiments were responsible for home defence when the regular army was abroad; they were not called upon to serve abroad themselves. The militia was in almost permanent existence during this period. Each county had to provide a quota of officers and men to serve in it. The Commander-in-Chief was usually a landowner of the county and officers came from the gentry. The Oxfordshire Militia was based in East Anglia protecting the exposed eastern coastline of England. Henry managed, for several years, to combine his military duties with his college Fellowship. A letter written by Eliza de Feuillide to her cousin Philadelphia Walter describes him at this time:

> Henry is now rather more than Six Foot high I believe. He also is much improved, and is certainly endowed with uncommon Abilities, which indeed seem to have been bestowed, tho' in a different way, upon each Member of this Family.[22]

Although married, Eliza enjoyed flirting with her male cousins. She had a soft spot for her handsome and talented – though as events were to reveal, somewhat unstable – cousin Henry.

Frank Austen, who was a much steadier character than his brother Henry, returned home in December 1793 after five years' absence, to await his next posting. Frank, now a mature and confident young man, had been promoted to the rank of Lieutenant the year before. His nephew later remembered him as a dignified man of 'great firmness of character, with a strong sense of duty.'[23] Cassandra and Jane were pleased to have their brother home again and to hear about his life at sea. Frank was a kind and affectionate brother, with a warm heart and a good sense of humour. Jane remembered her conversations with Frank about his naval career and later used some of this information in her novels.

Around this time the Austen sisters went to stay with a cousin of their father's, John Butler-Harrison, and his wife Elizabeth, who lived in St Mary's, a suburb of Southampton. Cassandra and Jane attended a ball at the Assembly Rooms at the Dolphin Inn while staying there,[24] which marked Jane's 'coming out' into society. It is not known when Cassandra 'came out', but it would probably have been shortly before Jane did; a young lady was not allowed to enter society before an older sister. Coming out was an important rite of passage for all young ladies of the gentry and aristocracy; it was the first step on the path to finding a husband. Jane's first engagement after entering society was the annual ball held by Lord Portsmouth at his home, Hurstbourne Park. The sisters enjoyed their increasingly busy social lives, especially Jane, who became very fond of dancing, as her nephew James Edward noted in his *Memoir.*

> There can be no doubt that Jane herself enjoyed dancing, for she attributes this taste to her favourite heroines; in most of her works, a ball or a private dance is mentioned, and made of importance.[25]

Throughout the early 1790s Jane continued to write in the privacy of the sitting room she shared with her sister. Cassandra encouraged Jane, and read and listened to the early evidence of her talent. By June 1793 Jane's *Juvenilia* was completed. The final piece, *Ode to Pity*, was dedicated to Cassandra, making a total of four pieces dedicated to her. Jane's three copy books contained a considerable quantity of work. James Edward noted in his *Memoir* that the later pieces of the *Juvenilia* marked a development in his aunt's progress as a writer:

> But between these childish effusions, and the composition of her living works, there intervened another stage of her progress, during which she produced some stories, not without merit, but which she never considered worthy of publication. During this preparatory period her mind seems to have been working in a very different direction from that into which it ultimately settled. Instead of presenting faithful copies of nature, these tales were generally burlesques, ridiculing the improbable events and exaggerated sentiments which she had met with in sundry silly romances... It would seem as if

> she were first taking note of all the faults to be avoided, and curiously considering how she ought **not** to write before she attempted to put forth her strength in the right direction.[26]

James Edward also observed that 'however puerile the matter' Jane's *Juvenilia* was 'always composed in pure simple English, quite free from the over-ornamented style which might be expected from so young a writer'.[27]

In some of the longer works of this period, Jane moved away from nonsensical stories mocking contemporary novels to more realistic stories of eighteenth-century life. With their domestic settings, themes of courtship, love and marriage, as well as their clever drawing of character, they provided a foretaste of Jane's mature works. Jane was moving towards writing domestic novels – the same genre as those by Fanny Burney and Maria Edgeworth, which she and Cassandra enjoyed reading.

The most significant literary achievement of the eighteenth century was the invention of the novel. There was a huge demand for novels of all genres, despite the fact that the novel was regarded by some as an inferior form of literature. To cater for this demand, most towns and watering-places had libraries. Mrs Austen subscribed to a library in Steventon;[28] so that she and her daughters had a ready supply of novels and other literature. Many of the novels that filled libraries were written by women, as writing was one of the few occupations deemed acceptable for them. It must have been a source of great pleasure and satisfaction to George Austen to see his clever daughter putting her knowledge of English history and literature to such good use. How gratifying for him to observe her budding writing talent and, particularly, to see her learning from such great writers as Richardson, that excellent delineator of character, as she developed her own writing style. The many hours he had devoted to her academic education had not been wasted.

5

STEVENTON

1794–1797

In January 1793 Louis XVI of France was guillotined by the revolutionaries. The Austen family were worried about events across the Channel because Eliza's husband, the Comte de Feuillide, was in the centre of the revolution in Paris. They had good reason to be concerned as the Comte was arrested a year later on a bogus charge of suborning witnesses in the case of his friend the Marquise de Malboeuf, who was also under arrest. He was accused of conspiring against the Republic and both he and the Marquise went to the guillotine.[1]

The whole family were extremely upset at the fate of the Comte, and were very anxious about Eliza. She had now lost both her mother and her husband, and was left with a sickly child to bring up alone. Jane was particularly distressed by this turn of events, which haunted her for many years, and resulted in her developing a deep hatred of Republican France. This tragedy brought the full horrors of the French Revolution directly into the lives of the Austen family; until then the political turmoil in France had not really affected them. In the same month in which the Comte was executed, Republican France declared war on Great Britain and Holland. Frank and Charles Austen both became involved in this long war, which became a cause of much concern for their family.

Visits to relatives in other parts of the country gave Cassandra and Jane an occasional change of scenery and a break from their normal routine. In the summer of 1794 they travelled to Adlestrop in Gloucestershire to stay with their kind uncle Thomas Leigh, who used to visit them at Reading Abbey School, and his wife Mary. A neighbour who met them during their stay described them as 'very charming young women'.[2] Cassandra and Jane enjoyed the freedom of going away without their parents, but this was not always easy as it was not considered either appropriate or safe for young women to use public transport without either a man or an older woman as escort. When they travelled together the sisters were reasonably safe, but an escort was still advisable.

The trip to Adlestrop was followed later that summer by a visit of several weeks' duration to Edward and Elizabeth in Kent. On this occasion the sisters went to Kent together, but they usually went separately thereafter. Staying with Edward was always a great pleasure because their kind, attentive and affectionate brother was good company. Edward had a lively, fun-loving side to his personality and was a thoughtful host who took trouble to ensure that his guests had an enjoyable time. One of the highlights of this visit for Cassandra and Jane was meeting their new nephew Edward, who was then three months old.

Cassandra had, by this time, developed a close bond with her sister-in-law and always looked forward to seeing her, but Jane did not share the same closeness with her. Anna Austen, some years later, observed that Elizabeth 'much preferred' Cassandra and thought that this was because 'a little talent went a long way with the Goodneston Bridgeses of that period, & much must have gone a long way too far.'[3] By 'talent' Anna was probably referring to Jane's cleverness, as her literary talent remained a secret during Elizabeth's lifetime. Elizabeth may also have been put off by Jane's quick wit and ironic sense of humour, which were not to everyone's taste.

While in Kent, the Austen sisters met their brother's friend Edward Taylor of Bifrons Park, near Canterbury, for whom Jane seems to have developed romantic feelings. She described him as having 'beautiful dark eyes'[4] and, when passing Bifrons two years later, Jane 'contemplated with a melancholy pleasure, the abode of Him, on whom I once fondly doated.'[5]

Now that both her daughters had 'come out' into society, Mrs Austen accompanied them to social events. Young ladies had to be chaperoned on such occasions, either by their mother or another older female relative. This was one of the many rules that governed the behaviour of young unmarried women in order to protect their reputations. The chaperones at balls and dances chatted among themselves, and played cards, while they kept an eye on the dancing. Nothing went unnoticed by the vigilant chaperones, whose presence ensured that the code of conduct governing the behaviour of young people on the lookout for potential marriage partners was observed.

Cassandra and Jane began to attend the county balls, which were held at Basingstoke Assembly Rooms once a month, on a Thursday evening, through the season. Balls were held in public assembly rooms at the time of the full moon, when travelling was safer. Mrs Austen once composed a rhyme describing a ball that Cassandra and Henry attended when Jane was away from home. This is interesting to read as an example of Mrs Austen's habit of expressing herself in humorous rhyme and also for the indication it gives of the numerous and varied members of the local nobility and gentry who formed the Austen family's extensive social circle. Jane must have been much amused by this rhyme, which reads as follows:

> I send you here a list of all
> The company who graced the ball
> Last Thursday night at Basingstoke;
> There were but six and thirty folk;
> Altho' the Evening was so fine.
> First then, the couple from the Vine;
> Next, Squire Hicks and his fair spouse –
> They came from Mr Bramston's house,
> With Madam, and her maiden Sister;
> (Had she been absent, who'd have miss'd her?)
> And fair Miss Woodward, that sweet singer,
> For Mrs Bramston liked to bring her;
> With Alethea too, and Harriet
> They came in Mrs Hicks' chariot;
> Perhaps they did, I am not certain.
> Then there were four good folk from Worting;

For with the Clerks there came two more
Some friends of theirs, their name was Hoare
With Mr, Mrs, Miss Lefroy
Came Henry Rice, that pleasant boy;
And lest a title they should want,
There came Sir Colebrook and Sir Grant.
Miss Eyre of Sherfield and her Mother;
One Miss from Dummer and her brother.
The Mother too as chaperon;
Mr and Mrs Williamson;
Charles Powlett and his pupils twain;
Small Parson Hasker, great Squire Lane;
And Bentworth's rector, with his hat,
Unwillingly he parts from that.
Two Misses Davies with two friends –
And thus my information ends.
P.S. It would have been a better dance
But for the following circumstance –
The Dorchesters, so high in station,
Dined out that day, by invitation,
At Heckfield Heath with Squire Le Fevre;
Methinks it was not quite so clever
For one Subscriber to invite
Another, on the Assembly night;
But 'twas to meet a General Donne,
His Lordship's old companion;
And as the General would not stay
They could not fix another Day.[6]

The Austen sisters also paid social calls on friends and neighbours, sometimes accompanied by their mother. They were often returning calls paid to them. It was social etiquette to return calls received from others as soon as possible and, if the person was not at home, to leave a calling card.

The people with whom the Austens mixed were traditional Tories, like themselves – mostly the sort of cultured, well-connected people who shared their values and traditions. The Austen family's extensive social circle consisted of the type of large landowners and lesser gentry who feature in Jane's novels. The former included Lord Dorchester of Kempshott Park and Lord Bolton of Hackwood Park, both near Basingstoke, and Lord Portsmouth, a former pupil of George Austen who lived at Hurstbourne Park, 5 miles from Andover. Also in their social circle were William Chute and his family of The Vyne, a grand country house near Basingstoke. Chute, the Tory M.P. for Hampshire and Master of the Vyne Hunt was, with his florid complexion and powdered wig, the archetypal image of a Tory squire. Their gentry friends included the Bramston, Mildmay, Heathcote and Bigg-Wither families.[7] The three daughters of Lovelace Bigg-Wither became close friends of the Austen sisters. Jane occasionally went to the Basingstoke balls with Catherine Bigg (only the male members of her family used the double-barrelled surname), usually when Cassandra was away, and stayed the night at Manydown House, her friend's home.

The Austens also mixed with members of the *nouveaux riches*, who had risen up the social scale into the gentry through trade and business. William and James Holder of Ashe Park, not far from Steventon, who had made their fortunes in the West Indies, fitted into this category. Friends belonging to the lesser gentry included the Digweeds, Harwoods and Terrys of Steventon, Deane and the nearby village of Dummer respectively.[8] Cassandra and Jane took an interest in these members of their local community, and kept up to date with events in their lives.

In 1794 Jane began work on a short story which she named *Lady Susan*. It was written in the popular letter form, with which Jane had been familiar since she started reading contemporary fiction. The story is about a cruel mother who tries, but fails, to force her daughter into an unwanted marriage. The idea for the story is believed to have come from the sad tale, known to both Jane and Cassandra, of the unhappy childhood of Mrs Lloyd, mother of their friends Martha and Mary. Mrs Lloyd and her sisters were badly mistreated by their mother.[9] Jane never wrote such a sad story again; she made the conscious decision to write only on happy themes, as befitted her positive and cheerful personality. As she later explained in *Mansfield Park,* Jane decided not 'to dwell on guilt and misery' – other writers could deal with such unpleasant matters.

George Austen realised early on that Jane had a talent for writing, and always encouraged and supported her. On 5 December 1794 he bought her a portable writing desk from a shop in Basingstoke, which was described in the sales particulars as 'a Small Mahogany Writing Desk with 1 long Drawer and Glass Ink Stand Compleat.'[10] The desk cost twelve shillings. Jane later took it with her whenever she went to stay in Kent.

George Austen may well have encouraged his daughter to develop her writing talent because he knew that her marriage prospects would be limited by his inability to provide her with a dowry. He may have thought that writing was Jane's best chance of acquiring an independent income if she failed to find a husband to support her. As previously mentioned, women made money from writing the books, especially novels, which filled the circulating libraries to be found in most towns and pleasure resorts.

Soon after completing *Lady Susan* Jane started work on *Elinor and Marianne*, an early version of the novel later published as *Sense and Sensibility*. This was the first of the novels that Jane described as 'pictures of domestic life in country villages'.[11] *Elinor and Marianne,* like *Lady Susan*, was written in letter form, but this was changed to a straightforward narrative by the time the novel had evolved into *Sense and Sensibility*.

As with all her other writing, this novel was written in the peace and quiet of Cassandra's and Jane's private sitting room, with her sister nearby – probably reading, drawing or sewing. Cassandra was the first person to read the novel, or listen to Jane reading it to her, as it progressed. She laughed over the comic scenes and characters, became involved in the plot and, probably, as she had with Jane's *Juvenilia*, made some helpful observations. Her sister's enjoyment of her work was all the encouragement Jane needed to keep writing.

The relationship between the characters Elinor and Marianne, two close and loving sisters, was central to their lives and the novel, just as the relationship between the Austen sisters was central to theirs. Jane drew on her deep emotional connection with Cassandra when she wrote this novel. There are some similarities between Elinor and Cassandra; they are both wise and sensible older sisters who kept their own emotions under control, and looked after and supported their sisters. Jane could not, however, be likened to the impulsive and over-emotional Marianne although she did, as will be seen, sometimes need guidance from her 'wiser and better' older sister.

Jane's fictional characters are so true to life that many readers have been tempted to surmise that they were real people. Her intention, however, as she clearly stated herself, was to create and not to reproduce. In his *Memoir* her nephew James Edward repudiated this accusation when he observed that 'She did not copy individuals, but she invested her own creations with individuality of character... Her own relations never recognised any individuals in her characters...' Jane herself said that she was 'too proud of my gentlemen to admit that they were only Mr A. or Colonel B'.[12]

Elinor and Marianne contains a number of scenes set in London, which are so detailed and topographically accurate that it is likely that Jane went there while she was writing this work. She may have gone to visit her cousin Eliza and observed London life and society for herself. By this time Jane was actively looking out for material to use in her writing and nothing missed her acute observation.

Cassandra and Jane continued to enjoy long walks in the countryside. If they were not busily occupied in their sitting room, they were most likely to be found in the country lanes around Steventon and Deane. They often walked as many as 6 miles in one day, if the weather was good. When the country lanes were muddy they wore wooden overshoes resembling clogs, called pattens, to lift their clothes out of the dirt. Only very wet weather, which Jane referred to as 'dirty weather', prevented them from going out. Jane was responsible for walking to the village of Popham, 2 miles away, to collect the family's post and Cassandra, no doubt, frequently went with her. As the sisters were nearly always together, they were often treated as a unit. George Austen was sometimes heard to ask, when his daughters disappeared on one of their long walks, 'Where are the girls? Are the girls gone out?'

The Austen family suffered another bereavement in May 1795 when James' wife Anne died suddenly. Anne had just finished eating a meal with her husband when she became ill. A doctor was called but he could do nothing to help her and she died a few hours later. The doctor thought the cause of death was probably a ruptured liver.[13] Anne was buried in the churchyard of St Nicholas' Church, Steventon and a memorial tablet was placed on the south side of the chancel.

Anna Austen, who was only two years old when her mother died, kept asking for her mama. James, who was trying to deal with his own grief, sent his daughter to Steventon Rectory to be comforted and cared for by her grandparents and aunts. Anna spent most of the next two years at Steventon and developed a strong, lasting closeness to both Cassandra and Jane. Anna loved listening to the stories her Aunt Jane made up to amuse her. A little cherry-wood chair was bought for her use, at the cost of half a crown.[14] In later life, Anna's only memory of her mother was of 'a tall and slender lady dressed in white.'[15]

Cassandra and Jane's Christian faith was central to their lives, and helped to sustain them when they were affected by adversities such as the death of a family member. They were both confirmed into the Anglican Church. The date of Cassandra's confirmation is not known, but it is thought that Jane was confirmed at the age of eighteen, as a prayer book still exists with her name written in it and the date 24 April 1794. The sisters attended services at their father's church twice every Sunday, with their mother and any brothers who were at home. The family also gathered in the rectory for prayers every day, including Sundays. Their daughters' strong faith was undoubtedly due to the example set by George and Cassandra Austen, as well as the moral and religious education they had received since early childhood.

In a description which also fits Cassandra, Henry Austen wrote that Jane was 'thoroughly religious and devout' and that 'her opinions accorded strictly, with those of the Established Church.'[16] Their deep faith was something else the sisters shared and which drew them close together. Jane expressed her beliefs and demonstrated her piety in a number of prayers that she wrote for her father to use in his services. One of these prayers, which still hangs on the wall of Steventon Church, contains the following lines:

> Give us almighty Father, so to pray as to deserve to be heard, to address thee with our hearts, as with our lips. Thou art everywhere present, from thee no secret can be hid. May the knowledge of this teach us to fix our thoughts on thee, with reverence and devotion that we pray not in vain.

Cassandra, not being inclined to reveal her deepest feelings, was unlikely to have expressed her beliefs openly.

The faith which underpinned their lives was reflected in their actions. As children the sisters accompanied their mother when she visited the needy of Steventon and Deane. As adults, like the daughters of other clergymen, they visited the poor and sick of their father's parish, and made and collected clothes for those who needed them.

Among the Steventon villagers helped by Cassandra and Jane were Betty Dawkins, Mary Hutchins, Mary Steevens, Elizabeth Kew, Elizabeth Staples and their families.[17] Jane later drew on her experience of visiting the poor when she created the chaotic, overcrowded conditions in which the Price family lived in *Mansfield Park*. This experience probably also inspired her concern for the poor, and the belief that they should be treated kindly and respectfully, which is expressed in *Emma*.

Since their engagement, Cassandra and Tom Fowle had kept in touch by letter and visits. They had waited a long time for him to be offered a better-paid living to enable them to marry. They were still waiting in the autumn of 1795 when a good opportunity arose for Tom to make some money. He was offered, and accepted, the position of private chaplain to his kinsman Lord Craven, who was the commanding officer of the 3rd Regiment of Foot.[18] In January 1796 Tom accompanied Lord Craven to the West Indies when his regiment was sent there as part of a military expedition led by Sir Ralph Abercromby. After he left Cassandra began to put together her trousseau and think about her wedding clothes but, apart from these preparations, life went on as usual.

The main source of information about the Austen sisters is Jane's surviving correspondence, which dates from January 1796 until a few weeks before she died. This correspondence consists of a considerable portion of her letters to Cassandra and some to other people. Jane's letters were so well written and interesting that her family and friends were always pleased to receive them.

Jane's letters to Cassandra provide an unfiltered insight into their lives and the things that mattered to them. As adults, the sisters spent weeks, and occasionally months, apart when they stayed at the homes of family members, usually their brothers Edward and Henry. As she was not always in the best of health, Mrs Austen liked to have one of her daughters at home with her, for company and to help run the household. For this reason the sisters rarely went away together and the only way to keep in contact was by letter. They exchanged letters every few days, providing a continuous commentary on what they were doing. As paper and postage were expensive, Jane occasionally followed the common practice of cross writing, when the writer turned the completed page around ninety degrees and wrote over it in the opposite direction. For the same reason she also rarely used paragraphs.

Jane's letters contain the sort of details lacking from the record of their earlier lives, which has been pieced together largely from family memoirs – most of which were written many years later – and the letters of other people. The same incisive wit, ironic humour and brilliant pen portraits that are found in her novels are also present in her letters. In both novels and letters Jane uses her pen to describe a person or a scene in the same way that an accomplished artist uses a few deft strokes of a brush.

The letters are written in a lively, chatty style and they reflect the writer's happy, positive outlook on life. They bring Cassandra up-to-date with news of family, friends and neighbours, as well as the minutiae of domestic life. Jane's letters also provide a fascinating insight into gentry life in late Georgian and Regency England. Jane occasionally makes cruel or unkind comments in her letters about neighbours and acquaintances. Her family always insisted that these comments were never intended to hurt. The sisters were so close and in tune with one another that they could write things that they could be certain would go no further. The following observations were made on the matter by William and Richard Austen-Leigh, Jane's great-nephew and his nephew, the authors of *Jane Austen, Her Life and Letters, A Family Record* –

> ... the correspondence was between sisters who knew, each of them, what the other was thinking, and could feel sure that nothing one might say would be misapprehended by the other; and the sort of freemasonry which results from such a situation adds to the difficulty of perfect comprehension by outsiders.[19]

A common observation about Jane's letters to her sister is that they make very few references to politics and national events, such as the Napoleonic Wars. This was because the purpose of Jane's letters was to convey family news and therefore only dealt with matters of relevance to family members and home life. Other matters are only mentioned when they concern family and friends. Writing anything irrelevant to the purpose of the letters would have been a waste of precious paper. It was also not normal for women to discuss national and political affairs, as these were considered to be the preserve of men. If Jane and Cassandra had any political views, they would have shared the moderate Tory inclinations of the men of the family. The Tory party was the party of the English country gentleman and the establishment.

Regrettably, Jane's surviving letters to Cassandra are only part of one side of their correspondence and reveal only what happened when they were apart. Cassandra's half of the correspondence did not survive because, shortly before her death, she destroyed all her letters to her sister. She also destroyed some of Jane's letters to her and cut portions out of others. These were the parts which Cassandra, who was a very private person, did not want future generations of her family to read.

Some of the earliest surviving letters from Jane to Cassandra contain details of her first romantic attachment with a young man she met in December 1795. Jane had already attracted the admiration of a few local men, but had shown no interest in them. Tom Lefroy, however, was different. This shy, fair-haired young man was the nephew of the Austen family's friend the Reverend George Lefroy. Tom, who lived in Ireland, had recently been awarded a degree in law by Trinity College, Dublin. He was invited to Ashe Rectory for Christmas and New Year, and danced with Jane at three balls during his stay. It soon became obvious that the young couple were developing an affection for each other.

Cassandra, who was staying with her fiancé's family in Berkshire, found out about Jane's budding romance and became alarmed. Having inherited her mother's unerring common sense and sound judgement, Cassandra was worried that if Jane was not careful people may start to gossip about her. It was essential to observe the strict code that governed the behaviour of young people of marriageable age. If a couple danced together too often, instead of dancing with a number of different partners, and spent too much time together between dances, it could be assumed that they had reached an 'agreement'. A stain on the reputation of an unmarried woman could seriously harm her chances of finding a husband.[20]

Jane's chaperone at these balls could not have been very watchful, as it seems that she got rather carried away. Cassandra, who was also worried that her sister might get hurt, scolded her in a letter. Jane's reply, which clearly shows that she was aware of her inappropriate behaviour, contains the following paragraph:

> You scold me so much in the nice long letter which I have this moment received from you, that I am almost afraid to tell you how my Irish friend and I behaved. Imagine to yourself everything most profligate and shocking in the way of dancing and sitting down together. I **can** expose myself, however, only **once more**, because he leaves the country soon after next Friday, on which day we **are** to have a dance at Ashe after all. He is a very gentleman-like, good-looking, pleasant young man, I assure you. But as to our having ever met, except at the last three balls, I cannot say much; for he is so excessively laughed

> at about me at Ashe, that he is afraid of coming to Steventon, and ran away when we called on Mrs Lefroy a few days ago.[21]

In the second part of this letter Jane added:

> After I had written the above, we received a visit from Mr Tom Lefroy and his cousin George. The latter is really very well-behaved now; and, as for the other, he has but **one** fault, which time will, I trust, entirely remove – it is that his morning coat is a great deal too light. He is a very great admirer of Tom Jones [the eponymous hero of the novel by Henry Fielding] and therefore wears the same coloured clothes, I imagine, which **he** did when he was wounded.[22]

In her last letter on the subject, dated 14–15 January 1796, Jane told Cassandra that she would be meeting Tom the following night at a ball at Ashe. She rather intriguingly continued:

> I look forward with great impatience to it, as I rather expect to receive an offer from my friend in the course of the evening. I shall refuse him, however, unless he promises to give away his white Coat.[23]

The next day Jane added,

> At length the Day is come on which I am to flirt my last with Tom Lefroy, & when you receive this it will be over. – My tears flow as I write, at the melancholy idea.[24]

Cassandra was not the only person to have been alarmed, as the Lefroys had also noticed the growing attachment between Tom and Jane. Tom was an impecunious young man who was planning a career in the legal profession. His education was being paid for by a wealthy uncle, and the Lefroys feared that if he became engaged to a young lady without a dowry he would lose the support of his benefactor. The Lefroys therefore acted quickly to bring the romance to an end, and early in the new year Tom left Ashe Rectory earlier than expected.

When she heard of Tom's departure Cassandra was very relieved. Jane's light-hearted letters suggest that she did not really expect a proposal from him. There seems however to be an underlying sadness in her last letter and a suspicion that she really did shed tears when he left Ashe, despite her description of this attachment as no more than a flirtation and that she did not care for Tom. It was not long before Tom Lefroy met and married a wealthy heiress, which would seem to confirm that Jane's first romance was, indeed, halted because of her lack of a dowry. Tom went on to enjoy a glittering legal career, which culminated in his appointment as Lord Chief Justice of Ireland.

The only person who knew Jane's real feelings about Tom was Cassandra. If Jane was hurt Cassandra would have consoled her and made sure she kept her pain to herself, to avoid adding to any gossip she may have occasioned. Jane did not forget Tom quickly. Several references to him in her letters show that she was interested to hear about him for some years after they parted, but there is no record of her reaction to his marriage. Many years later Tom Lefroy's nephew was recorded as saying that his uncle had been in love with Jane but that 'it was a boyish love'. The story of Jane's first romantic attachment illustrates how her older and wiser sister protected and guided Jane even if, on this occasion, she did not seem to be prepared to listen.

It may have been Jane's flirtatious behaviour with Tom Lefroy that led to the accusation by Mrs Mitford, wife of a former rector of Ashe and mother of the author Mary Russell Mitford, that she was 'the prettiest, most affected husband-hunting butterfly' that she ever remembered. The Austen family always vehemently rejected this accusation, pointing out that Mrs Mitford left Ashe when Jane was only ten years old.[25] The Mitfords remained in the area, however, and Mrs Mitford may well have witnessed Jane's behaviour or heard reports of it from other people.

Both of Cassandra and Jane's sailor brothers were progressing through the ranks of the navy. There are many references to their careers in Jane's letters. After arriving home at the end of 1793, Frank remained there until his next posting, which came three months later. For the next two years he was based in English waters and was able to see his family more often. In September 1796 Frank was appointed commander of HMS *Triton,* a new frigate, which was launched at Deptford.[26] His steady character and strong sense of duty contributed to his rapid progression.

After leaving the Royal Naval Academy at the age of fifteen Charles became a Midshipman on HMS *Daedalus* under the command of Captain Thomas Williams, his cousin Jane's husband. He then served under Williams on HMS *Unicorn,* which, in the summer of 1796, was involved in a battle with the French ship *La Tribune*.[27] The *Unicorn* was victorious and her captain was rewarded with a knighthood. Cassandra and Jane were pleased for both Charles and Williams, whom Jane thereafter referred to as 'his royal highness Sir Thomas Williams'.[28]

In August 1796 Jane went to Kent without her sister. She was accompanied on the journey by her brothers Edward and Frank. The journey was broken by a stop in London, which Jane described memorably as 'this scene of Dissipation and vice'.[29] As usual the sisters corresponded throughout the period of their separation and Jane's letters contain a continuous report on her stay. The weather in Kent was insufferably hot and Jane complained of being 'in a continual state of Inelegance'.[30] In a letter dated 5 September Jane wrote:

> We dined at Goodnestone and in the Evening danced two Country Dances & the Boulangeries. – I opened the Ball with Edwd. Bridges; the other couples were Lewis Cage & Harriot, Frank & Louisa, Fanny & George ... We supped there, & walked home at night under the shade of two Umbrellas.[31]

By this time Edward and Elizabeth had three children – Fanny, Edward and the latest addition George, who was born the previous year. The presence of the children added to the pleasure of Jane's visit. She informed Cassandra that she had 'taken little George once in my arms since I have been here, which I thought very kind'.[32] George, who as a toddler referred to himself as 'itty Dordy', became a great favourite of Jane's.

Jane was anxious to hear about a ball her sister was due to attend in her absence, and she wrote that she hoped 'to receive so long & minute an account of every particular that I shall be tired of reading it.'[33] Jane, who wanted to be at home by the end of September, was faced with a dilemma when Frank had to leave Kent earlier than planned on suddenly receiving his posting to HMS *Triton*. Jane had been relying on Frank to take her home and she was afraid that her return would be delayed. Much as she enjoyed this and later visits to Kent she was glad to be taken home, presumably by Edward, and to be reunited with Cassandra. Their need to be in continuous contact when separated indicates the strength of their mutual dependence and their exceptionally close bond.

In October, soon after returning home from Kent, Jane began writing *First Impressions*, the original version of *Pride and Prejudice*. This novel was written, like her other works, in the privacy of the sitting rooms she shared with her sister. As with *Elinor and Marianne*, Cassandra was aware of the progress of the novel and, probably, made some helpful suggestions. At this stage no one else in the family knew that Jane was working on another novel, and would not know about it until it was completed.

A few weeks later, in November 1797, James Austen became engaged. He had been anxious for some time to find a second wife, partly because he wanted his daughter Anna to have a mother figure in her life. James had briefly courted his widowed cousin Eliza, but it seems that she never really considered marrying the serious, sometimes melancholy, James and was also put off by the fact that he was a clergyman. It is surprising that James ever considered that his flamboyant and pleasure-loving cousin would make him a suitable wife.

James then turned his attention to two women named Mary – a Mary Harrison of Andover and Mary Lloyd, his sisters' close friend.[34] He eventually decided on the latter, after getting to know her better when she stayed at Steventon Rectory in the autumn of 1787. James proposed to Mary in November and, much to his mother's delight, he was accepted. Mrs Austen's pleasure is evident in the following paragraph from a letter she wrote to Mary after being informed of the engagement.

> Mr Austen & Myself desire you will accept our best Love, and that you will believe us truly sincere when we assure you that we feel the most heartfelt satisfaction at the prospect we have of adding you to the Number of our very good Children. Had the Election been mine, you, my dear Mary, are the person I should have chosen for James' wife, Anna's Mother and my Daughter, being as certain, as I can be of anything in this uncertain world, that you will greatly increase & promote the happiness of each of the three.[35]

Eliza was pleased to hear about the engagement and immediately wrote to Philadelphia Walter to ask if she had heard the news.

> Has Cassandra informed You of the Wedding which is soon to take place in the family? James has chosen a Second Wife in the person of Miss Mary Floyd [sic] who is not either rich or handsome, but very sensible & good humoured – you have perhaps heard of the family for they occupied my Uncle's house at Deane six or seven years since, and the eldest Sister is married to Mr Fulwar Fowle who is Brother to Cassandra's intended. Jane seems much pleased with the match, and it is natural she should, having long known & liked the lady.[36]

Cassandra's feelings about the engagement are not recorded, but there is no reason to doubt that she too was pleased at the match between her brother and her good friend.

Sadly, Mary was badly scarred by smallpox, as Mrs Chute noted when James took her to meet the family at The Vyne. In a letter to her sister Mrs Chute wrote:

> … she is perfectly unaffected, and very pleasant; I like her. Was it not for the smallpox which has scarred and seamed her face dreadfully, her countenance would be pleasing; to my near-sighted eyes at a little distance she looked to advantage.[37]

The marriage of James and Mary took place at Hurstbourne Tarrant, in Hampshire, in January 1797. Mary moved back into

Deane Rectory, where she had previously lived with her mother and sister, and little Anna returned to her father's home. Steventon Rectory was a much quieter place after the lively child left. Her grandparents and aunts, whose lives she had brightened, must have missed her considerably. Unfortunately, Mrs Austen had been too hasty in predicting that Mary would increase the happiness of her family. Sadly, Mary's marriage to James would sour her relationship with Jane because it brought out an unpleasant side to her character, which had not previously been evident. Mary also resented her husband's closeness to his family, and did not turn out to be either a good or kind stepmother to Anna.

6

STEVENTON

1797–1799

In the spring of 1797 the Austens were deeply distressed to hear that Cassandra's fiancé, Tom Fowle, had died of yellow fever in San Domingo, just before he was due to return home, and had been buried at sea. Tom died in February but the news took time to reach England. It was a devastating blow to Cassandra to lose the man she loved and to have the future they had planned together so cruelly snatched away from her. In May, Eliza wrote about this tragedy in a letter to her cousin Philadelphia Walter:

> I have just received a letter from Steventon where they are all in great Affliction (as I suppose You have heard) for the death of Mr Fowle, the Gentleman to whom our Cousin Cassandra was engaged – He was expected home this Month, from St Domingo where he had accompanied Lord Craven, but Alas instead of his arrival news were received of his Death. –This is a very severe stroke to the whole family, and particularly to poor Cassandra for whom I feel more than I can express – Indeed I am most sincerely grieved at this Event & the Pain which it must occasion our worthy Relations. Jane says that her Sister behaves with a degree of resolution and Propriety which no common mind could evince in so trying a situation.[1]

Lord Craven, who was not aware of Tom and Cassandra's engagement, said that he would never have allowed him to go to the West Indies if he had known. Tom, who wrote his will leaving his fiancée £1,000 just before he set off,[2] knew the potential risks but had calculated that they were worth taking in order to bring forward his marriage. With outstanding courage and steely determination, Cassandra managed to stay outwardly strong. As always, even in the depths of her grief, she kept her feelings under control to avoid causing additional pain to her anguished family. Cassandra philosophically accepted her loss as the will of God and, strengthened and upheld by her faith, she held firmly to the belief that she would meet Tom again in the after-life. Despite her courage and stoicism, Cassandra was so traumatised by Tom's death that she never considered marriage again, although, according to her family, several men showed an interest in her over the next few years.[3] Only her beloved sister truly understood Cassandra's loss and grief. Their deep love for each other and their close bond helped Cassandra to endure her sorrow. Tom's death, like other setbacks in their lives, served to strengthen and deepen their emotional bond. In order to keep herself occupied Cassandra took over the management of the household, which her ailing mother had been struggling with for some time.

In August of that year Jane completed the manuscript of *First Impressions*, after ten months of writing. As with the main characters in *Elinor and Marianne,* she drew on her relationship with Cassandra when she created the heroine Elizabeth Bennet and her sister Jane. The relationship of the sisters is central to the novel and the older sister Jane, like Elinor, is more in control of her feelings and more restrained than the impulsive and spirited Elizabeth. Jane's young niece Anna, who was often at Steventon Rectory, was present when the novel was read aloud to the family. It did not occur to Jane that Anna would be listening, but the alert and clever child was listening intently, as she recalled many years later:

> Listen however I did with so much interest, & with so much talk afterwards about 'Jane & Elizabeth' that it was resolved for prudence sake, to read no more of the story aloud in my hearing. This was related to me years afterwards, when the Novel had been published; & it was supposed that the names might recall to my recollection that early impression.[4]

Jane was anxious from the outset to keep her writing a secret from all but her closest family, and she certainly did not want Anna to talk about her fictional characters outside the home. This desire for secrecy may have been because novels were looked down on as a form of literature, or from modesty, but also because Jane's novels were, at this time, written solely for the pleasure and entertainment of herself and her family.

George Austen thought so highly of *First Impressions* that he took it upon himself, without Jane's knowledge, to offer the manuscript to the London publisher Thomas Cadell. He sent him the following letter in November 1797:

> Sir,– I have in my possession a Manuscript Novel, comprising 3 Vols; about the length of Miss Burney's *Evelina*. As I am well aware of what consequence it is that a work of this sort should make its first appearance under a respectable name, I apply to you. I shall be much obliged, therefore, if you will inform me whether you choose to be concerned in it, what will be the expense of publishing it at the author's risk, and what you will venture to advance for the property of it, if on perusal it is approved of. Should you give any encouragement, I will send you the work.
>
> I am Sir, your humble Servant
>
> George Austen.[5]

A reply was sent by return of post declining the offer. Thomas Cadell thus, unwittingly, rejected the opportunity of publishing the novel that later became the world-famous *Pride and Prejudice* without reading it. This rejection, however, meant that Jane could revise the novel, as a mature writer, and improve it into a masterpiece. If *First Impressions* had been published, the finished and perfected *Pride and Prejudice* would never have come into existence.

Many years later Jane's niece Anna made the following comment to her brother about George Austen's attempt to get *First Impressions* published:

> The letter does not do much credit to the tact or courtesy of our good Grandfather for Cadell was a great man in his day,

> and it is not surprising that he should have refused the favor so offered from an unknown.[6]

It is not known whether Jane was aware of her father's action. However, it is unlikely that she would have been upset by this eminent publisher's refusal to read her novel as, at this stage, she was not seeking publication. If Jane was aware of this, it did not stop her from embarking on the rewriting of *Elinor and Marianne* as the narrative novel which was later published under the title of *Sense and Sensibility*.

Mrs Austen continued to suffer poor health so, in November 1797, she went to Bath, in the hope that taking the waters would help her. It was also an opportunity to visit her brother James and his wife Jane. Mrs Austen took her daughters with her. They travelled from Steventon to Bath via Andover and Devizes. It rained during the final part of the journey and their first view of the city was a wet and dismal one.

The Austens stayed with the Leigh-Perrots at 1, The Paragon, in the upper part of the city, not far from the Upper Assembly Rooms and the fashionable shops of Milsom Street. The Leigh-Perrots, who were devoted to each other, had a good relationship with Mrs Austen. Cassandra and Jane got on well with their uncle, but not so well with his wife. Jane Leigh-Perrot was a rather gloomy and negative character, who seemed to suffer from a perpetual cough, and the atmosphere at their home was not particularly relaxed or congenial. As Cassandra and Jane were both together in Bath there are no letters providing details of what they did there. We can, however, be sure that they went everywhere together, as much as possible, and that this visit at least gave them a change of scenery and a break from their usual routine at home.

Bath was still a fashionable resort in the last years of the eighteenth century, although it was gradually being replaced in popularity by Brighton. Bath had been transformed earlier in the century from an insignificant 'watering-place' into a capital of fashion. Its growing popularity led to a vast building programme, which included grand new crescents of houses to accommodate the increasing number of visitors and entertainment venues.

Among the many attractions on offer in the city were two Assembly Rooms, concert halls, pleasure gardens, libraries, a variety of shops and excellent walks in the surrounding hills. The Austen sisters met many of the Leigh-Perrots' friends and acquaintances, giving Jane ample opportunity to watch and analyse the behaviour of the people she met. Jane had by this time developed a novelist's frame of mind; she was able to adopt the viewpoint of an outsider, and she became a careful observer of the foibles, weaknesses, habits and manners of the people around her. Jane also acquired a good topographical knowledge of Bath, which she would soon use when she started work on the novel that became *Northanger Abbey*.

It is not known whether Mrs Austen used the Roman baths or just drank the healing spa-water, but she benefited from her stay in Bath. The Austen ladies returned home some time in December, a month after setting off. Before they left James Leigh-Perrot, who was a cultured man, gave Jane a copy of Hume's *History of England*.[7]

When Mrs Austen and her daughters reached home they received the not entirely unexpected news that Henry had become engaged to his cousin Eliza, in whom he had shown a romantic interest for some time. Henry's previous attachments, including a broken engagement, had come to nothing. For a long time Eliza, who was ten years older than Henry, had been unwilling to respond to his attentions. She did not want to give up her freedom, not least the freedom to flirt, by marrying again but, eventually, she agreed to become Henry's wife. George and Cassandra Austen were concerned about the engagement because Henry was not a very stable character, and marriage to the pleasure-loving Eliza was unlikely to have a steadying influence on him. As far as Jane was concerned, however, the union between her favourite brother and her much-loved cousin was good news. In a letter to her godfather Warren Hastings, Eliza described Henry as possessing an excellent 'Heart, Temper and Understanding'.[8]

The marriage took place on 31 December 1797 at Marylebone Parish Church. Henry continued to serve as a captain in the Oxfordshire Militia for some time after the marriage. His wife and step-son moved to East Anglia to be with him, but they eventually set up home in London. Visits to Henry and Eliza would open up a new area of experience for his sisters, especially Jane, who visited them more frequently than Cassandra.

Earlier that month Mrs Lefroy had introduced Jane to a young man whom she thought would make her a good husband. She may have been trying to make up for putting an end to Jane's romance with her husband's nephew nearly two years before. Samuel Blackall, a clergyman and fellow of Emmanuel College, Cambridge, stayed with the Lefroys over Christmas. Jane did not take to Blackall at all, finding him both pompous and self-centred. She was relieved when he left Hampshire, but this was not to be the last she would hear of him.

At the end of 1797, Edward Austen came into his inheritance when his adoptive mother Catherine Knight, who had been a widow for three years, handed over the extensive Knight estates and properties to him. Managing the estates had become too much for her so she retired to live at Whitefriars, a house near Canterbury. Edward, Elizabeth and their four children moved from Rowling to Godmersham House, a grand Palladian-style building with a beautiful classical interior, built in 1732 by Thomas Knight I. The following description of Godmersham House and estates, taken from Hasted's *History of Kent* (1798) gives an idea of the vast lands and property that Edward inherited:

> It lies in the beautiful Stour valley, a situation healthy and pleasant to the extreme, the river Stour glides through it from Ashford, in its course towards Canterbury; Godmersham House and park are the principal objects in it, both elegant and beautiful, the Ashford high road encircles the east side of the park, along which there is a sunk fence, which affords an uninterrupted view of the whole of it, and adds greatly to the beauty of this elegant scene, and leads through the village of Godmersham close to it, the whole village which contains about twenty houses, belongs to Mrs Knight, excepting one house, as does the greatest part of the parish, excepting the lands belonging to the dean and chapter of Canterbury. There are about twenty more houses in the parish, and about two hundred and forty inhabitants in all. The church, and vicarage, a neat dwelling, pleasantly situated, stand at a small

> distance from the village, on the left side of the road, with the ancient manor-house near the former, close to the bank of the river; the meadows in the vale are exceeding fertile, the uplands are chalk, with some gravel among them, the hills rise high on each side, those on the west being the sheep walks belonging to Godmersham-house, the summits of which are finely cloathed with wood, at proper intervals; the opposite ones are the high range of unenclosed pasture downs of Wye and Brabourne.

Cassandra and Jane would pay many happy visits to Godmersham House and, later, to Chawton House, the property Edward inherited in Hampshire.

The Austens suffered another bereavement in August 1798 when Mrs Austen's niece Jane Williams was killed in a carriage accident. Jane had been driving herself in a light whiskey carriage in Newport on the Isle of Wight, when a runaway dray horse crashed into her. She was thrown out of her carriage and died a few hours later. Jane had frequently stayed at Steventon Rectory, including a visit before her marriage and, more recently, when her husband was away at sea in 1796. Cassandra and Jane were shocked and distressed at the news of the death of their childhood companion.

Cassandra's and Jane's first recorded visit to Godmersham took place at this time. They set off for Kent with their parents on 24 August. Unfortunately, as the sisters were there together, there are no letters describing how they spent their time in Kent. They no doubt enjoyed the company of their young niece and nephews; a fifth child, William, was born during their stay. Jane particularly liked spending time with two-year-old George and, after returning home, she drew pictures to send to him. Jane probably also did some writing, as she took her writing desk containing her work with her. She may have finished *Sense and Sensibility* while in Kent and started work on the novel originally called *Susan*, which was eventually published as *Northanger Abbey*.

This stay at Godmersham gave Cassandra and Jane a chance to compare the lives of the Kent aristocracy with those of the corresponding class in Hampshire. It also gave Jane the opportunity to gather more raw material for her writing. The insider's view of life in an English country house, which Jane acquired on this and subsequent visits to Godmersham, was put to good use when she wrote *Mansfield Park*. The sisters enjoyed the luxurious surroundings, fine food and lavish social events which were part of country house life, and which Jane referred to as living '*a la* Godmersham'.[9] Jane later wrote that 'Kent is the only place for happiness. Everybody is rich there,' unlike in Hampshire, where everybody was 'so horridly poor and economical.'[10]

The sisters attended the Ashford Assembly Rooms, a few miles from Godmersham, where they met members of the east Kent aristocracy, who belonged to Edward's and Elizabeth's social circle. Like all large country houses, Godmersham was the centre of the local community, with visitors arriving and departing all the time. The busy life of Godmersham was a novelty for Cassandra and Jane on their first visit, but Jane would later find the social life, entertaining and constant stream of callers exhausting.

Edward proudly showed his family around the Godmersham estates. The features in the landscaped grounds included two summer houses, one in the form of a Greek temple and the other a Gothic hermitage, and a river walk with a bathing house. As a fellow farmer, George Austen took a particular interest in his son's sheep and pigs. Like every good country house owner of the period, Edward was improving his house and grounds.

Jane and her parents left Godmersham on 24 October, leaving Cassandra behind to help Elizabeth, who was still recovering from her recent confinement. The first part of their journey was easy, apart from the discomfort of a crowded carriage. They stopped overnight at the Bull and George inn in Dartford, where they were well looked after by the landlord Mr Nottley. This inn was to be a regular stopping place on future journeys to and from Kent. Jane nearly lost her precious writing desk and all its contents at Dartford, as she explained in a letter to Cassandra written at the Bull and George:

> After we had been here a quarter of an hour it was discovered that my writing and dressing boxes had been by accident put into a chaise which was just packing off as we came in, and were driven away towards Gravesend in their way to the West

> Indies. No part of my property could have been such a prize before, for in my writing-box was all my worldly wealth, 7 pounds... Mr Nottley immediately despatched a man and horse after the chaise, and in half an hour's time I had the pleasure of being as rich as ever; they were got about two or three miles off.[11]

The second part of their journey home was prolonged, taking three days, and very uncomfortable. Mrs Austen became unwell, probably due to the excessive swaying of the carriage. Once home Jane dosed her mother with dandelion tea and laudanum drops, prescribed by Dr Lyford of Basingstoke. Jane had to nurse her mother for five weeks, as well as doing the housekeeping in the absence of her sister. Jane enjoyed what she described as 'experimental housekeeping',[12] especially choosing the family meals. James Austen called in at Steventon Rectory soon after the travellers returned, in defiance of his wife's wishes.[13] This was the first indication of Mary's overbearing and domineering behaviour. As time went by Mary increasingly controlled her husband, which led to a strained relationship between Jane and her sister-in-law. Whether Cassandra was also irritated by Mary's behaviour is not known but if she was, she would have kept her feelings well hidden.

James and Mary Austen's first child, James Edward, was born in November 1798. In contrast to the birth of Anna, when she had walked through the country lanes at night to attend her first daughter-in-law, Mrs Austen was so worried that she asked not to be informed of the birth of this baby until after the event. Mary was attended by her friend Miss Debary, and the baby arrived safely. Jane informed Cassandra, who was at Godmersham, in a letter dated 17–18 November:

> Sunday – I have just received a note from James to say that Mary was brought to bed last night, at eleven o'clock, of a fine little boy, and that everything is going on very well.[14]

Showing how justified Mrs Austen was in her fears for her daughter-in-law, Jane also told Cassandra that two of their neighbours had recently died in childbirth. This news was wisely kept from Mary.[15] In her next letter, written a few days later, Jane described their nephew to Cassandra:

> I had only a glimpse at the child, who was asleep; but Miss Debary told me that that his eyes were large, dark and handsome.[16]

The new baby was christened at Deane Church on the first day of the new year. Although he was christened James Edward, he was always known in the family as Edward, to avoid confusion with his father. He would be much loved by both his aunts and was to play an important part in their lives. James Edward would also be significant as the author of the first biography of Jane Austen, which contains information on Cassandra as well as Jane, and has been used as a source by every biographer since.

It is clear from Jane's letters that she and Cassandra followed the careers of their sailor brothers with great interest. They exchanged letters with them, but regular correspondence was not easy when Frank and Charles were away at sea. Both brothers were keen to get on, and their father sought the help of family connections on their behalf. Knowing the right people was essential for promotion in the army and navy at that time. George Austen wrote to Admiral Gambier, a connection of General Mathew, the father of James Austen's first wife. As a result of Gambier's influence, Frank was promoted to the rank of Commander. In a letter dated 28 December 1798 Jane informed Cassandra of this good news; her excitement and pride are palpable.

> ... Frank is made.– He was yesterday raised to the Rank of Commander, & appointed to the Petterel Sloop, now at Gibraltar.– A Letter from Daysh [clerk at the Navy Office] has just announced this, & as it is confirmed by a very friendly one from M^{r}. Mathew to the same effect transcribing one from Admiral Gambier to the General, We have no reason to suspect the truth of it.[17]

Charles, who was still serving on the small ship HMS *Scorpion,* was anxious to be transferred to a larger vessel and more arduous duties. His father also wrote to Admiral Gambier on his behalf and received a reply stating that he needed to stay longer on the *Scorpion* to gain more experience.[18]

Just before Christmas Jane attended a ball with her friend Catherine Bigg, which she described in a letter to Cassandra. Being attractive, of neat appearance and with a lively and friendly personality, Jane always had a dancing partner. She told Cassandra that: 'There were twenty Dances & I danced them all, & without any fatigue.'[19] Reading this, and knowing that Jane was not short of admirers, may have caused Cassandra to fear that she may lose her beloved sister, on whom she was becoming increasingly emotionally dependent since the death of her fiancé.

In December 1798 there was a sequel to Mrs Lefroy's attempt the previous year to find a husband for Jane. The Reverend Samuel Blackall was invited to pay another visit to the Lefroys, when he would have been likely to meet Jane and her family again. He had clearly decided that Jane would make him a suitable wife because in his letter replying to the invitation he wrote

> It would give me particular pleasure to have an opportunity of improving my acquaintance with that family [the Austens] – with a hope of creating to myself a nearer interest. But at present I cannot indulge any expectation of it.[20]

Jane was relieved to hear this, as she explained to Cassandra:

> This is rational enough; there is less love and more sense in it than sometimes appeared before, and I am very well satisfied. It will all go on exceedingly well, and decline away in a very reasonable manner. There seems no likelihood of his coming into Hampshire this Christmas, and it is therefore most probable that our indifference will soon be mutual, unless his regard, which appeared to spring from knowing nothing of me at first, is best supported by never seeing me.[21]

This episode seems to have been no more than a source of amusement to Jane, although she was interested to hear, some years later, that Samuel Blackall had found himself a wife.

Jane's letters to her sister reveal that, like most young women, they were interested in clothes and fashion. The many detailed and colourful descriptions of clothes make fascinating reading and add to the picture Jane's letters present of the world in which she lived. Unlike their sisters-in-law Elizabeth and Eliza, Cassandra and Jane could not afford the latest fashions or to buy new clothes regularly. They had to manage on a small dress allowance from their father, which did not go very far. The sisters were often unable to afford basic items of clothing, such as stockings. They did their best to look respectable and fashionable by adding new accessories and trimmings to their clothes, or by dyeing them. When their dresses were too shabby to wear any longer they were turned into petticoats. Cassandra and Jane also borrowed clothes from each other, as the following extract from a letter dated 18–19 December 1798 illustrates:

> I took the liberty a few days ago of asking your Black velvet Bonnet to lend me its cawl, which it very readily did, & by which I have been enabled to give a considerable improvement of dignity to my Cap, which was before too **nidgetty** to please me. – I shall wear it on Thursday, but I hope you will not be offended with me for following your advice as to its ornaments only in part – I still venture to retain the narrow silver round it, put twice round without any bow, & instead of the black military feather shall put in the Coquelicot one, as being smarter; – & besides Coquelicot is to be all the fashion this winter. – After the Ball, I shall probably make it entirely black.[22]

Like many women, the sisters made a lot of their own clothes, including caps, and, when they could afford it they bought fabric and paid a dressmaker to make it up for them. Their fabrics were bought either from a pedlar selling door to door, or from a draper's shop in Basingstoke owned by a Mrs Davis.

It took time for the latest trends to reach the countryside, but Cassandra and Jane could see them when visiting Bath and London. If they had access to the popular women's periodicals, such as Heidelhoff's *Gallery of Fashion* and *The Lady's Monthly*

Museum, they would have seen the coloured fashion plates for which they were renowned. The sisters could not afford to subscribe to these publications themselves, but they may have seen them at Godmersham House or in a library. Fashion plates were also published in diaries and pocket books. There is no evidence that Cassandra and Jane were embarrassed by or resented the fact that they did not have much money for clothes. Like most people of their time they accepted their God-given lot in life, knowing that their lives were comparatively easy and comfortable, and that they were richer in other ways.

Early in 1799 Jane attended a ball at Kempshott House given by Lady Dorchester. She wrote to Cassandra on the day of the ball.

> I am not to wear my white sattin cap tonight after all; I am to wear a Marmalouc cap instead, which Charles Fowle sent to Mary, & which she lends me. – It is all the fashion now, worn at the Opera, & by Lady MIldmays, at Hackwood Balls.[23]

The craze for Egyptian style clothes, such as the cap referred to by Jane, was started in England following the Battle of the Nile in August 1798.

Jane told Cassandra the names of the men she danced with at the ball and added, 'One of my gayest actions was sitting down two Dances in preference to having Lord Bolton's eldest son for my Partner, who danced too ill to be endured.'[24]

Cassandra's letters to Jane seem to have been as amusing as Jane's to her. In January 1799 Jane wrote 'You must read your letters over five times in future before you send them & then perhaps you may find them as entertaining as I do. – I laughed at several parts of the one which I am now answering.'[25] After reading another of her sister's letters Jane described her as a 'comic genius'.

Towards the end of Cassandra's stay in Kent, Jane was longing to see her and was weary of waiting for her to come home. No sooner had Cassandra and Jane been reunited in March, however, than they were separated again. On 16 May, Edward Austen, who was unwell, set off for Bath to take the waters accompanied by Elizabeth, their eldest two children Fanny and Edward, Mrs Austen and Jane. It was wet when they arrived and the streets were full of umbrellas. Jane wrote to Cassandra as soon as they arrived to report on their journey which 'went off exceedingly well' and to describe their lodgings at 13, Queen Square – not far from the famous Royal Crescent.

> We are exceedingly pleased with the House; the rooms are quite as large as we expected, M[rs] Bromley [the landlady] is a fat woman in mourning, & a little black kitten runs about the Staircase, – Eliz: has the apartment within the Drawing room ; she wanted my Mother to have it, but as there was no bed in the inner one, & the stairs are so much easier of ascent or my Mother so much stronger than in Paragon as not to regard the double flight, it is settled for us to be above; where we have two very nice sized rooms, with dirty [this should possibly read dimity] Quilts, & everything comfortable.
>
> I like our situation very much – it is far more chearful than Paragon, & the prospect from the Drawingroom window at which I now write, is rather picturesque, as it commands a perspective veiw of the left side of Brock Street, broken by three Lombardy Poplars in the Garden of the last house in Queen's Parade.[26]

The arrival of Edward and Elizabeth Austen of Godmersham Park and their relatives would have been announced in the list of arrivals published in the Bath newspaper, and recorded in the visitors' books in all the places the Austens visited. Edward took the waters while the ladies enjoyed the pleasures and entertainments which Bath had to offer, including Sydney Gardens, the theatres and the fashionable shops in Milsom Street. There is no record of them attending any balls in the Assembly Rooms, of which there were two in Bath. The Austens called on Mrs Austen's brother and sister-in-law at 1, The Paragon, where Mr Leigh-Perrot was confined due to a bad attack of gout.

Jane had plenty of opportunities to gather fresh material for her writing and to memorise details of Bath to use in her novel *Susan*. The following excerpts from Jane's letters provide some interesting details of her visit and a fascinating snapshot of Bath, which was to become a significant place for the Austen sisters, at the end of the eighteenth century.

Sunday 2nd June 1799
What must I tell you of Edward? –Truth or Falsehood? – I will try the former, & you may chuse for yourself another time.– He was better yesterday than he had been for two of three days before, about as well as while he was at Steventon.– He drinks at the Hetling Pump, is to bathe tomorrow, & try Electricity on Tuesday; – he proposed the latter himself to Dr Fellowes, who made no objection to it, but I fancy we are all unanimous in expecting no advantage from it.

I saw some Gauzes in a shop in Bath Street yesterday at only 4*s*. a yard, but they were not so good or so pretty as mine. – Flowers are very much worn [as headwear] & Fruit is still more the thing. – Eliz. has a bunch of Strawberries, & I have seen Grapes, Cherries, Plumbs & Apricots.

I spent Friday evening with the Mapletons & was obliged to submit to being pleased inspite of my inclination. We took a very charming walk from 6 to 8 up Beacon Hill, & across some fields to the Village of Charlcombe, which is sweetly situated in a little green Valley, as a Village with such a name ought to be ... There is to be a grand gala on Tuesday evening in Sydney Gardens; – a Concert, with Illuminations & fireworks; – to the latter Eliz. and I look forward with pleasure, & even the Concert will have more than its usual charm with me, as the Gardens are large enough for me to get pretty well beyond the reach of its sound.[27]

Tuesday 11th June 1799
We walked to Weston one evening last week, & liked it very much. Liked **what** very much? – Weston? – no – **walking** to Weston – I have not expressed myself properly, but I hope you will understand me. – We have not been to any public place lately, nor performed anything out of the common daily routine of No. 13 Queen Square, Bath–. But to day we were to have dashed away at a very extraordinary rate, by dining out, had it not so happened that we do not go.[28]

> Wednesday 19th June 1799
> Last Sunday We all drank tea in Paragon; my Uncle is still in his flannels, but is getting better again. – On Monday, Mr Evelyn [a friend of Edward's] was well enough for us to fulfil our engagement with him; – the visit was very quiet & uneventful; pleasant enough. – We met only another Mr Evelyn, his cousin, whose wife came to Tea. – Last night we were in Sidney Gardens again, as there was a repetition of the Gala which went off so ill on the 4th. – We did not go till nine, & then were in very good time for the Fire-works, which were really beautiful, & surpassing my expectation; – the illuminations too were very pretty. – The weather was as favourable, as it was otherwise a fortnight ago. – The Play on Saturday is I **hope** to conclude our Gaieties here, for nothing but a lengthened stay will make it otherwise.[29]

Jane enjoyed her stay in Bath but, as their leaving date drew near, she hoped that nothing would occur to postpone it. She was missing her sister who, as always, had kept her informed of all that was happening at home. Jane, being a country girl at heart, was probably missing the Hampshire countryside as well. Exciting as Bath was, nothing could compare with the tranquillity and security of home. The Austens' departure was not delayed and they left Bath on 24 June, after an enjoyable stay, and with Edward's health improved. There was no time for Jane to write when she was in Bath, but it is believed that she finished her novel *Susan* soon after her return. The manuscript was then put away to be revised later; it remained untouched for nearly four years.

This busy year continued for Cassandra and Jane when they accompanied their parents on three excursions to see relatives. Travelling around the country was a popular pastime for the better-off classes, including the Austens. Improvements in roads and transport encouraged people to travel for pleasure as well as from necessity. In late summer of this year the Austens visited the Leighs of Adlestrop in Gloucestershire and the Coopers at Harpsden in Oxfordshire. The latter were about to move to Hamstall Ridware in Staffordshire, where Edward Cooper had been offered a living by his relative Mary Leigh. The Austens also visited Jane's godfather Samuel Cooke and his family at Great Bookham in Surrey. The extensive travelling undertaken by the Austens in 1799, and the varied scenes they encountered, disprove the claims of some of Jane's early biographers that she led a sheltered life, largely confined to rural Hampshire.

Another myth about Jane Austen, which was started by some of her early biographers including her nephew, was that she led a calm and untroubled life. The Austen family, like most others, had their share of trouble and tragedy. In addition to the family bereavements previously described, an event occurred in December 1799 which caused the Austens much distress. Mrs Austen's sister-in-law, Jane Leigh-Perrot, was accused of stealing a piece of lace from a shop in Bath. This was an attempt to extort hush money from her wealthy husband. James Leigh-Perrot, however, refused to pay up and his wife was committed to Ilchester Gaol, with no bail granted, to await trial the following March. James Leigh-Perrot was able to pay for special treatment, so his wife was allowed to stay in the gaol-keeper's house, instead of the gaol itself, and her husband was allowed to stay with her. The couple were forced to suffer the indignity and discomfort of living in an overcrowded, noisy and squalid house. None of her family or friends doubted Mrs Leigh-Perrot's innocence but, because of the harsh penal code, if she was found guilty the punishment would have been severe. Due to the value of the lace the most lenient punishment would have been transportation. Not knowing how to help, Mrs Austen offered, presumably with their consent, for one or both of her daughters to stay with their aunt during her house arrest and to be at her side throughout her trial. Fortunately for Cassandra and Jane, the offer was refused, with Mrs Leigh-Perrot saying that she could not allow 'those elegant young women' to stay in such conditions and 'to have two young creatures gazed at in a public court would cut me to the very heart.' The Austens were greatly relieved when Mrs Leigh-Perrot was acquitted at her trial after just 15 minutes deliberation by the jury. She was invited to stay at Steventon Rectory to recover from her ordeal.[30]

The remainder of the year was largely uneventful for Cassandra and Jane. In October Edward Austen and his six-year-old son Edward visited Steventon and Cassandra returned with them to

Kent, where she remained for three months. Jane enjoyed the first balls of the new season at Basingstoke Assembly Rooms. At one of these balls she told Cassandra: 'I wore ... your favourite gown, a bit of muslin of the same round my head ... & one little Comb.'[31] Jane also attended Lord Portsmouth's ball at Hurstbourne Park with Charles, who drove from Gosport to accompany her there.

In November Jane went to Ibthorpe to stay with Martha Lloyd, where she was made welcome and spent her time 'very pleasantly'.[32] She told Cassandra that Martha would be returning to Steventon with her 'and our plan is to [have] a nice black frost for walking to Whitchurch, & there throw ourselves into a postchaise, one upon the other, our heads hanging out of one door, & our feet at the opposite.'[33] When Jane set off home with Martha in early December she had no idea of the news that awaited her. They were barely through the front door of the rectory when Mrs Austen greeted them with the announcement 'Well, girls, it is all settled. We have decided to leave Steventon and go to Bath.'

Jane was so shocked to hear this that she fainted.[34] Her distress was witnessed by Mary Austen, who was there to meet her sister Martha. Jane was also informed that her father would retain the living of Steventon and would employ James as his curate to look after the parish in his absence. James, Mary and their family would move into the rectory.

7

STEVENTON AND BATH

1800–1802

As Jane's reaction to the news shows, the decision to move to Bath was a sudden one. Only a few weeks earlier George Austen had been planning changes to the rectory garden, including the planting of new trees. It was a shock to Jane to be told that she would be leaving her home of twenty-five years and exchanging the peaceful countryside of north Hampshire, which she loved so much and which her nephew described as 'the cradle of her genius',[1] for the streets of one of the busiest places in England.

There is no record of Cassandra's reaction to the news, which she received at Godmersham. She must, however, have had similar feelings to her sister, as she too was deeply attached to her childhood home and the surrounding countryside. Cassandra and Jane had not been consulted about the move but, as financially dependent unmarried women, they had no choice but to go wherever their parents took them.

There were a number of possible reasons why George Austen and his wife chose Bath as their place of retirement. It was a familiar place and they knew a number of people who lived there as well as the Leigh-Perrots. Bath was full of retirees and catered for older people. Mrs Austen's poor health may have been a factor in their choice of Bath, with all its medical facilities. Bath was also a renowned hunting ground for husbands and the Austens may have felt that living there would increase the chance of their daughters finding suitable men to marry. Women in their middle to late twenties, like Cassandra and Jane, were in danger of being written off as 'old maids', and being stigmatised for not fulfilling their expected destiny in life.

Jane suspected that her sister-in-law Mary had played a part in her father's sudden decision to retire, because she was eager for James to succeed him at Steventon. Jane felt that she and James were pushing them out of their home. George and Cassandra Austen tried to soften the blow of the move for their daughters by offering the inducement of future holidays in the West Country and Wales.

Cassandra, with her philosophical attitude to life, would probably have accepted the move more easily than Jane did. She would, as usual, have suppressed her feelings and put on a brave face. No letters survive for the few weeks after the move was announced, which would have provided an insight into the feelings of both sisters, but it is inconceivable that Jane did not write to Cassandra, who remained at Godmersham, at this crucial time. The most likely explanation is that Jane's letters were so full of her distress at the move that they were among those that Cassandra destroyed a few years before she died, as being too private for anyone else to read. Cassandra probably sent a number of letters encouraging Jane to keep her feelings to herself. She no doubt reminded Jane that their duty to their parents required them to go along with their wishes without demur. In Jane's next surviving letter, dated 3–5 January 1801, which was written in her usual lively and cheerful style, she was clearly coming to terms with the sudden change in her life.

> I get more & more reconciled to the idea of our removal. We have lived long enough in this Neighbourhood, the Basingstoke Balls are certainly on the decline, there is something interesting in the bustle of going away, & the prospect of spending future summers by the Sea or in Wales is very delightful. – For a time we shall now possess many of the advantages which I have often thought of with Envy in the wives of Sailors or Soldiers. – It must not be generally known however that I am not sacrificing a great deal in quitting the

Country – or I can expect to inspire no tenderness, no interest in those we leave behind.[2]

Jane's positive outlook and cheerful temperament meant that she was never downcast for long. It must have been a relief for Cassandra to read these lines and, with Jane in a better frame of mind, to look forward to the move herself. Jane even began to plan the clothes she would need for Bath. On 25th January she wrote:

> I shall want two new coloured gowns for the summer, for my pink one will not do more than clear me from Steventon. I shall not trouble you, however, to get more than one of them, [in London where Cassandra was going to stay on her way home] and that is to be a plain brown cambric muslin, for morning wear; the other, which is to be a very pretty yellow and white cloud, I mean to buy in Bath. Buy two brown ones, if you please, and both of a length, but one longer than the other – it is for a tall woman. Seven yards for my mother, seven yards and a half for me; a dark brown, but the kind of brown is left to your own choice, and I had rather they were different, as it will be always something to say, to dispute about which is the prettiest. They must be cambric muslin.[3]

Jane now busied herself in helping her parents with preparations for the move. Decisions had to be made about which furniture and effects they would take to Bath, and which they would sell. The furniture and other items being left behind were valued by Mr Bayle, a cabinet maker and auctioneer from Winchester, at more than £200.[4] These included 500 books belonging to George Austen, some books of Jane's and her piano.

Jane described in a letter to Cassandra dated 14–16th January how a group of local ladies, including her sister-in-law and friends, arrived at the rectory to look at Mrs Austen's poultry with a view to buying them –

> ... & soon afterwards a party of fine Ladies issuing from a well-known, commodious green Vehicle, their heads full

> of Bantam-Cocks and Galinies [hens], entered the house – Mrs Heathcote, Mrs Harwood, Mrs James Austen, Miss Bigg and Miss Jane Blachford.[5]

Presumably the 'well-known commodious green vehicle' was James and Mary's carriage. Jane also wrote, with more than a hint of bitterness –

> My father's old Ministers are already deserting him to pay their court to his Son; the brown Mare, which as well as the black was to devolve on James at our removal, has not had patience to wait for that, & has settled herself even now at Deane... everything else I suppose will be seized by degrees in the same manner.[6]

It seems that Jane was so put out by her sister-in-law's apparent eagerness to move into Steventon rectory that she declined an invitation to a party held to celebrate James' and Mary's fourth wedding anniversary.

By the end of January, after a lengthy separation, Jane was longing to see Cassandra again. In her letter of 25th she complained about the length of her sister's absence:

> Neither my affection for you nor for letter-writing can stand out against a Kentish visit. For a three months' absence I can be a very loving relation and a very excellent correspondent, but beyond that I degenerate into negligence and indifference.[7]

At the end of January Jane had a break from the house moving preparations when she went to stay with Catherine and Alethea Bigg at Manydown. Cassandra was by this time in London, where she spent three weeks with Henry and Eliza at their new home in Upper Berkeley Street, off Portman Square. According to Philadelphia Walter they lived 'quite in style' with a French cook and a new carriage. They had become part of a social circle that included a number of French émigrés. Henry had recently resigned his commission in the Oxfordshire Militia and had set up in business in London as a banker and army agent, with an army friend. In a letter written before leaving for Manydown Jane wrote to Cassandra:

> I hope you will see everything worthy notice, from the Opera House to Henry's office in Cleveland Court; and I shall expect you to lay in a stock of intelligence that may procure me amusement for a twelvemonth to come.[8]

Cassandra probably had items to buy for other family members as well as the dress fabric Jane had requested. There was a much better selection of goods in the London shops than could be found in country towns like Basingstoke, and whenever Cassandra or Jane went to London they took a shopping list with them.

In February the sisters were reunited at Steventon, where preparations for the move to Bath continued. The Austens received farewell visits from friends, neighbours and parishioners, who were all sorry that they were leaving. Edward and Elizabeth, Frank and Charles also paid farewell visits while, as Jane put it, 'Steventon is ours.'[9]

The Austens left Steventon at the beginning of May 1801. Mrs Austen and her daughters went to the Lloyds' home, while George Austen went to London and then to Godmersham with Frank. After staying for two days at Ibthorpe, Mrs Austen and Jane went on to Bath, leaving Cassandra behind. Jane wrote to her sister as soon as they arrived at the Leigh-Perrots' home, where they were to stay while they found somewhere to live.

> Our Journey here was perfectly free from accident or Event; we changed Horses at the end of every stage, & paid at almost every Turnpike; – we had charming weather, hardly any Dust, & were exceedingly agreable, as we did not speak above once in three miles. – Between Luggershall & Everley we made our grand Meal ... We had a very neat chaise from Devizes; it looked almost as well as a Gentleman's, at least as a very shabby Gentleman's –; inspite of this advantage however We were above three hours coming from thence to Paragon, & it was half after seven by Your Clocks before we

> entered the house. Frank, whose black head was in waiting in the Hall window received us very kindly; and his Master & Mistress did not shew less cordiality.[10]
>
> The first veiw of Bath in fine weather does not answer my expectations; I think I see more distinctly thro' Rain. – The Sun was got behind everything, and the appearance of the place from the top of Kingsdown, was all vapour, shadow, smoke & confusion.[11]

Mrs Austen and Jane started looking for suitable, reasonably priced accommodation soon after their arrival. This was not easy as there were problems with every property they viewed and the Austens, who had discussed house-hunting before leaving Steventon, could not agree on where they wanted to live in the city. Jane wanted a house near Sydney Gardens, so she and Cassandra could walk in the labyrinth every day. Some properties viewed by Mrs Austen and Jane were 'very desirable in size and situation' but were found to be 'putrifying'.[12]

Jane often accompanied her uncle on his daily visits to the Pump Room to drink the healing spa-water. It was always busy in the Pump Room, where attendants in mob caps filled glasses with mineral water and handed them around. Jane, who described herself as 'a desperate walker', found it frustrating to walk with her uncle who walked slowly with the aid of a stick. Sometimes Mr Leigh-Perrot went with his niece to view properties.

The first few weeks in Bath were busy ones for Jane. She went to church twice on Sundays, probably at Bath Abbey in the medieval part of the city, and walked in the famous Crescent Fields, where people liked to promenade in their fashionable clothes. Jane accompanied her aunt and uncle when they made social calls and, just a week after arriving in Bath, she was taken to a ball at the Upper Assembly Rooms. In a letter to Cassandra she wrote

> In the evening I hope you honoured my Toilette & Ball with a thought; I dressed myself as well as I could, & had all my finery much admired at home. By nine o'clock my Uncle, Aunt & I entered the rooms & linked Miss Winstone to us. – Before tea, it was rather a dull affair; but then the before tea

did not last long, for there was only one dance, danced by four couple. – Think of four couple, surrounded by about an hundred people, dancing in the upper rooms at Bath! – After tea we **cheered up**; the breaking up of private parties sent some scores more to the Ball, & tho' it was shockingly & inhumanly thin for this place, there were people enough I suppose to have made five or six very pretty Basingstoke assemblies.[13]

Jane chatted to a Mr Evelyn, a friend of Edward's who lived in Kent, and amused herself by observing the people around her to report back to Cassandra.

The following evening the Leigh-Perrots held a party at home, which Jane found dull and boring, as she informed her sister.

> Another stupid party last night; perhaps if larger they might be less intolerable, but here there were only just enough to make one card table, with six people to look over, & talk nonsense to each other. Ly Fust, M[rs] Busby & a M[rs] Owen sat down with my Uncle to Whist within five minutes after the three old Toughs came in, & there they sat with only the exchange of Adm. Stanhope for my Uncle till their chairs were announced.[14]

Fortunately, the party Jane attended the following evening was 'not quite so stupid'.

Later in the month Jane went on two long walks in the countryside surrounding Bath with an acquaintance named Mrs Chamberlayne, who was dull company but just as energetic a walker as Jane. Mr Evelyn, whom Jane had met at the ball, invited her for a ride in his phaeton. Jane described him as a 'harmless' man who enjoyed feeding birds. They went for a ride to the top of Lansdowne Hill in Mr Evelyn's 'very bewitching Phaeton & four'.[15]

On her return from the ride there were two letters waiting for Jane on the hall table, one from Cassandra and the other from Charles. Her brother informed her that he had received £30 in prize money following the capture of the French privateer *La Furie* and expected £10 more. He had bought his sisters a gold chain and topaz cross each with this money, which led Jane to exclaim to Cassandra – 'but of what avail is it to take prizes if he lays out the produce in presents to his Sisters. He has been buying Gold chains & Topaze Crosses for us; – he must be well scolded...'[16] Charles's gifts to his sisters inspired the episode in *Mansfield Park,* when Fanny Price's sailor brother William buys her an amber cross with some prize money.

In a letter to her sister dated 21–22 May Jane referred to the sale of the furniture and effects left behind at Steventon. She considered that Mr Bent, the auctioneer, had put too low a valuation on some items, including the books that James was buying. Jane wrote:

> Mr Bent seems <u>bent</u> upon being very detestable, for he values the books at only 70£. The whole World is in a conspiracy to enrich one part of our family at the expence of another.[17]

The search for a new home came to an end when the *Bath Chronicle* advertised a short lease on 4, Sydney Place.[18] This house was opposite Sydney Gardens, in the location favoured by Jane, close to open countryside but within walking distance of the centre of Bath. It only needed to be redecorated before new tenants could move in and was the prefect home for the Austens.

At the beginning of June George Austen and Cassandra arrived in Bath, which made Jane much happier. The sisters could settle down together and help each other to adapt to their new lives. One of the most difficult things for them to adjust to was the busyness and noise of Bath, after the tranquillity of Steventon. This must have been particularly difficult for Jane, as she was very sensitive to noise. The following contemporary description of the main shopping street in Bath, written by Pierce Egan, gives some idea of the surroundings to which Cassandra and Jane had to adapt.

> Milsom Street is the very magnet of Bath, the centre of attraction and, till the hour of dinner-time, the peculiar resort of the beau monde – where the familiar nod and the

> 'how do you do' are repeated fifty times in the course of the morning. All is bustle and gaiety, numerous dashing equipages passing and repassing, others gracing the doors of the tradesmen; sprinkled here and there with the invalids in the comfortable sedans and easy two-wheeled carriages. The shops are capacious and elegant. Among them the visitors find libraries to improve the mind, musical repositories to enrich their taste and science, confectioners to invite the most fastidious appetite, and tailors, milliners, &c. of the highest eminence in the fashionable world, to adorn the male and decorate the female, so as to render the form almost of statuary excellence.[19]

Jane soaked up the atmosphere of Bath and added to her knowledge of its topography and architecture, which helped her as she revised *Susan* and later wrote *Persuasion*.

While their new home was being redecorated the Austens went to Devon for a holiday. They are believed to have gone to Sidmouth and then to stay with Richard Buller, a former pupil of George Austen, who was vicar of Colyton, a small town between Sidmouth and Lyme Regis. It may have been while on this holiday that Jane met a man with whom she had a brief romance. This remained a secret until, many years after Jane's death, Cassandra broke her habit of reticence and spoke about it to her niece Caroline. The details were related by James Edward Austen-Leigh in his *Memoir* of Jane.

> She [Cassandra] said that, while staying at some seaside place, they became acquainted with a gentleman, whose charm of person, mind and manners was such that Cassandra thought him worthy to possess and likely to win her sister's love. When they parted, he expressed his intention of soon seeing them again; and Cassandra felt no doubt as to his motives. But they never again met. Within a short time they heard of his sudden death. I believe that, if Jane ever loved, it was this unnamed gentleman; but the acquaintance had been short, and I am unable to say whether her feelings were of such a nature as to affect her happiness.[20]

Recalling her conversation with Cassandra about this 'charming man' Caroline wrote 'I never heard Aunt Cass. speak of any one else with such admiration – she had no doubt that a mutual attachment was in progress between him and her sister.' She considered that her aunt's attachment to this man had not 'overclouded her happiness for long', however, as it 'had not gone far enough to leave misery behind'.[21] If Jane had, like Cassandra, met a man she felt she could marry only to lose him, her sister was the best person to help her to deal with her grief and recover her equilibrium. Cassandra, as usual, was close by to comfort and support Jane. She would have encouraged her sister to hide her feelings for the sake of those around her, and to be strong, as she herself had been when her fiancé died.

It is thought that Jane may have used this experience when writing *Persuasion,* in which the heroine Anne Elliot suffers for years after breaking off her engagement to Frederick Wentworth, but never forgets her feelings for him. When Anne says 'All the privilege I claim for my own sex (it is not a very enviable one; you need not covet it), is that of loving longest, when existence or when hope is gone,' is she expressing the author's own pain? Jane surely could not have written her six love stories without having known the experience of love herself.

After their holiday in Devon Mr and Mrs Austen and their daughters went to Steventon for a brief stay in their old home with James and Mary. It must have been difficult for Jane to see her sister-in-law running the rectory in her mother's place, and possibly painful for her parents and sister too. Cassandra and Jane spent one day at Ashe Rectory with the Lefroys, who took them back to Steventon and stayed for dinner. By 5 October the Austens were back in Bath, where they moved into their new home.

Unfortunately, only one of Jane's letters survives for the period May 1801 to January 1805. This may have been because Cassandra and Jane were together for much of this time. It is unlikely, however, that they were not separated occasionally and only able to communicate by letter. It is very likely, for example, that Cassandra was at Godmersham in 1801 and 1803, when her niece Marianne and her nephew Charles were born, as Edward and Elizabeth relied on her help when their babies arrived. The explanation for the gap in Jane's correspondence is a mystery, but the result is that little is known about the Bath period of the Austen sisters' lives.

It is known from other sources that James, Mary and nine-year-old Anna visited his parents and sisters in Bath in April 1802. This must have been another awkward time for Jane, given her suspicion that Mary was responsible for her father's decision to retire. If Cassandra shared Jane's feelings about Mary, only Jane would have known. With her characteristic self-control, Cassandra would not have allowed any hint of her feelings to escape to anyone else.

Cassandra and Jane would both have been pleased to see their brother and delighted to see Anna, who remembered this visit to Bath clearly in later life. She recalled that her grandparents

> ... seemed to enjoy the cheerfulness of their Town life, and especially perhaps the rest which their advancing years entitled them to, which, even to their active natures, must have been acceptable.[22]

Anna also recorded the following memory of her still-handsome grandfather:

> At the time when I have the most perfect recollection of him he must have been getting on hard, as people say, for 70. His hair in its whiteness might have belonged to a much older man; it was very beautiful & glossy, with short curls above the ears ... I can well remember at Bath, where my Grand Father latterly resided, what notice he attracted, when on any public occasion he appeared with his head uncovered.[23]

Following the Peace of Amiens in March 1802, which briefly ended hostilities between Great Britain and France, Charles Austen returned to England. He joined his parents and sisters on their summer holiday, which was spent in Dawlish and Teignmouth in Devon. Some years later Jane recalled that the library at Dawlish was 'particularly pitiful and wretched',[24] but nothing else is known about this holiday in Devon. The five Austens then went on a tour of Wales, which included Tenby and Barmouth.

Cassandra and Jane spent the autumn of that year with Charles on a brief visit to James and Mary at Steventon, followed by a longer one to Edward and Elizabeth at Godmersham. After returning to Steventon, Cassandra and Jane went to stay with the Bigg sisters at Manydown for two weeks. It was while staying there that Jane received her only known offer of marriage. This unexpected proposal came from Harris Bigg-Wither, the twenty-one-year old younger brother of her friends, who was the heir to a considerable estate. Jane accepted this offer, which was made on the evening of the 1 December, but she had second thoughts overnight and withdrew her acceptance the following morning.

Jane had been briefly tempted by the material and other advantages that marriage to Harris Bigg-Wither would have provided. Despite these advantages, Jane quickly decided that she could not marry a man she did not love. As her novels illustrate, Jane believed that a woman's best chance of happiness was to be found in a happy marriage to a man she loved and respected, and who loved and respected her in return. She also believed that a couple needed to know each other well before they made the momentous decision to marry. Jane knew she could not risk marrying a man she barely knew and did not love.

On the morning of 2 December, Mary Austen was surprised to see the Bigg-Wither family carriage pull up in front of Steventon Rectory. She watched as her sisters-in-law and their friends emerged and tearfully said goodbye to each other, before Catherine and Alethea got back into the carriage and departed. Jane, who was agitated and upset, told Mary that they needed James to take them home to Bath immediately. Mary tried to persuade them not to go back so soon, no doubt thinking of the inconvenience this would cause her husband, who had a service to conduct on Sunday. Cassandra backed Jane's urgent entreaties, but they refused to offer an explanation. It was most unlike them to be so demanding, but James acceded to their wishes.[25]

When Mary Austen heard what had happened at Manydown, she reputedly expressed her disapproval of Jane's refusal of such an eligible young man. It is inconceivable that any other member of Jane's family would have wanted her to risk her happiness by marrying a man she did not love. In his biography of Jane her nephew James Edward described this incident in the following words:

> In her youth she had declined the addresses of a gentleman who had the recommendations of good character, and connections, and position in life, of everything, in fact, except the subtle power of touching her heart.[26]

Jane's niece Caroline also commented on this affair. She wrote:

> To be sure she should not have said yes – over night – but I have always respected her for the courage in cancelling that yes – the next morning – All worldly advantages would have been to her, & she was of an age to know **this** quite well – My Aunts had very small fortunes & on their Father's death they & their Mother would be, they were aware, but poorly off – I beleive most young women so circumstanced would have taken Mr W & trusted to love after marriage.[27]

Cassandra was by Jane's side when she hastily retreated from Manydown and was there, as she always was when Jane needed her, to support her sister until the drama subsided. Fortunately, their long-standing friendship with the Bigg sisters was not spoiled by Jane's rejection of their brother. Two years later Harris Bigg-Wither married a lady by the name of Anne Howe-Frith. There would be five sons and five daughters; none of the daughters would marry.

8

BATH

1803–1806

A year after the Peace of Amiens was signed Henry and Eliza decided to travel to France and attempt to reclaim the confiscated property of her first husband. Eliza's frail son Hastings, who would have inherited his father's property, had died in 1801 at the age of fourteen. While Henry and Eliza were in France, Napoleon broke the terms of the peace treaty and hostilities started again. Orders were issued in France for the detention of all British nationals. Henry and Eliza only managed to escape arrest and internment because Eliza's excellent French enabled them to pass as a French couple.[1] This was, naturally, a worrying time for Cassandra, Jane and the rest of the Austen family.

In the winter of 1802 to 1803 Jane revised the manuscript of her novel *Susan,* with a view to trying to get it published. It is not known why Jane changed her mind about seeking publication for her work, but it is possible that her brother Henry may have influenced her. Unlike Cassandra, Jane had no money of her own and perhaps she simply wanted some financial independence. She may also have realised that her chances of finding a man she loved enough to marry were diminishing and if she ever needed to make her own living, becoming a published author would be a good way of doing so. Whatever her reasons, early in 1803 Jane sold her revised manuscript to the London publisher Richard Crosby for £10. Henry's business associate, Mr Seymour, dealt with the publisher on Jane's behalf and stipulated that the novel be published soon.[2] Crosby advertised the forthcoming publication of *Susan* in the literary journal *The Flowers of Literature*[3] but, for some unknown reason, he did not publish it. The manuscript was filed away in the publisher's office and Jane did not pursue the matter for the time being.

Cassandra and Jane's sailor brothers were recalled to active service after hostilities resumed between Great Britain and France. Charles rejoined the *Endymion* as First Lieutenant[4] and Frank moved to Ramsgate in Kent to lead the Sea Fencibles, a volunteer unit set up to defend the east coast against the threat of French invasion.[5] Jane, and possibly Cassandra, visited him in Ramsgate in the summer of 1803. While he was in Ramsgate the deeply religious Frank became known as 'the officer who knelt in church'.[6] It was also while working in Ramsgate that Frank met Mary Gibson, who was to become his first wife and a much-loved sister-in-law to Cassandra and Jane. Frank remained in Ramsgate until the following May, when he was appointed Commander of the fifty-gun flagship HMS *Leopard* stationed off Boulogne. The following year he was transferred to HMS *Canopus*.[7]

In the spring of 1804 Mrs Austen, who seems never to have been in good health, became ill. The nature of her complaint is not known but it was serious enough to require the attention of William Bowen, an apothecary based in Argyle Buildings, Bath. Cassandra and Jane nursed their mother during her illness and Mrs Austen celebrated her recovery by writing the following humorous verses entitled *Dialogue between Death and Mrs A.*

Says Death,
'I've been trying these three weeks and more
To seize an old Madam here at Number Four,
Yet I still try in vain, tho' she's turned of three score;
To what is my ill success owing?'

'I'll tell you, old Fellow, if you cannot guess,
To what you're indebted for your ill-success –
To the prayers of my husband, whose love I possess;
To the care of my daughters, whom Heaven will bless,
To the skill and attention of Bowen.'[8]

From this time onwards Mrs Austen became increasingly dependent on the care of her daughters.

In the autumn of this year Cassandra and Jane went with their parents to Godmersham and then they went, alone, to stay with the Lefroys at Ashe. In November they all had a holiday together at Lyme Regis, in Dorset. This was their first visit to the seaside resort, which was to provide the setting of important scenes in Jane's novel *Persuasion*.

Around this time Jane started to write another novel named *The Watsons,* but she lost interest in it after writing five chapters and the work was never completed. The unfinished manuscript was written neatly on small sheets of paper, which could be easily covered up if any unexpected visitor disturbed her, as she was still very secretive about her writing.[9] There are a number of possible reasons for Jane's inability to compose any new writing while she lived in Bath. Her great-niece Mary Augusta Austen-Leigh suggested that the loss she suffered when she left Hampshire was one explanation for this:

> She had lost her youth. At the age of twenty-five, while still a young woman, she had left her native place, her earliest friends, and every well-loved scene associated with the first overflowings of her happy girlish fancies. It was the birthplace, not of herself alone, but of many creations, born to a far longer existence than hers was destined to be upon earth – all those characters that live and move for us throughout the pages of her first three novels.[10]

Unhappiness over the death of the man she met in Devon may also have been a contributory factor. Nevertheless, Jane continued to gather material, which she used later when she took up writing again. She continued to watch the people around her, noting mannerisms, expressions and conversations, and to analyse their behaviour. Bath gave her the opportunity to study a variety of people of different types and from different social classes. Jane continued to add to her knowledge of the streets and architecture of Bath, and soaked up its atmosphere to add to her store of raw material for future novels.

In the summer of 1804 Henry and Eliza went with his parents and sisters on holiday back to Lyme Regis. It is believed that they stayed at Pyne House in Broad Street. On one of their walks in the countryside around Lyme, Cassandra made a watercolour sketch of Jane, showing a back view of her sitting on a hillside, with the strings of her bonnet hanging loose. It may have been on this holiday that Jane visited the pretty villages of Charmouth, Uplyme and Pinny, which she later described in *Persuasion*. Some time in September Henry, Eliza and Cassandra went on to Weymouth, which they found a dull and disappointing place. Jane and her parents stayed in Lyme, where they moved into smaller lodgings. Cassandra wrote to Jane to tell her about Weymouth and Jane replied in the only surviving letter from this period to update Cassandra, who had moved on to Ibthorpe, on what she was doing:

> We are quite settled in our Lodgings by this time, as you may suppose, & everything goes on in the usual order. The servants behave very well & make no difficulties, tho' nothing certainly can exceed the inconveniences of the Offices, except the general Dirtiness of the House & furniture, & all its Inhabitants. – Hitherto the weather has been just what we could wish; – the continuance of the dry Season is very necessary to our comfort. – I endeavour as far as I can to supply your place, & be useful & keep things in order.[11]

Jane described bathing in the sea and attending balls at the Assembly Rooms, from the windows of which could be seen 'only sea and sky'. She described in detail the ball she attended on 13 September with her parents.

> The Ball last night was pleasant, but not full for Thursday. My Father staid very contentedly till half past nine – we went a little after eight – & then walked home with James & a Lanthorn, tho' I believe the Lanthorn was not lit, as the Moon was up. But this Lanthorn may sometimes be a great convenience to him. – My Mother & I staid about an hour later. Nobody asked me the two first dances – the two next I danced with Mr Crawford – & had I chosen to stay longer might have

danced with M[r] Granville, M[rs] Granville's son – whom my dear friend Miss Armstrong offered to introduce to me – or with a new, odd looking Man who had been eyeing me for some time, & at last without any introduction asked me if I meant to dance again.– I think he must be Irish by his ease, & because I imagine him to belong to the Hon[ble] Barnwalls, who are the son & son's wife of an Irish Viscount – bold, queerlooking people, just fit to be Quality at Lyme.[12]

Jane was not short of company in her sister's absence. She enjoyed spending time with Miss Armstrong, her friend from Bath, with whom she went walking on the Cobb. The holiday ended when Jane and her parents returned to Bath on 25 October, and the sisters were reunited after several weeks' separation. The family, who had given up the last three weeks of their lease on 4, Sydney Place, now moved to Green Park Buildings, which they had rejected as a place to live when they first moved to Bath. Their new home was on the outskirts of Bath near green fields and the River Avon, and not far from Beechen Cliff.

In December the Austens learned of the sudden death of their friend Anne Lefroy, who had been particularly close to Jane. On 16 December, Jane's twenty-ninth birthday, Mrs Lefroy had set off on her horse, accompanied by a servant, to go shopping in the village of Overton. On their way they met James Austen, who noticed that she was struggling with her horse. At the top of Overton Hill the horse started to run away, possibly due to being startled by something. Mrs Lefroy threw herself off the horse but sustained fatal injuries as a result. James Austen conducted her funeral service on 21 December.[13] The death of their old friend was deeply upsetting for the Austen family. On the fourth anniversary of her friend's death Jane wrote a poem in her memory, showing how affected she was by the loss. This poem, which contained eleven verses opened with the following lines.

The day returns again, my natal day;
What mix'd emotions in my mind arise!
Beloved Friend, four years have passed away
Since thou were snatched for ever from my eyes.

The day commemorative of my birth,
Bestowing life, and light, and hope to me,
Brings back the hour which was thy last on earth,
O! Bitter pang of torturing memory![14]

In the new year the family suffered an even more grievous loss when George Austen died at the age of seventy-three. He had not been in the best of health for some time, but his death was sudden. George had felt unwell on 19 January, but the following morning he was feeling better and got up to have breakfast. Later that day he became unwell again, and his condition gradually deteriorated. He died at twenty past ten on the morning of 21 January. Jane immediately wrote the following letter to Frank, who was on board HMS *Leopard* at Dungeness, informing him of the sad news and describing their father's last hours:

> Monday 21st January 1805
> Green Park Bldgs.
> My dearest Frank,
>
> I have melancholy news to relate, & sincerely feel for your feelings under the shock of it. – I wish I could better prepare You for it. – But having said so much, Your mind will already forestall the sort of Event which I have to communicate. – Our dear Father has closed his virtuous & happy life, in a death almost as free from suffering as his Children could have wished. He was taken ill on Saturday morning, exactly in the same way as heretofore, an oppression in the head with fever, violent tremulousness, & the greatest degree of Feebleness. The same remedy of Cupping, which had before been so successful, was immediately applied to – but without such happy effects. The attack was more violent, & at first he seemed scarcely at all releived by the Operation. – Towards the Evening however he got better, had a tolerable night, & yesterday morning was so greatly amended as to get up & join us at breakfast as usual, walk about with only the

> help of a stick, & every symptom was then so favourable that when Bowen saw him at one, he felt sure of his doing perfectly well. – But as the day advanced, all these comfortable appearances gradually changed; the fever grew stronger than ever, & when Bowen saw him at ten at night, he pronounc'd his situation to be most alarming. – At nine this morning he came again – & by his desire a Physician was called; – Dr Gibbs – But it was then absolutely a lost case – Dr Gibbs said that nothing but a Miracle could save him, and about twenty minutes after Ten he drew his last gasp. – Heavy as is the blow, we can already feel that a thousand comforts remain to us to soften it. Next to that of the consciousness of his worth and constant preparation for another World, is the remembrance of his having suffered, comparatively speaking, nothing. – Being quite insensible of his own state, he was spared all the pain of separation, & went off almost in his Sleep. – My Mother bears the Shock as well as possible; she was quite prepared for it, & feels all the blessing of his being spared a long illness. My Uncle & Aunt have been with us, & shew us every imaginable kindness. And tomorrow we shall I dare say have the comfort of James's presence, as an Express has been sent to him. – We write also of course to Godmersham & Brompton [where Henry and Eliza now lived]. Adieu my dearest Frank. The loss of such a Parent must be felt, or we should be Brutes. – I wish I could have given you better preparation – but it has been impossible.
>
> Yours Ever Affecly
>
> J.A.[15]

A second letter had to be sent to Frank the following day, as his ship had moved on to Portsmouth before he could receive the first one. The later letter included a few additional sentences, including the following:

> His tenderness as a Father, who can do justice to? ... The Serenity of the Corpse is most delightful! – It preserves the sweet, benevolent Smile which always distinguished him.[16]

James and Henry hurried to Bath on hearing the news, but Edward was unable to leave Godmersham. Charles could not be contacted easily as he was a long distance away in Halifax, Nova Scotia, commanding HMS *Indian*. James tried to persuade his mother to return with him to Steventon, but Mrs Austen decided to stay in Bath.

George Austen's funeral was held on 26 January at St Swithin's Church, Walcot, Bath, where he was married in 1764. He was buried in the church crypt under a tablet bearing the following inscription:

> Under this stone rest the remains of the Rev George Austen, Rector of Steventon and Deane in Hampshire, who departed this life the 21st January 1805, aged 73 years.[17]

Cassandra and Jane felt the loss of their father deeply. Jane had always been closer to him than to her mother. As with previous bereavements their strong faith helped them to bear the loss and their firmly held belief that they would be reunited with their father in the afterlife also sustained them.

Mrs Austen and her daughters were placed in a difficult financial position following the death of George Austen. James became rector of Steventon and Deane on his father's death and the income from these livings passed to him.[18] The small annuity, which had supplemented George Austen's church income, ceased on his death. Mrs Austen's sons, except Charles, offered their mother an annual sum, according to their means, to support her and their sisters. These pledges doubled their income leading Mrs Austen to exclaim 'Never were children so good as mine.'[19] It is clear from Jane's letters that she felt guilty about her financial dependence on her brothers, two of whom had families to support, and Cassandra probably felt the same. Unfortunately, financial dependence was the lot of the majority of women of their social class in England at that time.

Two months after George Austen's death Mrs Austen and her daughters moved from Green Park Buildings to 25, Gay Street, one of the busiest thoroughfares in Bath. Their new home was in a more fashionable part of the city, near the elegant terraced houses of the Circus and the famous Royal Crescent, and the Crescent Fields.

In April Cassandra went to stay with the Lloyds at Ibthorpe. Mrs Lloyd was seriously ill and Cassandra probably went to help and support her friend Martha. Many letters must have been exchanged during the six weeks in which the sisters were separated, but only two of Jane's letters to Cassandra survive. These letters show that Jane's spirits were recovering following the death of her father and she was enjoying a busy social life once more. Jane and her mother received lots of callers and made calls themselves. 'What request we are in!'[20] Jane exclaimed to her sister. They also enjoyed walks in the fine spring weather and spent time with Mrs Austen's cousin Cassandra Cooke, her husband Samuel and two of their children, who were staying in Bath. A visit to watch her friend Miss Chamberlayne 'look hot on horseback' at a riding school reminded Jane of a visit to the same riding school seven years earlier. 'What a different set are we now moving in! But seven years I suppose are enough to change every pore of one's skin, & every feeling of one's mind.'[21]

By 21 April, when Jane began the second letter, Mrs Lloyd had died and a reference is made to Martha moving to Bath to live with the Austens. This letter also contains the following amusing description of a visit to Lady Leven, the mother of Lord Balgonie, a lieutenant in the navy and a friend of Charles Austen.

> On receiving a message from Lord & Lady Leven thro' the Mackays declaring their intention of waiting on us, we thought it right to go to them. I hope we have not done too much, but the friends & admirers of Charles must be attended to. – They seem very reasonable, good sort of people, very civil, & full of his praise. – We were shewn at first into an empty Drawing-room, & presently in came his Lordship, not knowing who we were, to apologise for the servant's mistake, & tell a lie himself, that Lady Leven was not within. – He is a tall, gentlemanlike looking man, with spectacles, & rather deaf; – after sitting with him ten minutes we walked away; but Lady L. coming out of the Dining parlour as we passed the door, we were obliged to

> attend her back to it, & pay our visit over again. – She is a stout woman, with a very handsome face. – By this means we had the pleasure of hearing Charles's praises twice over; – they think themselves excessively obliged to him, & estimate him so highly as to wish Ld Balgonie when he is quite recovered, to go out to him – The young man is much better, & is gone for the confirmation of his health, to Penzance. – There is a pretty little Lady Marianne of the party, to be shaken hands with & asked if she remembers Mr Austen.[22]

As this letter shows, Jane kept Cassandra informed in minute detail of all that she was doing in her absence. Jane viewed her letters as a continuous conversation with her sister, as illustrated when she observed to Cassandra 'I have now attained the true art of letter-writing, which we are always told, is to express on paper exactly what one would say to the same person by word of mouth.'[23]

From the beginning of 1804 there is another source of information on the lives of the Austen sisters, in the form of a diary kept by their niece Fanny. For Christmas 1803 Elizabeth Austen gave her daughter a copy of *The Ladies Compleat Pocket Book,* a blank diary in which she began to make daily entries, often in considerable detail. Fanny kept a diary from then until nearly the end of her long life. The early diaries, which record the daily activities and comings and goings at Godmersham, provide a fascinating insight into life in an English country house in the late Georgian and Regency periods. There are frequent references to Cassandra and Jane, and descriptions of how they spent their time when they stayed with Edward and his family in Kent.

The first such visit recorded by Fanny is the one made by her grandmother and aunts in the summer of 1805. The Austen ladies stopped to collect Anna from Steventon on their way to Kent. Anna's stepmother was due to give birth to her second child and, presumably, they took Anna with them to help Mary. Fanny recorded their arrival on Wednesday 19 June. Two days later she noted the birth of James and Mary's daughter Caroline Mary Craven Austen.

Fanny's diary shows that life at Godmersham was as busy as ever. Edward and Elizabeth now had nine children, following the birth of Louisa the year before. Cassandra and Jane, as usual, delighted in the company of their young nephews and nieces. They enjoyed the fun and pleasure of being aunts, as the following diary entries illustrate:

> Tuesday 25th June
> We had a whole holiday [from lessons]. Aunts and G.Mama played at school with us. Aunt C. was Miss Teachum, the Governess, Aunt Jane was Miss Popham, the teacher, Aunt Harriot [Bridges], Sally the Housemaid, Miss Sharpe [Fanny's governess], the Dancing Master, the Apothecary & the Sergeant, Grandmama, Betty Jones the Pie Woman & Mama the Bathing Woman. They dressed in character & we had a most delightful day. – After dessert we acted a Play called *Virtue Rewarded*. Anna was Duchess St Albans, I was the Fairy Serena & Fanny Cage a shepherdess Mona. We had a Bowl of Syllabub in the evening.
>
> Tuesday 30th July
> Aunts C. & Jane, Anna, Edward, George, Henry, William & myself acted *The Spoilt Child* & *Innocence Rewarded*, afterwards we danced & had a most delightful evening.

Anne Sharp, Fanny's governess, who was mentioned in the earlier entry, became Jane's close friend and remained so until Jane's death.

Fanny's diary entries for just a few days show how busy her aunts were during their stay, with outings and social engagements nearly every day:

> 8th August
> Mama, Aunt Jane, George and I went in the chaise to Canterbury.
>
> 9th August
> Papa, Mama & Aunts dined at Lees Court.

12th August
Aunts Cass. and Jane walked to Eggerton with Willm ,Lizzy & I.

16th August
Mama and Aunt Jane went in the evening to the ball at Canterbury.[24]

Later in the month Cassandra and Jane took it in turns to visit Elizabeth's mother, who was now widowed, and her family at Goodnestone. During Jane's visit, Elizabeth's brother Edward paid her a lot of attention. In a letter to Cassandra dated 27 August Jane wrote

> It is impossible to do justice to the hospitality of his attentions towards me; he made a point of ordering toasted cheese for supper entirely on my account.[25]

This attention and a reference in a later letter to 'an invitation' that Jane had received from him but could not accept, seems to suggest that Edward may have tried to propose to her.[25] A gap in the surviving correspondence between these two letters makes it impossible to be certain about this.

At the end of August Mrs Austen and Anna left Godmersham, while Cassandra and Jane stayed on. They were going to Worthing with Edward and Elizabeth the following month. Fanny recorded the journey to Sussex in her diary.

16th September
Papa, Mama, Aunts Cass. & Jane & I set off from Godmersham for Battel, where we arrived about 4, & finding no accommodation we proceeded to Horsebridge where we slept. We saw the abbey at Battel.[26]

The party arrived at Worthing the following day. Fanny's diary shows that she delighted in the company of her aunts as much as they did in hers, and that she was becoming increasingly close to them. They went for long walks together and enjoyed 'delicious dips in the sea'. Fanny also recorded that Jane won a prize of 17*s* in a raffle one evening. When Fanny and her parents returned to Godmersham her aunts remained in Worthing, where they were joined by their mother and Martha for a holiday that lasted until November. While they were there, the Battle of Trafalgar was fought. Reference to this epic battle was hidden amongst family news in Fanny's diary. On 17 November, sixteen days after the event, Fanny wrote 'We heard of a very great Victory we had obtained over the French, but that Lord Nelson was killed.'

Frank Austen, who had been recognised by Nelson as 'an excellent young man',[27] had hoped to be put in command of a frigate under the great admiral. To his great disappointment, however, Frank's ship HMS *Canopus* was involved in the Blockade of Cadiz and other duties when the Battle of Trafalgar took place.[28] His sisters shared his disappointment in playing no part in that glorious victory. A few weeks later Frank's involvement in the victory over the French at San Domingo helped to compensate him for missing the Battle of Trafalgar. He received a gold medal and a silver vase as a reward, as well as the gratitude of both Houses of Parliament.[29] Cassandra and Jane were both proud of his achievement and delighted in the recognition he received. Frank, who had been engaged to Mary Gibson for two years, was now in a secure enough financial position to plan his wedding.

In January 1806 the Austen ladies and Martha moved to Trim Street in a poorer part of the city, where accommodation was cheaper. This was a street in which Cassandra had been determined never to live, but the move was necessary owing to the need to economise. This was to be their last home in Bath. Around this time Cassandra's and Jane's financial situation improved when they received a bequest of £50 each in the will of Mrs Lillingston, a friend of their aunt Jane Leigh-Perrot, whom they had got to know during their time in Bath. This bequest was a considerable sum and must have been very welcome; Jane used it to cover her personal expenses for the next year.[30]

Financial considerations were also behind Mrs Austen's determination to move away from the expensive city of Bath as soon as possible. Frank and Mary suggested that they combined households after their forthcoming wedding, and Mrs Austen gladly accepted the offer. The plan was to find a home in Southampton, which was a pleasant and fashionable location as well as being convenient for Frank, who needed to be near Portsmouth when he was on shore leave.

On 2 July 1806 Mrs Austen, her daughters and Martha finally left Bath. Cassandra and Jane, who had been feeling restless for some time, left with what Jane described as 'happy feelings of escape'.[31] Although they had enjoyed some aspects of life in Bath, they were ready for a change. Before leaving Jane wrote a neat copy of the manuscript of her juvenile piece *Lady Susan* and added a conclusion. This was the only satisfactory writing she achieved during these unsettled years, but she had accumulated a valuable store of impressions and memories to use when she began to write again. Both sisters looked forward with pleasure to a return to their native county.

9

SOUTHAMPTON

1806–1809

After leaving Bath Mrs Austen and her daughters embarked on a series of visits to relatives, while Martha went on holiday to Harrogate. The Austen ladies' first stop was Adlestrop Rectory in Gloucestershire to stay with Mrs Austen's cousin, Thomas Leigh. It was twelve years since Cassandra and Jane had last visited their great-uncle, who was now a widower. In early August Thomas took his guests to Stoneleigh Abbey in Warwickshire, which he had recently inherited under the terms of the complicated will of the previous owner. The purpose of this visit was for Mr Leigh to stake his claim to the property.

Stoneleigh Abbey was originally a Cistercian monastery, founded in 1155. It had passed to the Leigh family at the time of the Dissolution of the Monasteries during the reign of Henry VIII. The Leigh family had built a new house with the stones of the old abbey and made other alterations. Charles I stayed there on his way to Nottingham at the start of the Civil War. Stoneleigh Abbey was a fascinating place in which to stay, especially for Jane, with her interest in history and her sympathy for the royal House of Stuart. Mrs Austen wrote a letter to her daughter-in-law Mary, describing this visit.

> And here we all found ourselves on Tuesday (that is yesterday sennight) Eating Fish, venison & all manner of good things, at a late hour, in a Noble large Parlour, hung round with

> family Pictures – every thing is very Grand & very fine & very Large – The House is larger than I could have supposed – we can **now** find our way about it, I mean the best part, as to the offices (which were the old Abby) Mr Leigh almost dispairs of ever finding his way about them – I have proposed his setting up directing Posts at the Angles ... I expected to find everything about the place very fine & all that, but I had no idea of its being so beautiful, I had figured to myself long Avenues, dark rookeries & dismal Yew Trees, but here are no such melancholy things; The Avon runs near the house amidst Green Meadows, bounding by large and beautiful Woods, full of delightful Walks... We walk a good deal, for the Woods are impenetrable to the sun, even in the middle of an August day. I do not fail to spend some part of every day in the kitchen garden, where the quantity of small fruit exceeds anything you can form an idea of... Our Visit has been a most pleasant one. We all seem in good humour, disposed to be pleas'd, and endeavouring to be agreable, and I hope we succeed.[1]

The only irritation during the Austens' stay was the presence of Elizabeth Twisleton (Lady Saye and Sele), who was distantly related to the Leigh family. Mrs Austen described her as 'rather tormenting' but she was 'sometimes amusing, and affords Jane many a good laugh'.[2] Jane probably also made a mental note of the behaviour of this eccentric lady, to add to her store of material for future novels.

On leaving Stoneleigh Abbey Mrs Austen and her daughters travelled to Hamstall Ridware in Staffordshire, stopping at Kenilworth and Warwick Castles on their way. Hamstall Ridware was the home of Mrs Austen's nephew Edward Cooper, who was rector of St Michael's Church, his wife Caroline and their eight children. This may have been a trying time for Jane, as there is a hint in her letters that she found Edward rather irritating. Edward was an enthusiastic evangelical preacher, who had recently published a book of sermons. Jane did not like the fanaticism displayed by the Evangelicals, as she regarded faith as a private matter. To make matters worse, Edward's eldest son, also named Edward, who was then twelve years old, was in the habit of imitating his father by preaching pompously to his younger brothers and sisters. The Austens stayed for five weeks, during which time all the Cooper children developed whooping cough. Unfortunately, Jane caught it from them and it took her many weeks to recover.

In October 1806 the Austen ladies and Martha moved into temporary lodgings in Southampton, with the newly married Frank and Mary. Jane was in uncharacteristically low spirits following the move. Her mood was not improved by Cassandra leaving for a visit to Godmersham. While Cassandra was away a permanent home was found in Castle Square. This house, which had a wide-ranging view of the Solent, belonged to John Henry Petty, the 2nd Marquis of Lansdowne. In a letter dated 8–9 February 1807 Jane described to her sister the preparations being made to the property prior to them moving in.

> The alterations & improvements within doors too advance very properly, & the Offices will be made very convenient indeed. – Our Dressing-Table is constructing on the spot, out of a large Kitchen Table belonging to the House, for doing which we have the permission of Mr Husket, Lord Lansdown's Painter, – domestic Painter I shd call him, for he lives in the Castle – Domestic Chaplains have given way to this more necessary office, & I suppose whenever the Walls want no touching up, he is employed about my Lady's face.[3]

Jane also described the changes she and her mother were supervising in the garden.

> Our Garden is putting in order, by a Man who bears a remarkably good Character, has a very fine complexion & asks something less than the first. The Shrubs which border the gravel walk he says are only sweetbriar & roses, & the latter of an indifferent sort; – we mean to get a few of a better kind therefore, & at my own particular desire he procures us some Syringas. I could not do without a Syringa, for the sake of Cowper's Line. – We talk also of a Laburnum – The Border under the Terrace Wall, is clearing away to receive

> Currants & Gooseberry Bushes, & a spot is found very proper for Raspberries.[4]

The garden was bounded on one side by the old city walls, which were wide enough to walk along. An attractive and productive garden was very important to the new tenants.

Jane was impatient for her sister's return not only because she missed her but also because she needed her to help with preparations for the move. Frank and Mary were also anxious for Cassandra's return, as Jane informed her:

> Frank & Mary cannot at all approve of your not being at home in time to help them in their finishing purchases, & desire me to say that, if you are not, they shall be as spiteful as possible & chuse everything in the stile most likely to vex you. Knives that will not cut, glasses that will not hold, a sofa without a seat, & a Bookcase without shelves.[5]

Jane described Frank, who was good with his hands, making a fringe for the drawing-room curtains. She also told Cassandra, 'We hear that we are envied our House by many people, & that the Garden is the best in the Town.'[6]

Having had enough of the busy social life of Bath, Cassandra and Jane decided that they would lead a quiet life after moving into their new home. They wanted to limit their social circle to Frank's naval friends and acquaintances, and declined offers of introductions to new people. One person Jane was pleased to be introduced to, however, was the small daughter of one of Frank's naval colleagues, whose visit she described in a letter to her sister.

> The morning was so wet that I was afraid we should not be able to see our little Visitor, but Frank who alone could go to Church called for her after Service, & she is now talking away at my side & examining the Treasures of my Writing-desk drawer; – very happy I beleive; – not at all shy of course. – Her name is Catherine & her Sister's Caroline – She is something like her Brother, & as short for her age, but not so well-looking. – What is become of all the Shyness in the World?

> … Our little Visitor has just left us, & left us highly pleased with her; – she is a nice, natural, openhearted, affectionate girl, with all the ready civility which one sees in the best Children of the present day; – so unlike anything that I was myself at her age, that I am often all astonishment & shame – Half her time here was spent at Spillikins; which I consider as a very valuable part of our Household furniture, & as not the least important Benefaction from the family of Knight to that of Austen.[7]

This is an interesting description because Jane's obvious pleasure in Catherine's company does not accord with the accusations of some of her early biographers that she did not like children. This myth seems to have derived from her description of the spoilt and disagreeable Middleton children in *Sense and Sensibility*. Jane and Cassandra, as their close relationship with their young nephews and nieces shows, both liked children immensely and delighted in their company. It was only badly behaved children that Jane disliked.

James, Mary and their little daughter Caroline stayed at Southampton at the beginning of 1807. This was an awkward time for Jane, not only because she found Mary's company difficult, but also because she had to entertain them without the help of Cassandra, who was once again at Godmersham. Bad weather made going out difficult, causing James to be restless and irritable, as he did not like being confined indoors. Jane suggested the popular Austen pastime of reading aloud together in the evenings, but Mary did not like the books Jane had chosen. Jane could not wait for her brother and sister-in-law to leave. She wrote to Cassandra expressing her relief when they left.

> When you receive this, our guests will be all gone or going; and I shall be left to the comfortable disposal of my time, to ease of mind from the torments of rice puddings and apple dumplings and probably to regret that I did not take more pains to please them all.[8]

Jane told Cassandra that Mary had asked her to return with them to Steventon, adding 'I need not give my answer.'[9] Later, following another visit from James and Anna, Jane, who rarely had cause to be irritated by any of her brothers, observed to her sister:

> I am sorry & angry that his [James'] Visits should not give one more pleasure; the company of so good & so clever a Man ought to be gratifying in itself; – but his Chat seems all forced, his Opinions on many points too much copied from his Wife's, & his time here is spent I think in walking about the House & banging the Doors, or ringing the Bell for a glass of Water.[10]

Marriage to Mary seemed to have changed James. It had also become noticeable that Mary did not get on well with her step-daughter Anna, who could sometimes be rebellious, and that James appeared to favour the children of his second marriage over Anna.[11] This must have been distressing for both Cassandra and Jane, whose close and affectionate relationship with Anna dated back to the time when they looked after her following the death of her mother.

Another niece arrived in April 1807, when Frank's wife Mary gave birth to their first child Mary-Jane, after a difficult delivery. Earlier that year, Frank had taken command of HMS *St Albans*[12] and was not at home for the birth of his daughter. Fortunately Mrs Austen, Cassandra, Jane and Martha were on hand to help Mary. The new father returned home for a month's leave at the beginning of June, and was present at the baby's christening.

In May, soon after Cassandra and Jane moved into Castle Square, they heard of the marriage of their brother Charles to Frances (Fanny) Palmer, the seventeen-year-old daughter of John Grove Palmer, a former Attorney General of Bermuda. Since 1804 Charles had been serving on the North American station commanding HMS *Indian*,[13] which was tasked with keeping neutral countries from trading with France. Charles was a highly respected commander who, as Cassandra proudly noted, was 'looked up to by everybody in all America'.[14]

In early August, Edward Cooper and his three eldest children visited their relatives in Southampton. When they left, Mrs Austen and her daughters joined a large family gathering at Chawton

House, Edward's residence in Hampshire, which had recently been vacated by tenants. James, Mary and their children were also invited. This was the first of many happy visits Cassandra and Jane were to make to the house. Chawton House, always referred to as Chawton Great House by the Austens, was a Tudor mansion with mullioned windows and an impressive porch. It was situated on rising ground in the village of Chawton, overlooking the grey stone church of St Nicholas, which was in a hollow nearby.

This was also Fanny Austen's first visit to the house, which she described in a letter to her former governess.

> This is a fine large old house, built long before Queen Elizabeth I believe, & here are such a number of old irregular passages &c &c that it is very entertaining to explore them, & often when I think myself miles away from one part of the house I find a passage or entrance close to it, & I don't know when I shall be quite mistress of all the intricate, & different ways. It is very curious to trace the genealogy of the Knights & all the old families that have possessed this estate, from the pictures of which there are quantities, & some descriptions of them have been routed out, so that we are not at a loss for amusement. There are quantities of Trees about the house (especially Beech) which always make a place pretty, I think.[15]

Cassandra and Jane, who were always happy to join in with the activities of their nephews and nieces, probably joined Fanny in her exploration of the house and grounds. The family enjoyed a number of activities and it may have been at this time that Mrs Austen, her daughters and daughters-in-law amused themselves by writing 'verses to Rhyme with "Rose".'[16] These verses show that Mrs Austen was not the only family member to excel at writing doggerel verse.

In September Edward and Elizabeth took their children to Southampton to stay with their Austen relatives. The following entries in Fanny's diary show some of the activities that were enjoyed during this visit.

Sunday 13th September
We all went to church & afterwards walked to the Polygon (an area of Southampton).

Monday 14th September
In the evening Papa, Aunts C & J, Wm. & I went to the play. They performed *The Way to Keep Him.*

Tuesday 15th September
We went in a hired boat to Hythe to call on Mrs Palmer (Charles Austen's mother-in-law) who called on us the day before. Mama, to everybody's astonishment, was of the party & not at all sick. In the evening Uncle Henry A. came. Aunts C & J walked in the High Street till late.

Wednesday 16th September
We all, excepting Mama, took a boat and went to Netley Abbey, the ruins of which are beautiful. We eat there of some biscuits we had taken and returned quite delighted. Aunt Jane & I walked in the High Street till late.[17]

They also enjoyed a trip to Lyndhurst and Lymington in the New Forest. Edward, Elizabeth and their children left Southampton some time in September.

From January to March 1808, Cassandra and Jane were away from home on a series of visits. As the sisters were together there are no letters describing exactly what they did while they were away. They stayed first with James and Mary at Steventon Rectory. This would have been easier for Jane than when James and Mary stayed at Southampton the previous year, because of the presence of Cassandra. She would have been a calming influence on Jane and helped her to rise above any irritation she felt in the company of her brother and sister-in-law. They would have enjoyed seeing their nephew and nieces, and having the opportunity to walk in the familiar, much-loved country lanes around their old home, if the weather permitted.

Cassandra and Jane then went to stay with their friends at Manydown, which would probably have been a more pleasurable visit for them. All three of the Bigg sisters were at Manydown at this time, as the now-widowed Elizabeth had returned with her young son to live in her father's house. The second sister, Catherine, was soon to marry the Reverend Herbert Hill, the uncle of the poet Robert Southey. There had been no ill-feeling following Jane's rejection of Harris Bigg-Wither's offer of marriage, and she is unlikely to have seen the now married Harris during their stay.

The sisters' final visit was to Kintbury in Berkshire to stay with Fulwar Craven Fowle, the brother of Cassandra's late fiancé Tom, and his wife Eliza, the sister of Mary Austen and Martha Lloyd. Fulwar, an old friend of James Austen, was the vicar of St Mary's Church in Kintbury and also Lieutenant Colonel of the rifleman section of the Berkshire Volunteers. Fulwar and Eliza had six children, one of whom, Tom, was a midshipman on HMS *Indian* under Charles Austen.[18] Many years after the Austen sisters visited Kintbury, Fulwar William, the eldest son of the Fowles, remembered Jane and left the following description of her at this time.

> She was pretty – certainly pretty – bright & a good deal of color in her face – like a doll – no that would not give at all the idea for she had so much expression – she was like a child – quite a child very lively & full of humor – most amiable – most beloved.[19]

In May, Jane went to London to stay with Henry and Eliza, who were then living at Brompton but were about to move to Sloane Street in Chelsea. By this time another of Henry's army friends had joined his banking business, which was now called Austen, Maunde & Tilson, and was based in Henrietta Street, Covent Garden. Henry was also an associate of the banking firm Austen, Gray and Vincent of Alton in Hampshire. Jane's visits to London were always pleasurable, not only because of her closeness to Henry and Eliza, but also because of the cultural opportunities the capital offered. Henry made sure his sisters went to the theatre and art galleries whenever they were in London. On this occasion Jane had the additional pleasure of seeing the ladies going to Court on 4 June for the king's birthday celebrations.

In June 1808 Jane went with James, Mary, James Edward and Caroline to Godmersham. This was James' and Mary's first visit there for ten years. Anna, who had recently caused consternation in the family by having her hair cut short, was left in Southampton with Cassandra. James travelled to Kent by horse to make space in the carriage for his sister. After receiving a warm welcome from Edward, Elizabeth and their children, Jane's first thought, as usual, was to write to Cassandra. 'Where shall I begin?' she wrote. 'Which of all my important nothings shall I tell you first?' She described the long, hot journey to Kent and how they 'drove, drove, drove' to get there. Jane was already missing Cassandra and told her that being at Godmersham without her seemed 'odd'.[20] This suggests that they made more visits there together than are known about. Jane's letters can only provide information about the times they were separated.

Jane was concerned that Elizabeth, who was expecting her eleventh child, did not look well. As the mistress of a grand country house, Elizabeth's work was far more onerous and demanding than that of the traditional wife, mother and housekeeper. Jane offered to do what she could to help her, including listening to her young nieces read. The following extracts from Jane's letters give an idea of how she spent her time at Godmersham:

15th–17th June 1808
Yesterday passed quite *a la* Godmersham: the gentlemen rode about Edward's farm, and returned in time to saunter along Bentigh with us; and after dinner we visited the Temple Plantations, which, to be sure, is a Chevalier Bayard of a plantation. James and Mary are much struck with the beauty of the place. To-day the spirit of the thing is kept up by the two brothers being gone to Canterbury in the chair. I cannot discover, even through Fanny, that her mother is fatigued by her attendance on the children. I have, of course, tendered my services, and when Louisa [Elizabeth's sister] is gone, who sometimes hears the little girls read, will try to be accepted in her stead.[21]

30th June–1st July
Our Tuesday's Engagement went off very pleasantly; we called first on Mrs Knight, & found her very well; & at dinner had only the Milles of Nackington in addition to Goodnestone &

> Godmersham & Mrs Moore ... In the Even^{g} came Mr Moore, Mr Toke, D^{r} & Mrs Walsby & others; – one Card Table was formed, the rest of us sat & talked, & at half after nine we came away.[22]

Jane also visited Mrs Knight in Canterbury who gave her 'a very agreeable present of some money' which she said 'would make her circumstances quite easy'. Mrs Knight sent her love to Cassandra, who had also received a gift of money from her on a previous occasion. Both sisters enjoyed an affectionate relationship with Edward's adoptive mother.

Jane noticed that James Edward enjoyed playing with his lively cousins, but Caroline found them rather overwhelming. Edward got on well with his young nephew and 'talked nonsense to him most delightfully'. James Edward later recorded that his uncle was a 'very amiable man, kind and indulgent to all connected with him', and that he 'possessed also a spirit of fun and liveliness, which made him especially delightful to all young people'.[23] Edward's easy company was one reason Jane enjoyed staying at Godmersham so much. On this visit all she needed to complete her happiness was the presence of Cassandra, although she was pleased when her sister-in-law Eliza arrived for a brief stay.

Jane asked Cassandra to write in minute detail of all that was happening at home. She became concerned when Cassandra took Anna to the Isle of Wight that she may be tiring herself too much. Despite all the pleasures and comforts of country house life, Jane was anxious to be home with her sister again. When she finally arrived home in July, after a stay of several weeks, Jane had no idea that life at Godmersham was soon to change and would never be the same again.

The sisters were only briefly reunited before it was Cassandra's turn to go to Godmersham. She went to attend Elizabeth during her confinement, as she had with previous confinements, and to help run the house and look after the children while she recovered. Fanny, who had regretted Cassandra's absence in the summer, wrote in a letter to her old governess Miss Chapman:

> Aunt Cassandra I am happy to say is coming to stay here some time, it will be a great comfort to me to have her assistance in the lessons during Mama's confinement, as well as her company.[24]

Cassandra arrived on 28 September, but was a few hours too late to be present at the birth of her nephew Brook John. She wrote home to tell her mother and Jane of the baby's arrival and to report that Elizabeth and her son were both doing well. In her next letter Cassandra must have praised Fanny, as Jane responded;

> I am greatly pleased with your account of Fanny; I found her in the summer just what you describe, almost another Sister, & could not have supposed that a neice would ever have been so much to me. She is quite after one's own heart; give her my best Love & tell her that I always think of her with pleasure.[25]

Little did Jane or Cassandra, or even Fanny herself, realise that her excellent qualities would soon be put to the test.

Elizabeth seemed to be recovering well from her confinement, so it was a great shock to her family when, on 10 October, she suddenly and unexpectedly died. Fanny described what happened in her diary.

> Oh! The miserable events of this day! My mother, my beloved mother torn from us after eating a hearty dinner. She was taken violently ill & expired (God have mercy upon us) after ½ an hour!!! [26]

Jane, her mother and Martha heard the tragic news from James and Mary. This was followed by a detailed letter from Cassandra. In her reply Jane wrote;

> We have felt, we do feel for you all – as you will not need to be told – for you, for Fanny, for Henry [Bridges], for Lady Bridges & for dearest Edward, whose loss & whose sufferings

> seem to make those of every other person nothing. – God be praised! that you can say what you do of him – that he has a religious Mind to bear him up, & a Disposition that will gradually lead him to comfort. – My dear, dear Fanny! – I am so thankful that she has you with her! – You will be everything to her, you will give her all the Consolation that human aid can give. – May the Almighty sustain you all – & keep you my dearest Cassandra well – but for the present I dare say you are equal to everything.[27]

Jane concluded by saying,

> We need not enter into a Panegyric on the Departed – but it is sweet to think of her great worth – of her solid principles, her true devotion, her excellence in every relation of Life. It is also consolatory to reflect on the shortness of the sufferings which led her from this World to a better. – Farewell for the present, my dearest Sister. Tell Edward that we feel for him & pray for him.[28]

The strong and capable Cassandra suppressed her own emotions in order to deal with the aftermath of Elizabeth's death. Henry Austen and Henry Bridges hurried to Godmersham to offer their help. Jane's main concern was for Edward and his motherless children. She was particularly worried about Fanny who, as the eldest daughter, would now have to help care for her siblings, support her father and assume her mother's duties as mistress of a large country house at the tender age of sixteen. Fortunately Fanny, like other upper-class girls brought up in English country houses, had learnt the necessary skills by watching and helping her mother. Jane wrote:

> Dearest Fanny must now look upon herself as his prime source of comfort, his dearest friend; as the Being who is gradually to supply to him, to the extent that it is possible, what he has lost.[29]

The death of her mother was the end of Fanny's childhood and she would need the love and support of her aunts more than ever in the years to come.

Edward's eldest sons, Edward and George, were at school in Winchester when their mother died. They were brought to Southampton to be comforted by their grandmother and Aunt Jane. The latter occupied and distracted her nephews from their grief by playing games with them, taking them out for walks and on a boat trip. She also arranged for a local tailor to fit them out with mourning clothes, because she 'would not have them made uncomfortable by the want of what is usual on such occasions'.[30] Jane was helped by Martha, who did all she could to support her and the two boys. Cassandra and Jane supported each other by letter, and Jane reassured her sister by saying: 'You cannot write too often.'[31] Between them they were able to look after those most closely affected by Elizabeth's death.

Once again Cassandra's and Jane's strong faith, and their belief in life after death, helped to sustain them at this difficult time. When the initial shock had passed, life began to resemble something close to normality again, as Jane's letter to Cassandra dated 20 November suggests. The sisters had been amusing themselves by making romantic matches among members of their Kent and Southampton social circles. Jane wrote – 'I have a Southampton Match to return for your Kentish one, Capt. G. Heathcote & Miss A. Lyell; I have it from Alethea [Bigg] & like it, because I had made it before.'[32]

Jane's next letter shows that she was finding the frequent writing of long letters rather wearying, as she concludes with the words 'Distribute the affec^te^ Love of a Heart not so tired as the right hand belonging to it.'[33] She was finding the long separation from her sister hard to bear, even though she knew that Edward's need for Cassandra at that time was greater than her own. 'As to your lengthened stay,' Jane wrote, 'it is no more than I expected, & what must be, but you cannot suppose I like it.'[34] A few weeks later she wrote 'I am very glad to have the time of your return at all fixed, we all rejoice in it, & it will not be later than I had expected.'[35] She was desperate to be reunited with her sister, from whom she had been separated for most of the previous seven months. Cassandra finally returned to Southampton in February 1809, after an absence of more than four months. She would have been pleased to read a paragraph in a letter Fanny wrote to her former governess saying that her Aunt Cassandra had been 'the greatest comfort to us all'[36] in their time of affliction.

Shortly after Elizabeth's death, Edward offered his mother and sisters a new home. Frank and Mary had moved to a cottage in Alton, and they had been thinking about moving themselves. Edward offered them the choice of two properties – one in Wye near Godmersham and the other on his Hampshire estate, in the village of Chawton. The latter property was chosen.

Cassandra and Jane, who were proud of being 'Hampshire-born Austens', preferred to stay in their native county. They were delighted at the prospect of returning to north Hampshire. Jane's excitement is evident in her letters to her sister. She wrote:

> A larger circle of acquaintance & an increase of amusement is quite in character with our approaching removal. – Yes – I mean to go to as many Balls as possible, that I may have a good bargain. Every body is very much concerned at our going away, & every body is acquainted with Chawton & speaks of it as a remarkably pretty village & every body knows the House we describe – but nobody fixes on the right.[37]

Jane described a ball, which she and Martha attended at the Dolphin Inn, and observed:

> It was the same room in which we danced 15 years ago! – I thought it all over – & inspite of the shame of being so much older, felt with thankfulness that I was quite as happy now as then.[38]

The sisters made plans for their future at Chawton Cottage. In a letter to Cassandra dated 27–28 December 1808 Jane wrote:

> Mrs H. Digweed looks forward with great satisfaction to our being her neighbours – I w^{d} have her enjoy the idea to the utmost, as I suspect there will not [be] much in the reality.– With equal pleasure we anticipate an intimacy with her Husband's Bailiff & his wife, who live close by us, & are said to be remarkably good sort of people. – Yes, yes, we

will have a Pianoforte, as good a one as can be got for 30 Guineas – & I will practise country dances, that we may have some amusement for our nephews & neices, when we have the pleasure of their company.[39]

Jane seemed to be thinking once more about writing because before leaving Southampton she wrote the following letter, using a pseudonym, to Messrs Crosby & Co. in an attempt to get them to publish her novel *Susan*.

Wednesday 5th April 1809
Gentlemen,
In the Spring of the year 1803 a Ms. Novel in 2 vol. entitled *Susan* was sold to you by a Gentleman of the name of Seymour, & the purchase money £10 recd. at the same time. Six years have since passed, & this work of which I avow myself the Authoress, has never to the best of my knowledge, appeared in print, tho' an early publication was stipulated for at the time of Sale. I can only account for such an extraordinary circumstance by supposing the MS by some carelessness to have been lost; & if that was the case, am willing to supply You with another Copy if you are disposed to avail yourselves of it, & will engage for no farther delay when it comes into your hands. – It will not be in my power from particular circumstances to command this Copy before the Month of August, but then, if you accept my proposal, you may depend on receiving it. Be so good as to send me a Line in answer, as soon as possible, as my stay in this place will not exceed a few days. Should no notice be taken of this Address, I shall feel myself at liberty to secure the publication of my work, by applying elsewhere. I am Gentlemen &c &c
M.A.D.
Direct to Mrs Ashton Dennis
Post Office, Southampton [40]

Jane received the following disappointing reply to her letter.

Saturday 8th April 1809
Madam,
We have to acknowledge the receipt of your letter of the 5th inst. It is true that at the time mentioned we purchased of Mr Seymour a MS. Novel entitled *Susan* and paid him for it the sum of 10£ for which we have his stamped receipt as a full consideration, but there was not any time stipulated for its publication, neither are we bound to publish it. Should you or anyone else we shall take proceedings to stop the sale. The MS. shall be yours for the same as we paid for it.

For R.Crosby & Co
I am yours etc.
Richard Crosby.[41]

The reason for Crosby's failure to publish the novel in 1803 is unknown. When Jane wrote this letter, however, the Gothic novel it parodied had gone out of fashion, which may account for their refusal to publish it then. Jane did not have the money to buy back her manuscript and it therefore remained in the possession of R. Crosby & Co.

The move to Chawton was delayed because Mrs Austen became ill in March. By May she was well enough to travel with her daughters to Godmersham, where they planned to stay until Chawton Cottage was ready for them. Cassandra and Jane enjoyed the usual activities on offer at Godmersham, including visits to Canterbury and the Bridges family at Goodnestone. On 7 July Mrs Austen, her daughters and Martha finally moved into their new home, which marked the beginning of a happy and more settled period in the lives of the Austen sisters, and the start of a new creative period for Jane.

10

CHAWTON

1809–1812

Chawton Cottage was to be Cassandra's and Jane's home for the rest of their lives. It was to be the place most associated with Jane's career as a novelist as it was where she revised and prepared her early works for publication and created her last three novels. These were the happiest years of Jane's life, according to her family. They were happy years for Cassandra too, because when Jane was happy she was also.

Chawton Cottage was originally a roadside inn before it became the home of Edward's estate manager. Edward paid for the improvements and alterations necessary to make it a comfortable residence for his mother, sisters and Martha. He also paid for work to be done in the garden and for a delivery of firewood, as well as providing a donkey carriage for the use of his elderly mother.

Built in the seventeenth century, the cottage was an L-shaped, two-storey building constructed of whitewashed brick, with a tiled roof and sash windows. It was a larger building than its name suggests, although it was not as roomy as Steventon Rectory. On the ground floor were two parlours or sitting rooms, a dining room and the 'offices', which consisted of the kitchen, brewhouse and wash house. There were six bedrooms, and attic rooms for the servants to sleep in and for storage. The donkey carriage was kept in a small outhouse. As it was situated on a large corner plot, the house had gardens on three sides.

'The Cottage', as it was always called, opened straight onto the street. It was located at the end of the village of Chawton near a shallow pond, close to the place where a busy coach road from London divided into two. The left-hand road went on to Fareham and Gosport, and the right-hand road led to Winchester and Southampton. The nearest town was Alton, 2 miles away.

Caroline Austen described the interior of the house in *My Aunt Jane Austen, A Memoir.*

> Everything indoors and out was well kept – the house was well furnished, and it was altogether a comfortable and ladylike establishment, tho' I believe the means which supported it, were but small –
>
> The house was quite as good as the generality of Parsonage houses then – and much in the same old style – the ceilings low and roughly finished – **some** bedrooms very small – **none** very large but in number sufficient to accommodate the inmates, and several guests – [1]

The sitting room window looked directly onto the road, which was always busy. Among the travellers using the road were boys, including Edward's sons, on their way to and from Winchester School, at the beginning and end of every term. Mrs Austen, who liked to sit watching the passing traffic as she did her sewing and knitting, looked out for her grandsons when she knew they would be passing. They sometimes broke their journey at her house and called in to see their grandmother and aunts.

Caroline Austen described the constant traffic in her *Memoir*.

> Collyer's daily coach with six horses was a sight to see! and most delightful was it to a child to have the awful stillness of night so frequently broken by the noise of passing carriages, which seemed sometimes, even to shake the bed.[2]

People passing by in carriages and stagecoaches could see right into the house; Mrs Knight, who always liked to hear about the Austens, wrote in a letter to Fanny dated 26 October 1809:

> I heard of the Chawton Party, looking very comfortable at Breakfast, from a gentleman who was travelling by their door in a Post-chaise about ten days since. Your account of the whole family gives me the sincerest Pleasure, and I beg you will assure them all how much I feel interested in their happiness.[3]

The gardens, which were a particular source of pleasure to both Cassandra and Jane, contained a shrubbery, a vegetable garden, fruit trees, oak and beech trees and a variety of flowers. A wooden fence and hornbeam hedge separated the garden from the road.

The Austen ladies' new home was close enough to Steventon for James, Mary and their children to pay frequent calls. James and Anna liked to ride over together through the narrow country lanes. As these were not suitable for carriages Mary, James Edward and Caroline had to travel by the main roads, which were less direct. The cottage was very close to Chawton Great House where, after the tenants had vacated it, Edward and his children sometimes stayed. Later Frank and Charles and their families also stayed there from time to time. Being close to Alton, Henry could visit his mother and sisters easily when he was there on business. In April 1809 Frank's wife Mary and their daughter Mary-Jane moved into Rose Cottage in Alton, conveniently near to Chawton. It was at Rose Cottage that their second child, and first son, Frank William was born in July 1809. Jane wrote the following poem to commemorate the birth of her nephew in which she recalled Frank's childhood and which concluded with a verse about her new home.

> My dearest Frank, I wish you Joy
> Of Mary's safety with a boy,
> Whose birth has given little pain,
> Compared with that of Mary-Jane. –
> May he a growing Blessing prove,
> And well deserve his Parents' Love!
> Endow'd with Art's & Nature's Good,
> Thy name possessing with thy Blood;
> In him, in all his ways, may we
> Another Francis William see! –
> Thy infant days may he inherit,

Thy warmth, nay insolence of spirit; –
We would not with one fault dispense
To weaken the resemblance.
May he revive thy Nursery sin,
Peeping as daringly within,
(His curley Locks but just descried),
With 'Bet, my be not come to bide.'–
[a reference to something Frank said as a child]
Fearless of danger, braving pain,
And threaten'd very oft in vain,
Still may one Terror daunt his soul,
One needful engine of Controul
Be found in this sublime array,
A neighbouring Donkey's aweful Bray!
So may his equal faults as Child,
Produce Maturity as mild,
His saucy words & fiery ways
In early Childhood's pettish days
In Manhood shew his Father's mind
Like him considerate & kind;
All Gentleness to those around,
And eager only not to wound.
Then like his Father too, he must,
To his own former struggles just,
Feel his Deserts with honest Glow,
And all his Self-improvement know. –
A native fault may thus give birth
To the best blessing, conscious worth. –

As for ourselves, we're very well,
As unaffected prose will tell.
Cassandra's pen will give our state
The many comforts that await
Our Chawton home – how much we find
Already in it to our mind;
And how convinced that when complete
It will all other Houses beat
That ever have been made or mended,

With rooms concise or rooms distended.
You'll find us very snug next year;
Perhaps with Charles & Fanny near –
For now it often does delight us
To fancy them just over-right us.[4]

On returning from China, where he had been based for six months, Frank stayed with his family at Alton until his next posting. Another advantage of the move to Chawton was its proximity to Manydown, the home of the Bigg sisters.

Chawton was, and still is, a pretty country village surrounded by farmland and hop fields. Many of its 400 inhabitants were farm labourers or forest workers, some of whom worked on Edward's estate. The Austen ladies' new neighbours included the tenants of Chawton Great House – John Middleton, a widower with six children, and his housekeeper, Maria Beckford, who was also his sister-in-law.

The rector of Chawton was the Reverend John Papillon who lived, with his sister Elizabeth, near St Nicholas Church in the recently rebuilt rectory. Mrs Knight jokingly suggested that the rector would be a good husband for Jane. Jane, who was highly amused by this idea, responded by saying:

> I am very much obliged to Mrs Knight for such a proof of the interest she takes in me – & she may depend upon it, that I **will** marry Mr Papillon, whatever may be his reluctance or my own – I owe her much more than such a trifling sacrifice.[5]

The Prowting family – William Prowting, a magistrate and Deputy Lieutenant for Hampshire, and his two unmarried daughters – lived close to Chawton Cottage and became good friends of the Austens. Villagers later recalled seeing Jane climb over a stile and walk across the fields between her home and that of the Prowtings to visit them. Later one of the Prowting girls married and moved into the village.

Other neighbours included Mr and Miss Hinton, the inhabitants of Chawton Lodge, who were the children of a previous rector, and Miss Benn. The latter was a poor, middle-aged spinster who lived in a dilapidated cottage. She was the sister of the Reverend John Benn of the nearby village of Farringdon who, with a wife and twelve children to support, was unable to help his sister. Cassandra and Jane befriended Miss Benn and she was sometimes a guest at Chawton Cottage.

According to Caroline, her grandmother and aunts were only close to a few neighbours and were on friendly but somewhat distant terms with the rest. Cassandra and Jane took an interest in their neighbours and enjoyed hearing about them but, for most of them, this was as close as they became. Jane's letters show that the sisters enjoyed relaying and receiving information and gossip about their neighbours. Caroline made the following comment on Jane's interest in them.

> They sometimes served for her amusement, but it was her own nonsense that gave zest to the gossip – She never turned **them** into ridicule – She was as far as possible from being either censorious or satirical – she never abused them or **quizzed** them.[6]

Caroline remembered Chawton Cottage as a happy place, with visitors always coming and going. She also remembered it as being peaceful and tranquil.

> In the time of my childhood, it was a cheerful house – my Uncles, one or another, frequently coming for a few days; and they were all pleasant in their own family – I have thought since, after having seen more of other households, **wonderfully**, as the family talk had much of spirit and vivacity, and it was never troubled by disagreements as it was not their habit to argue with each other – There always was perfect harmony amongst the brothers and sisters, and over my Grandmother's door might have been inscribed the text 'Behold how good – and joyful a thing it is, brethren, to dwell together in unity.'[7]

Like most country dwellers the occupants of Chawton Cottage lived rather introspective lives. Caroline could not remember her aunts speaking about national events or anything outside the confines of their family and daily life. They were not unusual in this respect, as the latest news took a long time to reach remote country places like Chawton and country people were only affected by far-off events if members of their own families were involved. A comment written by Jane later, concerning the Peninsula War battle at Almeida illustrates this – 'How horrible it is to have so many people killed. – And what a blessing that one cares for none of them.'[8]

Apart from the few neighbours they befriended, the occupants of Chawton Cottage did not make any new acquaintances. This was partly due to their inability to travel far, but also because they chose not to engage in the sort of social activities that had occupied so much of their time in Steventon, Bath and their final months in Southampton. Mrs Austen, being elderly and not in good health, wanted a quiet and easy life. As far as Cassandra and Jane, and probably Martha, were concerned, they had now settled into spinsterhood and one of the main motivations for their previous busy social lives – the need to find a husband – no longer mattered to them.

Cassandra and Jane now assumed the ways and appearance of middle-aged spinsters – rather too soon according to Caroline, who wrote 'I believe my two aunts were not accounted very good dressers, and were thought to have taken to the garb of middle age unnecessarily soon.'[9] Jane also started to wear a cap, except when she was in London with her nieces, who refused to let her wear one. They made her curl her hair and tie it with a ribbon – a look that Jane did not particularly like, but which her nieces assured her looked charming.

According to Caroline Austen, life at Chawton Cottage was 'easy and pleasant'[10] with little variety in it. The Austen ladies and Martha became regular attenders at St Nicholas Church, a short walk from their home. Cassandra and Jane became involved in helping sick and needy parishioners, as they had done at Steventon. They also taught poor village children to read and write.

The sisters resumed their habit of taking long walks in the countryside, usually in the afternoons. The town of Alton, with its shops and circulating library, was close enough to reach on foot. As they did not have a carriage, Cassandra and Jane had to walk everywhere.

They took up the same indoor pastimes as they had enjoyed at Steventon, such as reading and needlework. Caroline remembered some of the beautiful pieces of needlework Jane made at Chawton Cottage, including an embroidered muslin scarf and a piece of embroidery that she made for Fanny, and they both helped their mother to make a large patchwork quilt. Cassandra resumed her hobby of drawing and watercolour painting, and took over from her mother as the family letter writer.

Cassandra, assisted by Martha, took charge of running the household, which included planning meals, supervising the servants and brewing beer. Martha put together a book of recipes and remedies for them to use. Many women compiled such books in the eighteenth century and they were often handed down to their daughters and granddaughters. Jane was put in charge of preparing breakfast for the family and looking after the stores of tea, sugar and wine. These expensive items, which were kept under lock and key, were used sparingly. Mrs Austen took on responsibility for looking after the large garden; when gardening she wore a round green smock, like those worn by land labourers.

Once Jane was settled in her new permanent home she began to think about writing again. Her sister's reassuring presence provided Jane with the emotional stability and peace of mind necessary for her creativity to flourish. Her limited housekeeping duties allowed Jane enough time to write. The only difficulty she encountered was the lack of a private space to work in. As she did not have a separate study or a private room of her own, Jane had to write in the family sitting room, in the midst of the daily activities of the household. She sat at a small writing table, placed by the window to give her sufficient light. Jane now wore spectacles when she was writing, as she suffered from weak eyes. As she still did not want any servants or visitors to know that she was a writer, Jane insisted that a creaking door between the sitting room and the offices should not be adjusted, as it gave her notice of anyone about to enter. She continued to write on small pieces of paper, which could be hastily put away or covered up with blotting paper.

The first thing Jane did was to go through the manuscript of *Sense and Sensibility* and make a few additions to it. In this, and Jane's subsequent novels, the heroine undergoes a journey of self-discovery. When this is completed and she has overcome a series of obstacles, the heroine marries the man who is right for her. Two important themes in all the novels are repentance and the importance of love in marriage.

When the manuscript had been tidied up, Jane's family, no doubt including Cassandra, encouraged her to try to get this novel published. According to her brother Henry:

> She became an authoress entirely from taste and inclination. Neither the hope of fame nor profit mixed with her early motives... It was with extreme difficulty that her friends, whose partiality she suspected whilst she honoured their judgement, could prevail on her to publish her first work.[11]

By 'friends' Henry meant family, as only family members, with one exception, knew of her secret life as a writer. With the encouragement of these 'friends' Jane sent the manuscript, either in late 1809 or early 1810, to the London publisher Thomas Egerton. Much to her delight, Egerton agreed to publish it at her expense. Jane was so sure, however, that she would not recover the expense of publication that she saved enough money from her small income to cover the expected loss. The title chosen for this novel is thought to have come from the popular *Lady's Monthly Museum* magazine. This title was a headline of an article entitled *Effects of Mistaken Synonymy*.[12]

Only a few people were aware that Jane was soon to be a published author. The people who knew were Cassandra, Mrs Austen, Martha, Jane's brothers and their wives, the Leigh-Perrots and Fanny. James Austen's three children were not in on the secret at this stage. Jane made it clear that she wanted the knowledge of her authorship to be limited to these people and

Cassandra helped her to keep the secret. Fanny noted in her diary that Cassandra had written to beg her and her father not to tell anyone that Jane had written *Sense and Sensibility*.

In October 1809 Edward, Fanny and her brother Charles came to stay at Chawton Cottage. Fanny recorded in her diary that her grandmother and aunts were all well. Over the next three weeks she spent a lot of time with Cassandra and Jane. They made a number of visits together to Mary and her two children at Alton. They all went to a jubilee celebration to mark the fiftieth anniversary of the accession day of the 'dear old king'. Fanny was not used to walking the sort of distances that her aunts walked and on Friday 27 October she recorded in her diary that she was 'as tired as a dog'.[13]

Around this time the Austen family became worried about Anna. Their anxiety was caused by her brief engagement to Michael Terry, son of Thomas and Elizabeth Terry, who lived in the village of Dummer near Steventon. Michael, a good-looking young man from a respectable and well-connected family, was a Cambridge-educated clergyman with the prospect of a comfortable family living. Despite these advantages, Anna's father and stepmother did not consider him a suitable match for her. Their reservations may have been due to the fact that he was eighteen years older than Anna. James and Mary refused to consent to the engagement and Anna was sent to Godmersham to put distance between her and Michael.

At the beginning of 1810, Michael's sister Charlotte wrote to the Austens to ask them to reconsider their opposition to the engagement. Cassandra then spoke to James and Mary on Anna's behalf with the result that they gave Michael permission to go to Godmersham to pay his addresses to her. Fanny is said to have liked him.

After returning home Anna went to stay with the Terrys at Dummer for three days, during which time she decided that Michael was not the right man for her after all and broke off the engagement. Much embarrassment was caused to both families and meeting each other socially became awkward. Cassandra and Jane supported Anna during this difficult time, and she was invited to stay at Chawton Cottage. Jane wrote a witty poem entitled *Mock Panegyric on a Young Friend*. This poem, which began with the lines 'In measured verse I'll now rehearse/ The charms of lovely Anna', warned about being too emotional.[14]

At the end of March 1811, while *Sense and Sensibility* was being printed, Jane went to London to stay with Henry and Eliza in Sloane Street. During this visit she checked the proofs of her novel, which was much easier to do there, as Henry's home was not far from her publisher's office in Whitehall.

Jane's next surviving letter to Cassandra, after a gap of twenty-one months, was written in Sloane Street between 18 and 20 April. As usual she was anxious to tell her sister what she had been doing since they parted. She begins by saying 'I have so many little matters to tell you of, that I cannot wait any longer before I begin to put them down.'[15] Jane goes on to describe meeting and spending time with her godfather Samuel Cooke, his wife Cassandra and her three cousins Mary, George and Theo, who were staying in London. She went with Mary to see the natural history exhibits at the Liverpool Museum in Piccadilly, followed by a visit to the Gallery of the British Institute in Pall Mall. These were good places to watch people, as she explained to Cassandra – 'I had some amusement at each, tho' my preference for Men & Women always inclines me to attend more to the company than the sight.' At the end of a busy day Henry collected her from the Cookes' lodgings in Bentinck Street and 'after putting Life & Wit into the party for a quarter of an hour, put himself and his Sister into a Hackney Coach.' Jane added, 'I bless my stars that I am done with Tuesday!'[16]

Wednesday was just as hectic, however. In the morning Jane went shopping with Manon, Eliza's maidservant. They went to Wilding & Kent, on the corner of Grafton Street and New Bond Street. Jane told Cassandra that this popular shop was so crowded that she had to wait 'full half an hour' to be served, but she came away 'very well satisfied' with her purchases of 'Bugle Trimming' and silk stockings.[17] This letter shows that, despite having adopted the dress of middle-aged women, Cassandra and Jane remained interested in clothes and that they still had to watch their money carefully. Jane wrote:

> I am sorry to tell you that I am getting very extravagant & spending all my Money; & what is worse for **you**, I have

> been spending yours too; for in a Linendraper's shop to which I went for check'd Muslin, & for which I was obliged to give seven shillings a yard, I was tempted by a pretty coloured muslin, & bought 10 ^{yds} of it, on the chance of your liking it; – but at the same time if it sh^{d} not suit you, you must not think yourself at all obliged to take it ; it is only 3/6 p^{r} y^{d}, & I sh^{d} not in the least mind keeping the whole – In texture it is just what we prefer, but its resemblance to green cruels [an embroidered fabric] I must own is not great, for the pattern is a small red spot.[18]

That afternoon Jane 'drank tea' with two of Henry's business associates and their wives, James and Frances Tilson and the Smiths. Jane met a number of other people during her stay, including some of Eliza's French émigré friends who had sought refuge in London during the French Revolution. She told Cassandra that she found 'all these little parties very pleasant'.[19]

In one of her letters to Jane, Cassandra, who was staying at Godmersham, enquired about the progress of the proofreading of *Sense and Sensibility*. She seems to have received the impression that her sister was so busy socialising that the proofs were being neglected. Jane replied:

> No indeed, I am never too busy to think of *S & S*. I can no more forget it, than a mother can forget her sucking child; & I am much obliged to you for your enquiries. I have had two sheets to correct, but the last only brings us to W.'s first appearance.[20]

Cassandra's concern about the proofs shows how closely involved she was in Jane's writing.

Jane's many social engagements while in London included a visit to the Lyceum Theatre to see the play *The Hypocrite* by Isaac Bickerstaffe, which she found very entertaining. She was disappointed, however, not to see her favourite actress Sarah Siddons. The highlight of Jane's stay was a grand musical party, which Eliza held on the evening of 23 April. Many of Henry's and Eliza's fashionable friends were invited, as well as their Cooke cousins. Among the sixty-six guests were a number of people Jane already knew. One of these acquaintances was Wyndham Knatchbull, Mrs Knight's brother who, Jane was later told, described her as 'a pleasing looking young woman'. Jane's response to this was:

> I depended upon hearing something of the Even^g from Mr W.K. – & am very well satisfied with his notice of me. 'A pleasing looking young woman'; – that must do; – one cannot pretend to anything better now, – thankful to have it continued a few years longer.[21]

Jane could not wait to tell Cassandra, in the usual minute detail, all about the party.

> The rooms were dressed up with flowers & c & looked very pretty. – A glass for the Mantelpiece was lent, by the Man who is making their own... At ½ past 7 arrived the Musicians in two Hackney coaches, & by 8 the lordly Company began to appear. Among the earliest were George & Mary Cooke, & I spent the greatest part of the even^g very pleasantly with them. – The Draw^g room being soon hotter than we liked, we placed ourselves in the connecting Passage, which was comparatively cool, & gave us all the advantage of the Music at a pleasant distance, as well as that of the first veiw of every new comer. – I was quite surrounded by acquaintance, especially Gentlemen... Including everybody, we were 66 – which was considerably more than Eliza had expected, & quite enough to fill the Back Draw^g room, & leave a few to be scattered about in the other, & in the passage. – The Music was extremely good... Between the Songs were Lessons on the Harp, or Harp & Piano Forte together – & the Harp Player was Wiepart, whose name seems famous, tho' new to me – There was one female singer, a short Miss Davis all in blue, bringing up for the Public Line, whose voice was said to be very fine indeed; – & all the Performers gave great satisfaction by doing what they were paid for; – & giving themselves no airs. – No Amateur could be persuaded to do anything – The

> House was not clear till after 12. – If you wish to hear more of it, you must put your questions, but I seem rather to have exhausted than spared the subject.[22]

Jane and Eliza spent the next day at home, recovering from the party, a report of which appeared in the *Morning Chronicle* two days later.

In this letter Jane referred to the birth of Frank and Mary's second son Henry Edgar, who had arrived a few days earlier. Frank was away at sea again, working as the flag captain to General Gambier on HMS *Caledonia*,[23] which was involved in blockading the French coast. Jane wrote, 'I give you joy of our new nephew, & hope if he ever comes to be hanged, it will not be till we are too old to care about it.'[24] Cassandra's and Jane's ever-growing number of nephews and nieces were a great delight to them and, as they grew up, were to play an increasingly important part in their lives.

Jane also reported to Cassandra that Anna was not causing any anxiety at Chawton, which must have been a relief to them both. She wrote:

> My Mother & Martha both write with great satisfaction of Anna's behaviour. She is quite an Anna with variations – but she cannot have reached her last, for that is always the most flourishing & shewey – she is at about her 3rd or 4th which are generally simple and pretty.[25]

Despite the anxiety Anna caused her aunts, she also amused them and they loved her dearly – a love which Anna returned.

Jane left London in May. On her journey home she stopped at Streatham to call on her friend Catherine Bigg, now Mrs Hill. As usual she had greatly enjoyed her stay in London and all the activities she had participated in, but she was glad to be back at her quiet home in Chawton. When Jane returned home only her mother and Anna were there. The garden had changed considerably since she went away and in her letter to Cassandra dated 29 May, Jane included the following delightful description of it as it was starting to fill out with summer flowers.

Above left: Jane Austen, painted by her sister.

Above right: Cassandra Austen.

Below left: Reverend George Austen, a miniature painted in 1801.

Below middle: Reverend George Austen.

Below right: Mrs Cassandra Austen.

Above left: James Austen.

Above right: Edward Austen, painted when he was on the Grand Tour.

Below left: Henry Austen. (Jane Austen House Museum, Chawton)

Below middle: Francis (Frank) Austen.

Below right: Charles Austen.

Above left: Thomas Knight, Edward Austen's adoptive father.

Above right: Catherine Knight, Edward Austen's adoptive mother.

Reverend George Austen presenting his son Edward to Thomas and Catherine Knight.

James Edward Austen, later Austen-Leigh, nephew of Cassandra and Jane, and author of the first biography of Jane.

Jane Austen, painted by her sister in 1804.

Steventon Church.

Steventon Rectory, a sketch by Anna Lefroy. (Colouring by the author)

Godmersham House, home of Edward Austen and his family.

Charing Cross, London. Cassandra and Jane often stayed with their brother Henry in London. (Yale Center for British Art, Paul Mellon Collection)

Covent Garden, London. Henry Austen lived in Henrietta Street near Covent Garden from 1813 to 1816. (Yale Center for British Art, Paul Mellon Collection)

Carlton House, London, home of the Prince Regent, which Jane visited in 1815. (Yale Center for British Art, Paul Mellon Collection)

Abbey Church, Bath, where the Austen family are believed to have worshipped.

Pulteney Bridge, Bath. Cassandra and Jane crossed this elegant bridge regularly in their walks around Bath.

The Holbourne Museum (originally the Sydney Hotel) in Sydney Gardens, Bath. Cassandra and Jane lived near here from 1801 to 1804.

Royal Crescent, Bath, the grandest of all the residential streets in Bath.

Queen Square, Bath, where Jane stayed in 1799.

The Pump Room, Bath, which Jane often visited with her uncle when he drank the waters there.

Pump Room, Bath, interior view.

25, Gay Street, Bath, home of Cassandra and Jane from 1805 to 1806.

The Roman Baths, Bath.

Dawlish, Devon, which Cassandra and Jane visited in 1802.

Stoneleigh Abbey, the ancestral home of Mrs Austen's family, the Leighs.

Southampton, home of Cassandra and Jane from 1806 to 1809.

Above: Village Scene by Thomas Rowlandson. All of Jane's novels are set in country villages such as this one.

Below: Chawton Cottage, home of Cassandra and Jane from 1809.

Above: The parlour in Chawton Cottage, where Jane wrote her last three novels.

Left: Plaque on Chawton Cottage.

Chawton House, Hampshire, unchanged since it was inherited by Edward Austen in 1797.

Cottages in the village of Chawton.

8, College Street, Winchester, where Jane died in July 1817.

Above: Winchester Cathedral, where Jane is buried.

Right: Jane's grave.

Left: The memorial to Jane near her grave in Winchester Cathedral.

Below: The graves of Cassandra Austen and her mother in the churchyard of St Nicholas Church, Chawton.

Some of the Flower seeds are coming up very well – but your Mignonette makes a wretched appearance... Our Young Piony at the foot of the Fir tree has just blown & looks very handsome; & the whole of the Shrubbery Border will soon be very gay with Pinks & Sweet Williams, in addition to the Columbines already in bloom. The Syringas too are coming out – We are likely to have a great crop of Orleans plumbs – but not many greengages – on the standard scarcely any – three or four dozen perhaps against the wall. I believe I told you differently when I first came home, but I can now judge better than I could then.[26]

A fascinating and detailed picture of daily life at Chawton Cottage and the domestic matters that occupied Cassandra and Jane can be put together from Jane's letters, as illustrated by the following extracts.

I will not say that your Mulberry trees are dead, but I am afraid they are not alive. We shall have pease soon – I mean to have them with a couple of Ducks from Wood Barn & Maria Middleton [daughter of the tenant of Chawton House] towards the end of next week.[27]

You cannot imagine – it is not in Human Nature to imagine what a nice walk we have round the Orchard. – The row of Beech look very well indeed & so does the young Quickset hedge in the Garden – I hear today that an Apricot has been detected on one of the Trees.[28]

Yesterday I had the agreable surprise of finding several scarlet strawberries quite ripe; – had **You** been at home, this would have been a pleasure lost. There are more Gooseberries & fewer Currants than I thought at first – We must buy currants for our wine.[29]

The chicken are all alive, & fit for the Table – but we save them for something grand.[30]

We began our China Tea three days ago & I find it very good.[31]

I continue to like our old Cook quite as well as ever – & but that I am afraid to write in her praise, I could say that

> she seems just the Servant for us – Her Cookery is at least tolerable; – her pastry is the only deficiency.[32]
>
> On Monday I had the pleasure of receiving, unpacking & approving our Wedgewood ware [which Jane had bought on her visit to London]. It all came very safely, & upon the whole is a good match, tho' I think they might have allowed us rather larger leaves, especially in such a Year of fine foliage as this. One is apt to suppose that the Woods about Birmingham [the area in which the china was made] must be blighted.[33]
>
> Have you remembered to collect peices for the Patchwork? – We are now at a standstill.[34]

As usual Jane was missing her sister and could not wait to see her again. Her letter of 31 May concludes with the words – 'God bless you – & I hope June will find you well & bring us together.'[35] As often happened, however, Jane was to be disappointed, as Cassandra's return was postponed for a week longer than had been planned. The delay seems to have been caused by transport arrangements.

Jane's letter to Cassandra dated 6 June mentions Anna, who was now much happier. She had been spending time with her friend Harriet, a niece of Miss Benn. Jane stopped writing her letter so that she could accompany Anna and her friend to Alton, where they were going to buy mourning clothes following the king's death, but Jane was glad to get back home again 'for the young Ladies had a great deal to do – & without much method in doing it.'[36]

Cassandra's visit to Godmersham had lasted from March to June. According to Fanny's diary her aunt spent a lot of time with her during her stay. They paid a number of social calls to family and friends, and went out for rides together in the countryside. Cassandra also went with Edward and Fanny on several trips to Canterbury. Edward's position as a magistrate involved regular trips there and Cassandra may have accompanied him on some of these. She also helped Fanny with her numerous duties as mistress of Godmersham House and with supervising the education of her younger siblings. It must have been a considerable help to Fanny to be relieved for a while of some of her heavy workload.

A few weeks after Cassandra returned home she and Jane went to stay with their friends at Manydown, from where they went one evening to dine with James and Mary at Steventon. Fulwar William Fowle was there and it may have been on this occasion that he heard Jane reading aloud. Many years later he recalled:

> She was a very sweet reader – She had finished the 1st Canto of *Marmion*, & I was reading the 2nd – when Mr W Digweed was announced. It was like the interruption of some pleasing dream the illusions of which suddenly vanish – [37]

In the summer of 1811 Charles returned to England from Bermuda with his wife Fanny and their two daughters, Cassandra and Harriet. His sisters were delighted at his return and were pleased to meet Fanny and their young nieces. In a letter to her cousin Philadelphia Walter, Cassandra wrote the following account of her brother's return:

> After an absence from England of almost seven years you may guess the pleasure which having him amongst us again occasion'd. He is grown a little older in all that time, but we had the pleasure of seeing him return in good health and unchanged in mind. His Bermudan wife is a very pleasing little woman, she is gentle & amiable in her manners and appears to make him very happy. They have two pretty little girls.[38]

Charles' next posting was as flag captain on the guard-ship *Namur*,[39] which was stationed at the Nore Station at Sheerness in Kent. This position involved regulating all the sailors recruited in the Thames and eastern ports, as well as responsibility for finding sailors to man the ships that were fitted out on the Thames and Medway. Charles and his family lived on board his ship.

The printing of *Sense and Sensibility* took longer than Jane expected, but it was finally published on 30 October 1811. The novel was published in three volumes at a cost of 15*s* for the set. It was advertised in two newspapers – the *Star* and the *Morning Chronicle* on 30 and 31 October;[40] these advertisements appeared for several weeks. To preserve Jane's anonymity the title page stated that it was written 'By a Lady'. The novel began to sell immediately and continued to sell steadily, and a number of short, but good, reviews appeared in the press. It became popular among members of high society including the Countess of Bessborough, sister of the famous Georgiana, Duchess of Devonshire, who wrote to Lord Granville Leveson-Gower – 'Have you read *Sense and Sensibility*? It is a clever novel. They were full of it at Althorp and tho' it ends stupidly I was much amus'd by it.'[41] The novel was also read by members of the royal family, including Princess Charlotte, who wrote:

> 'Sence and Sencibility' [sic] I have just finished reading; it certainly is interesting, & you feel quite one of the company. I think Maryanne & me are very like in disposition, that certainly I am not so good, the same imprudence, & C, however remain very like. I must say it interested me much.[42]

There was much speculation about who wrote the novel, but this was to remain a secret for another seven years.

Being a published author was very exciting and gratifying for Jane, and encouraged her to continue writing. The positive reaction to *Sense and Sensibility* was an additional boost to her confidence. Jane would probably have carried on writing even if her first published novel was not a success. She was a born writer who needed to exercise her creative talent. Cassandra was very proud of Jane's achievement and the public reaction to her first novel. Her encouragement and her delight in her sister's success spurred Jane on. The rest of the family also urged her to continue writing and in February Jane started to plan *Mansfield Park*. At the same time she embarked on an extensive revision of *First Impressions*, the novel that Thomas Cadell had considered not worth looking at, turning it into *Pride and Prejudice*.

As Jane worked on *Mansfield Park* and *First Impressions* she was living in two worlds concurrently – the real world and her imaginary world. William and Richard Austen-Leigh commented on this in *Jane Austen: Her Life and Letters, A Family Record*.

> But besides all these living objects of interest, Jane also had her own separate and peculiar world, peopled by the creations of her own bright imagination, which by degrees became more and more real to her as she found others accepting and admiring them.[43]

Only one person was allowed access to Jane's private imaginary world, and that was Cassandra. As she had from the time Jane started to write, she continued to share her stories as they were written and she got to know the characters as they were brought to life.

11

CHAWTON

1812–1813

All three of James Austen's children had happy memories of their childhood visits to Chawton Cottage and affectionate memories of their aunts. They wrote down their recollections in the 1860s, when James Edward was compiling his *Memoir* of Jane. Most of these are, therefore, of Jane, but there are a few references to Cassandra as well. Cassandra certainly contributed to the happy and tranquil atmosphere of Chawton Cottage, which her nephews and nieces enjoyed when they visited.

Anna, James Edward and Caroline all left detailed descriptions of Jane's appearance. The most comprehensive description was the following one, written by Anna.

> The Figure tall & slight, but not drooping; well-balanced, as was proved by her quick firm step. Her complexion of that rather rare sort which seems the peculiar property of light brunettes. A mottled skin, not fair, but perfectly clear & healthy in hue; the fine naturally curling hair, neither light nor dark; the bright hazel eyes to match, & the rather small but well shaped nose. One hardly understands how with all these advantages she could yet fail of being a decidedly handsome woman.[1]

Caroline's description of Jane's face was more complimentary. According to her Jane's 'was the first face that I can remember thinking pretty, not that I used that word to myself, but I know I looked at her with admiration.'[2] Her brother considered that Jane was 'not so regularly handsome as her sister, yet her countenance had a peculiar charm of its own to the eye of most beholders.'[3]

The only authenticated portrait of Jane as an adult is a watercolour picture by Cassandra, which dates from around 1810. This portrait cannot be relied on, however, as Anna described it as 'so hideously unlike'[4] Jane. Unfortunately, there is no detailed description of Cassandra as an adult. The only likeness is a silhouette of her as a young woman, which shows an attractive profile, a long aquiline nose and plenty of hair. Both sisters, according to Caroline, were 'particularly neat, and they held all untidy ways in great disesteem.'[5]

James' children also recalled some aspects of their aunts' characters and the differences between them. According to James Edward:

> They were not exactly alike. Cassandra's was the colder and calmer disposition; she was always prudent and well judging, but with less outward demonstration of feeling and less sunniness of temper than Jane possessed.[6]

James Edward added about Jane,

> ... but underneath them [her bright qualities] there lay the strong foundations of sound sense and judgment, rectitude of principle, and delicacy of feeling, qualifying her equally to advise, assist or amuse. She was, in fact, as ready to comfort the unhappy, or to nurse the sick, as she was to laugh, and jest with the light-hearted.[7]

Anna also remembered that underneath Jane's light-heartedness and 'her unusually quick sense of the ridiculous' she could be serious.

> ... when grave she was very grave; I am not sure but that Aunt Cassandra's disposition was the most equally cheerful of the two.[8]

Caroline remembered that despite Jane's 'cleverness and sharpness of mind' she never considered herself to be intellectually superior to other people and always, even as an adult, continued to regard Cassandra as a 'wiser and better person' than herself. In her *Memoir* Caroline wrote:

> When I was a little girl, she would frequently say to me, if opportunity offered, that Aunt Cassandra could teach everything much better than **she** could – Aunt Cass. **knew** more – Aunt Cass. could tell me better whatever I wanted to know – all which, I ever received in respectful silence – Perhaps she thought **my** mind wanted a turn in **that** direction but I truly believe she did always **really** think of her sister, as the superior to herself.[9]

Their nephew and nieces could see for themselves the intense, mutually sustaining relationship that their aunts shared and their great love for each other. In Anna's words:

> Their affection for each other was extreme; it passed the common love of sisters; and it had been so from childhood.[10]
>
> They were everything to each other. They seemed to lead a life to themselves within the general family life, which was shared only by each other. I will not say that their true, but their full feelings and opinions were known only to themselves. They alone fully understood what each other had suffered and felt and thought.[11]

Cassandra and Jane were devoted and much-loved aunts to the numerous children of their brothers. Being an aunt was important to both of them. Jane was Caroline's favourite aunt, as she recorded in the following paragraph taken from her *Memoir*:

> Of the two, Aunt Jane was by far my favourite – I did not **dislike** Aunt Cassandra – but if my visit had at any time chanced to fall out during **her** absence, I don't think I should have missed her – whereas, **not** to have found Aunt Jane at Chawton, **would** have been a blank indeed.[12]

Jane seemed to have a particular affinity with young children. Caroline remembered that, as a very young child, she was always creeping up on Jane and following her about the house and garden. Her mother eventually told her not to be a nuisance to her aunt, although Jane did not appear to mind. Caroline remembered the way children were attracted to Jane and how good she was at amusing and entertaining them.

> Her charm to children was great sweetness of manner – she seemed to love you, and you loved her naturally in return – This as well as I can now recollect and analyse, was what I felt in my earliest days, before I was old enough to be amused by her cleverness – But soon came the delight of her playful talk – Everything she could make amusing to a child – Then, as I got older, when cousins came to share the entertainment, she would tell us the most delightful stories chiefly of Fairyland, and her Fairies had all characters of their own –The tale was invented, I am sure, at the moment, and was sometimes continued for 2 or 3 days, if occasion served.[13]

Caroline remembered Jane joining in the imaginary games she played with her young cousins Cassy and Mary Jane. They were allowed to choose clothes from her wardrobe to dress up in. Caroline also recalled Jane playing Spillikins or Cup and Ball with them, and her skill in both games. James Edward remembered that Jane sometimes played Cup and Ball when she needed a rest from writing and she was so skilful that on one occasion she caught the ball more than a hundred times in succession.

According to Caroline, Jane was 'the delight of all her nephews and nieces' and that they 'valued her as always kind, sympathising and amusing.'[14] These affectionate memories contradict the view widely held among her early biographers that Jane did not like children; there can be no doubt that she did like children and greatly enjoyed their company. It was, as mentioned in an earlier chapter, unruly and badly behaved children that she disliked.

The Middleton children in *Sense and Sensibility* and Charles Musgrove's children in *Persuasion* are good examples of the spoilt, unpleasant children of whom Jane disapproved.

Anna did not agree with Caroline's claim that Jane was the favourite aunt of all her nephews and nieces. She thought that Cassandra was the favourite aunt of Edward's children, at least when they were younger. According to Anna:

> They liked her [Jane] indeed as a playfellow, & as a teller of stories, but they were not really fond of her. I believe that their Mother was not; at least that she very much preferred the elder Sister... This preference lasted for a good while, nor do I think there ever was any abatement in the love of that family for Aunt Cassandra. Time however brought, as it always does bring, new impressions or modifications of the old ones.[15]

Cassandra was at a disadvantage with her younger nephews and nieces because she did not possess the same inventive powers as Jane. She could not entertain them with ad hoc imaginary tales, but she was happy to join in their games, as Fanny's diary reveals. Cassandra was particularly close to Charles' daughter Cassy, who lived for a while at Chawton Cottage because seasickness prevented her from living on board her father's ship. Cassandra took charge of her little namesake and enjoyed teaching and looking after her.

The two aunts were always delighted to break from their daily routine when any nephews or nieces visited. This happened in April 1812 when Edward, Fanny and her cousin Fanny Cage came to stay. The young ladies went with Cassandra and Jane to visit neighbours and joined them on their regular walks in the countryside, including a walk to the village of Farringdon and back. Charlotte-Maria Middleton, the daughter of the tenant of Chawton Great House, went with them. Fanny had become closer to her aunts since her mother's death nearly four years previously and they enjoyed being together. The visit ended on 20 May when Edward, his daughter and his niece left for Winchester to visit

Fanny's brothers at college. They planned to finish their stay in Hampshire at Steventon Rectory.

On 18 June, not long after Edward and Fanny returned home, Henry and Cassandra arrived at Godmersham. The latter stayed for several weeks but, because none of Jane's letters survive from this time, few details are known about this visit. Fanny's diary records that she and her aunt attended a ball at Canterbury, where they met members of the Bridges family and paid a visit to the Bridges at Goodnestone. On 4 July Cassandra paid her brother Charles and his family a visit on board HMS *Namur,* stationed at The Nore in the mouth of the Thames. By this time Cassandra and Jane had spent nearly four weeks apart and must have been missing each other, especially Jane whose emotional dependence on her sister seemed to increase as they got older.

While Cassandra was in Kent, Jane and Mrs Austen went for a two-week stay at Steventon Rectory. They travelled to Basingstoke, where Mary picked them up in her carriage. This was the last time Mrs Austen stayed away from Chawton Cottage. According to her grandson she decided that her last stay away from home would be at Steventon Rectory, where she had spent so many happy years and where she had brought up her children. It was not that Mrs Austen was expecting to die soon, despite her indifferent health, but she seems to have decided that she was getting too old to travel any more and preferred to stay at home. Although she lived for another sixteen years, Mrs Austen kept her word and never spent another night away from Chawton Cottage.

When Jane and her mother left Steventon Rectory on 15 June, Anna went back to Chawton with them for three months. Anna's close relationship with her aunts had continued as she grew up – they enjoyed each other's company and had a shared interest in literature, especially novels. It was around this time that Anna grew especially close to Jane. As she explained to her half-brother James Edward this was

> ... the period of my own greatest share of intimacy [with Jane]; the two years before my marriage, & the two or three

> years after, when we lived, as you know almost close to Chawton when the original 17 years between us seemed to shrink to 7 – or to nothing.[16]

The following paragraph from her recollections shows what an easy and companionable relationship Anna had with both her aunts:

> It was my great amusement during one summer visit at Chawton to procure Novels from a circulating library at Alton, & after running them over to relate the stories to Aunt Jane. I may say it was her amusement also, as she sat busily stitching away at a work of charity, in which I fear that I took myself no more useful part. Greatly we both enjoyed it, one piece of absurdity leading to another, till Aunt Cassandra fatigued with her own share of laughter w[d] exclaim 'How **can** you both be so foolish?' & beg us to leave off.[17]

On one occasion when Anna was at Alton Library with her aunts a comical incident occurred. Anna came across a copy of *Sense and Sensibility* and, having no idea who the author was, threw it onto the counter contemptuously and exclaimed 'Oh that must be rubbish I am sure from the title.' Her aunts were greatly amused but did not divulge their secret. Anna was, at this time, attempting to write a novel herself and Jane was very supportive. This shared interest drew them even closer together.

On 14 October Edward Austen's adoptive mother Catherine Knight died at the age of sixty-one. Cassandra and Jane were saddened to hear of this, as they were both very fond of Mrs Knight. They were grateful to her for all the kindness and attention she had shown them and other members of the Austen family. She had shown much interest in Jane's writing and had looked forward to seeing *Sense and Sensibility* in print. Unfortunately, she died a few weeks before Jane's second and most famous novel was published.

On the death of Mrs Knight, Edward adopted the name of Knight and the family's coat of arms, which was a condition of his inheritance. Fanny did not like having to change her name and wrote in her diary, 'How I hate it!'[18] Jane declared that she would have to learn 'how to make a better K'.

Sense and Sensibility continued to sell steadily and Jane soon recovered her expenses. The first edition was sold out by August of this year – much to Jane's surprise and delight. Henry later recalled that Jane could hardly believe what she referred to as 'her great good fortune' at making a profit from her first published novel. 'Few so gifted,' he wrote, 'were so truly unpretending.' She regarded the money she made as a 'prodigious recompense for that which had cost her nothing'.[19] Cassandra, naturally, shared in her sister's success; it gave her much pleasure to see the novel, which she had known from its earliest conception, do so well in such a short space of time.

In the autumn of 1812 Thomas Egerton bought the copyright of *Pride and Prejudice*. Jane had to change the title of this novel from *First Impressions* because it was discovered that this title had already been used by another author. The idea for the new title came from Fanny Burney's novel *Cecilia,* in which the phrase appeared several times.

Martha was away from home when *Pride and Prejudice* was sold, so Jane told her the news in a letter.

> *P.& P.* is sold – Egerton gives £110 for it. – I would rather have had £150, but we could not both be pleased, & I am not at all surprised that he should not chuse to hazard so much. – Its being sold will I hope be a great saving of Trouble to Henry, & therefore must be welcome to me. – The Money is to be paid at the end of the twelvemonth.[20]

Jane's comment on the amount Egerton paid for the novel showed that she was still doubtful of her own ability. Egerton, however, had no doubt that *Pride and Prejudice* would be a success as he bought the copyright rather than offering to publish at Jane's expense, as he had with *Sense and Sensibility*.

Around the middle of November, Edward arrived for another stay at Chawton Cottage accompanied by Fanny, Lizzy and their cousin Mary Deedes. Jane was busy working on *Mansfield Park* and Cassandra was making preparations for Christmas. As usual, they were happy to break their routine to spend time with family visitors. Fanny noted in her diary that several people were invited for dinner at the cottage during their stay. Among these was Miss Benn, who remained a cause for concern to Cassandra and Jane. They did all they could to make her sad life more bearable. Edward gave his sisters some money to distribute among the poor of Chawton and, no doubt, Miss Benn was one of the recipients. Edward and the young ladies left Chawton on 25 November to call on the Knight boys at Winchester College and then planned to go on to Steventon Rectory. In a letter dated 29 November to Martha, who was away from home, Jane wrote:

> We have been quite alone, except Miss Benn, since 12 o'clock on Wednesday, when Edward & his Harem drove from the door; & we have since heard of their safe arrival & happiness at Winchester... The visit was a very pleasant one I really beleive on each side; they were certainly very sorry to go away, but a little of that sorrow must be attributed to a disinclination for what was before them.[21]

This comment suggests that Edward and his daughters preferred to stay at Chawton Cottage than Steventon Rectory.

Pride and Prejudice was published on 28 January 1813. It was published in three volumes and cost 18*s* for the set. To maintain Jane's anonymity it stated on the title page that it was written 'by the author of *Sense and Sensibility*'. An advertisement for the novel appeared in that day's edition of the *Morning Chronicle*, under the heading of 'Books Published This Day'.

Jane wrote excitedly to Cassandra at Godmersham informing her that she had received her copy from the publisher.

> I want to tell you that I have got my own darling Child from London; – on Wednesday I received one copy, sent down by Falknor [a coach company] with three lines from Henry to say that he had given another to Charles & sent a 3^{d} by the Coach to Godmersham; just the two Sets which I was least eager for the disposal of. I wrote to him immediately to beg for my other two Sets, unless he would take the trouble of forwarding them at once to Steventon & Portsmouth.[22]

Jane went on to describe how she and her mother read some of the first volume of *Pride and Prejudice* to Miss Benn, without her suspecting that Jane was the author.

> Miss Benn dined with us on the very day of the Books coming, & in the even^{g}. we set fairly at it & read half the 1st vol. to her – prefacing that having intelligence from Henry that such a work w^{d} soon appear we had desired him to send it whenever it came out – & I believe it passed with her unsuspected. – She was amused, poor soul! that she c^{d} not help, you know, with two such people to lead the way; – but she really does seem to admire Elizabeth. I must confess that I think her as delightful a creature as ever appeared in print & how I shall be able to tolerate those who do not like **her** at least, I do not know.[23]

Jane was eager to tell Cassandra of Miss Benn's approval. Fanny wrote to thank Jane for her copy of the novel and enclosed an amusing letter, supposedly written by Georgiana Darcy.

Jane's description of *Pride and Prejudice* as her 'own darling child' is interesting. She had previously told Cassandra that she could 'no more forget *Sense and Sensibility* than a mother could forget her sucking child'. Jane thought of her books as substitute children. According to a niece she often said that 'her books were her children, and supplied her sufficient interest for happiness.'[24] She was only too aware that if she had become a wife and mother, as was expected of women of her social class in Georgian England, it would almost certainly have ended her writing career. The demands of marriage, constant childbearing and motherhood would not have been compatible with writing.

Pride and Prejudice, like Jane's first novel, was well received by the literary world and the reading public. The first review, which appeared in the *British Critic* in February 1813, described it in glowing terms.

> It is very far superior to almost all the publications of the kind which have lately come before us. It has a very unexceptionable tendency, the story is well told, the characters remarkably well drawn and supported, and written with great spirit as

> well as vigour ... we have perused these volumes with much satisfaction and amusement, and entertain very little doubt that their successful circulation will induce the author to similar exertions.[25]

An equally positive article was published in the *Critical Review* in March. The author of this review considered that *Pride and Prejudice*

> ... rises very superior to any novel we have lately met with in the delineation of domestic scenes. Nor is there one character which appears flat, or obtrudes itself upon the notice of the reader with troublesome impertinence. There is not one person in the drama with whom we could readily dispense; – they have all their proper places; and fill their several stations with great credit to themselves, and much satisfaction to the reader.[26]

The novel was also well received by the reading public and several well-known people praised it. These included the dramatist Richard Sheridan, who thought it was 'one of the cleverest things he ever read' and Miss Milbanke, the future Lady Byron, described it as 'the most probable fiction I have ever read'.[27] There was much speculation about the identity of the author. Two of the people reputed to have written it were Mrs Boringdon, later the Countess of Morley, and the novelist Mrs Dorset, author of *The Peacock at Home*. One prominent literary gentleman, reflecting current notions about female intelligence, said 'I should like to know who is the author, for it is much too clever to have been written by a woman.'[28]

Jane was pleased to hear from Henry, who was on holiday in Scotland, that the novel was admired there, and also from her friend Anne Sharp, the former governess at Godmersham, that it was popular in Ireland. As with *Sense and Sensibility,* Jane was most concerned with the reaction of her family and friends. She wrote to Cassandra saying, 'I am exceedingly pleased that you can say what you do, after having gone thro' the whole work – &

Fanny's praise is very gratifying; my hopes were tolerably strong of **her**, but nothing like a certainty.'[29]

Cassandra noted details of the novel in a memorandum. She recorded that *First Impressions* was begun in October 1796 and finished in August 1797[30] and that it was published afterwards 'with alterations and contractions' under the title of *Pride and Prejudice*.

When *Pride and Prejudice* was published Jane was half way through writing *Mansfield Park*. In this novel she drew on her knowledge of the navy and even used the names of some of the ships her brother Frank had served on, with his permission. Cassandra helped Jane with her research for this novel by investigating the process of ordination and by finding out whether Northamptonshire, the setting for *Mansfield Park*, contained hedgerows.

Accuracy in minor details was important to Jane, who wanted her novels to be as realistic as possible. For the same reason, when she discovered from reading a travel book that there was in fact no Governor's house in Gibraltar, she changed her reference in the novel to a Commissioner's house.

Amidst all the excitement of *Pride and Prejudice* being published, life at Chawton Cottage went on as usual. Cassandra and Jane continued with their favourite pastimes of reading, sewing, taking long walks in the countryside, and paying and receiving the occasional visit. One visitor to the cottage was Charlotte-Maria Middleton, the daughter of the recent tenant of Chawton Great House. Charlotte-Maria recorded the following memory of Jane including a reference to Cassandra.

> I remember her as a tall thin spare person, with very high cheek bones great colour – sparkling Eyes not large but joyous and intelligent... her keen sense of humour I quite remember... We saw her often. She was a most kind and enjoyable person **to Children** but somewhat stiff & cold to strangers. She used to sit at Table at Dinner parties without uttering much probably collecting matter for her charming novels which in those days we knew nothing about – her

> Sister Cassandra was very lady-like but **very prim,** but my remembrance of Jane is that of her entering into all Childrens Games & liking her extremely...[31]

The description of Jane as 'stiff and cold' in the company of visitors suggests that she had not entirely lost her childhood shyness. It seems that it was only in the relaxed company of family and close friends that Jane's happy and warm personality really shone through. It seems that she hid behind Cassandra when strangers were present.

On 22 April Jane travelled to London where Eliza, who had been unwell for nearly two years, was dying. She may have suffered from breast cancer, the illness that killed her mother. Jane went to London to help nurse Eliza and to support her brother. As she sat at Eliza's bedside Jane may well have remembered her visits to Steventon Rectory and her admiration for her flamboyant older cousin, to whom she had dedicated *Love and Freindship*, one of her earliest pieces of writing. Jane was using her memories of the Austen family theatricals, in which Eliza had played such a prominent part, in the novel she was currently writing. The play put on by the young Bertrams was an important part of the plot in *Mansfield Park*.

Eliza died on 25 April and was buried in the churchyard of Hampstead parish church, beside her mother and son. The epitaph on her gravestone reads 'a woman of brilliant, serious and cultivated mind'.

When Jane returned home in early May, Edward and some of his children were in Hampshire. Godmersham House needed to be redecorated so they had come to stay at Chawton House, which the Middleton family had recently vacated. When his three sons joined them from Winchester College, Edward had all his children with him.

In May, Jane went back to London, having been collected by Henry in his curricle. One reason for this second visit was to help Henry to wind up Eliza's affairs. The day after she arrived in Sloane Street, Jane wrote to Cassandra. She described their journey at length, knowing that her sister would want to know every detail of what she had been doing since they parted.

> How lucky we were in our weather yesterday! – This wet morning makes one more sensible of it. We had no rain of any consequence; the head of the Curricle was put half-up three or four times, but our share of the Showers was very trifling, though they seemed to be heavy all round us, when we were on the Hog's back [a chalk ridge along the North Downs]; & I fancied it might then be raining so hard at Chawton as to make you feel for us much more than we deserved – Three hours & a q^{r} took us to Guildford, where we staid barely two hours & had only just time enough for all we had to do there, that is, eating a long comfortable Breakfast, watching the Carriages, paying Mr Herington [a grocer] & taking a little stroll afterwards. From some veiws which that stroll gave us, I think most highly of the situation of Guildford. We wanted all our Brothers & Sisters to be standing with us in the Bowling Green & looking towards Horsham.[32]

After Guildford their journey took them through the villages of Ripley, Cobham and Esher and the town of Kingston. They finally reached London at six-thirty in the evening after an 'enjoyable' 12-hour journey. Jane was very tired and glad to get to bed early.

The next day Jane began the usual round of visits and tea drinking with Henry's friends and neighbours. In her next letter to Cassandra, she described the peace and quiet of her brother's house.

> I am very snug with the front Drawingroom all to myself & would not say 'Thank you' for any Companion but You. The quietness of it does me good.[33]

Due to their state of mourning following Eliza's death, Henry did not take Jane to the theatre during this visit, but they did go to two picture galleries. At an exhibition held by the Society of Painters in Oil and Watercolours, Jane, whose mind was full of her fictional characters, spotted a portrait of a lady who looked just like Jane Bingley in *Pride and Prejudice*. She described her discovery to Cassandra.

> Henry and I went to the Exhibition in Spring Gardens. It is not thought a good collection, but I was very well pleased – particularly (pray tell Fanny) with a small portrait of M[rs] Bingley, excessively like her. I went in hopes of seeing one of her Sister, but there was no M[rs] Darcy; – perhaps however, I may find her in the Great Exhibition which we shall go to, if we have time; – I have no chance of her in the collection of Sir Joshua Reynolds's Paintings which is now shewing in Pall Mall, & which we are also to visit. – M[rs] Bingley's is exactly herself, size, shaped face, features & sweetness; there never was a greater likeness. She is dressed in a white gown, with green ornaments, which convinces me of what I had always supposed, that green was a favourite colour with her. I dare say M[rs] D. will be in Yellow.[34]

Jane later added:

> We have been both to the Exhibition & to Sir J. Reynolds', – and I am disappointed, for there was nothing like M[rs] D. at either – I can only imagine that M[r] D. prizes any Picture of her too much to like it should be exposed to the public eye. – I can imagine he w[d]. have that sort of feeling – that mixture of Love, Pride & Delicacy: – Setting aside this disappointment, I had great amusement among the Pictures; & the Driving about, the Carriage been [sic] open, was very pleasant. – I liked my solitary elegance very much, & was ready to laugh all the time, at my being where I was. – I could not but feel that I had naturally small right to be parading about London in a Barouche.[35]

This was the last time Jane stayed at the house in Sloane Street, as Henry was planning to move from the home he had shared with Eliza to live in rooms above his bank in Henrietta Street, Covent Garden. He moved there soon after Jane returned home.

Life was busy back in Chawton, especially when James and Charles arrived with their families. Presumably some of the new arrivals stayed at the Great House, as there would not have been much room at the cottage. There was much to-ing and fro-ing between the Great House and Chawton Cottage. The two households frequently dined together and met up for some part of every day. Cassandra and Jane enjoyed visiting the big house down the road, and Jane liked to sit in the small panelled room above the porch of the front door, from where she could watch people coming and going.

Jane and Fanny spent a lot of time together this summer. Fanny's diary contains such entries as 'Aunt Jane and I had a delicious morning together,' and 'Aunt Jane and I walked to Alton.'[36] They also read *Pride and Prejudice* together. Many years later Fanny's sister Marianne remembered them reading aloud and laughing in a bedroom, while she and her younger siblings listened at the door. This memory may have dated from this time. Marianne recalled hearing 'peals of laughter through the door' and thinking it 'very hard that we should be shut out from what was so delightful'.[37]

It was during this visit that Jane learned about Fanny's romantic attachment to John Pemberton Plumptre, a rather serious, but amiable, Cambridge graduate who lived at Fredville near Godmersham. Jane became the trusted confidante of her motherless niece. Fanny did not confide in Cassandra in the same way, despite the fact that she had seen more of her during her childhood, and Cassandra's closeness to both of Fanny's parents.

It was probably during this summer that James Austen's three children discovered the secret of their aunt's authorship. James Edward wrote a poem revealing his pleasure and surprise at the discovery, from which the following extract has been taken.

To Miss J. Austen
No words can express, my dear Aunt, my surprise
Or make you conceive how I opened my eyes,
Like a pig Butcher Pile has just struck with his knife,
When I heard for the very first time in my life
That I had the honour to have a relation
Whose works were dispersed through the whole of the nation.
I assure you, however, I'm terribly glad;

Oh dear! Just to think (and the thought drives me mad)
That dear Mrs Jennings good-natured strain
Was really the produce of your witty brain,
That you made the Middletons, Dashwoods, and all,
And that you (not young Ferrars) found out that a ball
May be given in cottages, never so small.
And though Mr Collins, so grateful for all,
Will Lady de Bourgh his dear Patroness call,
'Tis to your ingenuity really he owed
His living, his wife, and his humble abode.[38]

In July and September 1813 Jane wrote to her brother Frank, who was commanding HMS *Elephant,* which was stationed in the Baltic while on convoy duty. Among other family news Jane told Frank that Henry, who was expected soon at Chawton Cottage, had been promoted to Receiver General for Oxfordshire and that he seemed to be recovering well from the loss of Eliza. She wrote:

> Upon the whole his Spirits are very much recovered. – If I may so express myself, his Mind is not a Mind for affliction. He is too Busy, too active, too sanguine. – Sincerely as he was attached to poor Eliza moreover, & excellently as he behaved to her, he was always so used to be away from her at times, that her Loss is not felt as that of many a beloved Wife might be, especially when all the circumstances of her long & dreadful Illness are taken into the account. – He very long knew that she must die, & it was indeed a release at last.[39]

Henry, like Jane, was a buoyant character who could never be downcast for long. It was a relief to his sisters that Henry was enjoying life again. Jane also informed Frank that their great-uncle Thomas Leigh, the owner of Stoneleigh Abbey, had died at the age of seventy-nine. Cassandra and Jane remembered his visits to them at Reading Abbey School and his kindness to them.

In a postscript Jane brought Frank up to date regarding her books.

> You will be glad to hear that every Copy of *S. & S.* is sold & that it has brought me £140 – besides the Copyright, if that sh^{d} ever be of any value. – I have now therefore written myself into £250 – which only makes me long for more.[40]

This was a good profit for a first novel at that time. Jane also told Frank about the new book she was writing, which she hoped would sell well following the success of *Pride and Prejudice,* and asked if he minded her using the name of HMS *Elephant* and other ships he had served on in the novel.

In her second letter to Frank, Jane told him the latest news regarding Anna, who remained a cause for concern to her aunts. Anna had recently become engaged to Ben Lefroy, the son of Jane's late friend Anne Lefroy. This was not necessarily good news and Jane remained apprehensive, as she explained.

> It came upon us without much preparation; – at the same time, there was **that** about her which kept us in a constant preparation for something. – We are anxious to have it go on well, there being quite as much in his favour as the Chances are likely to give her in any Matrimonial connection. I believe he is sensible, certainly very religious, well connected & with some Independance. – There is an unfortunate dissimularity of Taste between them in one respect which gives us some apprehensions, he hates company & she is very fond of it; – This, with some queerness of Temper on his side & much unsteadiness on hers, is untoward.[41]

Jane told Frank the good news that there was to be a second edition of *Sense and Sensibility.* She also told him that Henry, 'in the warmth of his Brotherly vanity & Love', had revealed that she was the author of *Pride and Prejudice.* She thanked Frank and Mary for the 'superior kindness' they had shown her by keeping her secret.

The reason for the Austen family's concern about Anna's engagement was that, although Ben was in Jane's words 'a pleasant young man' and in many ways a good match for Anna, he had not yet decided what career he wanted to follow. There was concern that he would not be able to support Anna and a family. After the engagement was announced on 17 August, Anna went to stay at Chawton Cottage for three weeks. This suggests that her father and stepmother were not happy about the engagement.

The Knight family's stay at Chawton lasted for more than four months. They stayed longer than expected because the smell of paint at Godmersham took a long time to disappear. When they finally left in September, most of Edward's family and servants travelled in convoy back to Kent. This procession reminded Jane of the account in the Bible of St Paul's shipwreck in which the survivors all reached the shore by different means. The convoy consisted of two post-chaises containing eight people, a chair carrying two more, two people on horseback and the rest in a coach. Edward and his three eldest daughters were not part of the convoy, as they travelled by stagecoach with Jane to visit Henry in London. Cassandra, who remained at home with her mother and Martha, was expecting a visit from Alethea Bigg and her sister Elizabeth Heathcote.

Jane's letters to Cassandra from London dated 15–16 September 1813 are two of the most interesting and delightful of all her surviving letters. Henry was now settled in his new home in Henrietta Street, Covent Garden. Jane began her first letter at half-past eight in the morning after their arrival.

> Here I am, my dearest Cassandra, seated in the Breakfast, Dining, sitting room, beginning with all my might. Fanny will join me as soon as she is dressed & begin her Letter. We had a very good journey – Weather & roads excellent – the first three stages for *1s–6d* – & our only misadventure the being delayed about a q^r of an hour at Kingston for Horses, & being obliged to put up with a p^r belonging to a Hackney Coach & their Coachman, which left no room on the Barouche Box for Lizzy, who was to have gone her last stage there as she did for

> the first, consequently we were all 4 within, which was a little crowd; We arrived at a q^r past 4.[42]

There was not enough room at Henrietta Street for all of them, so Edward stayed at a nearby hotel. Jane described Henry's new home, where Eliza's French servants looked after him, as '…very nice. It seems like Sloane St. moved here.'[43]

Edward, Jane and the three young ladies had a long list of places to visit and things to do in London, so they got up early on the first morning to get started. Despite Anna's claim that Cassandra was the favourite aunt of the Godmersham children, it is evident from Jane's letters that Edward's daughters enjoyed an affectionate relationship with her and they all got on well with each other.

Henry took his visitors to the theatre several times during their stay, which they all enjoyed. Jane accompanied her nieces to the milliner's and dressmaker's shops and she seemed to revel in her role as an aunt. Jane was still as interested in fashion as she had been as a young woman. She reported to Cassandra that she had been highly amused to learn from the dressmaker's assistant that 'the stays now are not made to force the Bosom up at all; – **that** was a very unbecoming, unnatural fashion. I was really glad to hear that they are not to be so much off the shoulders as they were.'[44]

A hairdresser called at Henrietta Street to style the ladies' hair and Jane was persuaded by her nieces to dispense with her matronly cap and have her hair curled. It seems that the young ladies considered her cap too frumpy to wear in fashionable London. Cassandra must have been amused to read Jane's account of the hairdresser's visit.

> Mr Hall was very punctual yesterday & curled me out a great rate. I thought it looked hideous, and longed for a snug cap instead, but my companions silenced me by their admiration. I had only a bit of velvet round my head. I did not catch cold however.[45]

Jane was very anxious to inform Cassandra of some praise of *Pride and Prejudice* which had been passed on to her by Henry, who had also sent a copy to Eliza's godfather, and the Austen family's old friend, Warren Hastings. 'I long to have you hear Mr H's opinion of *P. & P.*' wrote Jane. 'His admiring my Elizabeth so much is particularly welcome to me.'[46]

While in London Jane had great pleasure in spending some of the money she had earned from the sale of *Pride and Prejudice,* which she described as her 'superfluous wealth'. Unsurprisingly, her first thought on receiving this money was to buy something for Cassandra. She and her nieces went to one of their favourite shops, Layton & Shears, which was conveniently situated at 9, Henrietta Street, next door to Henry's home. Jane treated herself and Cassandra to a length of poplin with which to make new gowns. 'I depend upon your being so kind as to accept it,' she wrote. 'It will be a great pleasure to me. Don't say a word. I only wish you could choose too.'[47] Jane also bought her sister a gown, which she sent on to Chawton. When Cassandra thanked her for the gown Jane's response was 'Remember that it is a present. Do not refuse me. I am very rich.'[48] It must have been a liberating experience for her to be able to spend money without having to think about it – at last she had some money she could call her own.

In contrast to Jane's enjoyable shopping expeditions with her nieces, she went with them and their father to the dentist's surgery. The girls had their teeth cleaned and filed, and Marianne had two teeth removed. 'Poor Marianne', wrote Jane 'had two taken out after all, the two just beyond the Eye teeth, to make room for those in front. – When her doom was fixed, Fanny, Lizzy & I walked into the next room, where we heard each of the two sharp hasty Screams... It was a disagreeable hour.'[49] This was followed by a much more pleasurable visit to Wedgewood's shop, where Edward and Fanny ordered a purple and gold dinner set decorated with the Knight family crest.

During Jane's absence Cassandra had a difficult time at home with her mother, who had been unwell again. She had been suffering from bad headaches and was treated by the application of leeches, a popular remedy based on the belief that illness was caused by an excess of blood in the body. Mrs Austen was becoming even more dependent on the care of her daughters and Martha. Cassandra had to manage without Jane for several more weeks as, when her visit to London ended on 22 September, Jane travelled to Godmersham with Edward and his daughters for what was to be her last stay there.

This visit to Godmersham was as busy as the previous ones had been. 'In this House there is a constant succession of small events, somebody is always going or coming,'[50] she wrote to Cassandra. Jane joined once more in the hectic social life of the east Kent aristocracy, but she sometimes found this tiresome. She described one dull visit to Cassandra.

> There was nothing entertaining, or out of the common way. We met only Tyldens and double Tyldens [another branch of the family with a double-barrelled name]. A Whist Table for the Gentlemen, a grown-up musical young Lady to play Backgammon with Fanny, & engravings of the Colleges at Cambridge for me.[51]

Of some other uninspiring visitors Jane wrote:

> Lady Eliz. Hatton & Annamaria called here this morn[g]. – Yes, they called, – but I do not think I can say anything more about them. They came & they sat & they went.[52]

She met some amusing people, however, such as Miss Milles of Canterbury.

> Miss Milles was queer as usual & provided us with plenty to laugh at. She undertook in **three words** to give us the history of M[rs] Scudamore's reconciliation, & then talked on about it for half an hour, using such odd expressions & so foolishly minute that I could hardly keep my countenance.[53]

Jane may have used some of Miss Milles' characteristics when she created Miss Bates in *Emma*.

Among the events Jane enjoyed was a ball, which she attended as Fanny's chaperone. Jane was now too old to dance at balls herself but there were some advantages to her new role, as she could sit on the sofa and drink as much wine as she liked. Jane was relieved not to have to go to another ball, which Fanny decided against attending at the last minute. 'I was very glad to be spared the trouble of dressing & going & being weary before it was half over, so my gown & my cap are still unworn,' she told her sister.[54]

Jane enjoyed dining at Chilham Castle, the home of the Wildman family, and several trips to Canterbury. On one such trip Jane accompanied Edward to Canterbury Jail when he went to inspect it in his capacity as a visiting magistrate. Jane had received a letter from Cassandra just before setting off and Edward read most of it to her on their journey.

To add to Jane's pleasure her brother Charles, his wife and their daughters arrived to spend a week at Godmersham. Jane told Cassandra that they had arrived after a difficult journey 'just like their own nice selves, Fanny looking as neat & white this morn^{g} as possible, & dear Charles all affectionate, placid, quiet, chearful good humour'.[55]

During her sister's absence Cassandra supervised a number of improvements that were being carried out at Chawton Great House, both inside and on the estate. Progress on the work was reported in her letters to Jane. In October, Cassandra left her mother and the house in Martha's care and went to London to see Henry. She was joined by her three friends Elizabeth, Catherine and Alethea, with whom she went out, visiting the sights of London in Henry's carriage.

Jane took her portable writing desk to Godmersham, as she had on previous visits, and found a quiet place in the library to write. She was probably putting the finishing touches to the manuscript of *Mansfield Park* or making notes for her next novel. Louisa Knight later remembered her aunt having sudden bursts of inspiration.

> I also remember how Aunt Jane would sit quietly working beside the fire in the library, saying nothing for a good while, and then would suddenly burst out laughing, jump up and run across the room to a table where pens and paper were lying, write something down, and then come back to the fire and go on quietly working as before.[56]

In October, while Jane was still at Godmersham, the second editions of both *Sense and Sensibility* and *Pride and Prejudice* were published by Thomas Egerton. A few weeks later, when Jane was staying with Henry again on her way home from Kent, *Mansfield Park* was accepted for publication by Egerton. He clearly did not rate this novel as highly as *Pride and Prejudice,* as he agreed to publish it on a commission-only basis.

Cassandra added to her memorandum about Jane's novels that *Mansfield Park* was begun in February 1811 and finished around June 1813.

12

CHAWTON

1814–1815

Cassandra recorded that Jane began to write *Emma* on 21 January 1814. Before starting, Jane said to her family 'I am going to take a heroine whom no one but myself will much like.' She worked on the novel throughout that year and into the beginning of the next. Jane wrote *Emma* more quickly than her first three novels, but it was no less polished. As she became more experienced at writing, she also became quicker.

Writing was an established part of her daily routine. A typical day at Chawton Cottage started with Jane getting up early to practise the piano. At nine o'clock breakfast was served, which Jane had prepared. In the morning Cassandra and Martha saw to the running of the house, Mrs Austen wrote letters, sewed or tended the garden, and Jane worked on her novel in the sitting room. Jane's nephew and nieces remembered how as young children, having no idea that she was writing a novel, they sometimes interrupted her. She never showed any irritation or impatience at being interrupted, but stopped writing, greeted them and turned her attention to them.

After lunch Cassandra and Jane went for a walk along the country lanes or to the shops in Alton. They sometimes visited neighbours, or called at Chawton Great House if any of their relatives were staying there. If there was no one in the house, they often took a stroll around the grounds.

During her years at Chawton Jane seemed to live in two worlds – the real world and her imaginary one. She was busy creating plots and characters in her head while carrying on her daily life. Her fictional characters were very real to her, as shown by the way she referred to two of her heroines as 'my Elinor' and 'my Elizabeth'.

Jane's characters were real to Cassandra as well; she had known them from their earliest conception and became well acquainted with them during the creative process. Cassandra's support and her interest in Jane's writing, in both the early and later creative periods, inspired her to continue. As can be seen by Jane's surprise at the amount of money she earned from writing *Sense and Sensibility*, she was not confident of her own ability. Without Cassandra's belief in her and her encouragement, Jane's novels may never have been written. Nor should Cassandra's contribution to her sister's happiness and peace of mind be under-estimated. Jane needed to be in the right frame of mind for her creativity to flourish, as shown by her inability to write during the unsettled years she spent in Bath and Southampton. When she returned to live in her beloved north Hampshire countryside, in a settled permanent home and with Cassandra by her side, she was able to write again.

Jane worked hard on *Emma* for the first two months of 1814 and then took a break when, on 1 March, she travelled by carriage to London with Henry. She had checked nearly all the proof sheets of *Mansfield Park* and Henry read a proof copy of the novel on the journey. Jane read *The Heroine, or Adventures of a Fair Romance Reader*, a novel by E. S. Barrett, and was 'very much amused by it.'[1] She was delighted at Henry's response to *Mansfield Park*. In her letter to Cassandra, written the day after her arrival, Jane shared her increasing pleasure in Henry's reaction to her novel.

> We did not begin reading till Bentley Green. Henry's approbation hitherto is even equal to my wishes; he says it is very different from the other two, but does not appear to think it at all inferior. He has only married Mrs R. I am afraid he has gone through the most entertaining part. – He took to Lady B. & Mrs N. most kindly, & gives great praise to the drawing of the Characters. He understands them all, likes Fanny & I think foresees how it will all be.[2]

Jane reported that they had 'a good journey' despite the weather.

> We had some Snowstorms yesterday, & a smart frost at night, which gave us a hard road from Cobham to Kingston, but as it was then getting dirty & heavy, Henry had a pair of Leaders put on from the latter place to the bottom of Sloane S^t^.– His own Horses therefore cannot have had hard work.[3]

Jane, with her interest in fashion, told Cassandra 'I watched for Veils as we drove through the Streets, & had the pleasure of seeing several upon vulgar heads.' The sisters wrote to each other almost every other day and Jane was often thinking of home. 'I hope,' she wrote, 'that you & my Mother could eat your Beefpudding. Depend upon my thinking of the Chimney Sweeper as soon as I wake tomorrow.'[4] Henry continued reading *Mansfield Park* after arriving home and Jane kept Cassandra informed of his admiration of it.

On 6 March Edward and Fanny arrived in London for a two-day stay, on their way home from Bath. They had endured an uncomfortable journey in the cold and sleet. Jane and Fanny ventured out into the snowy streets to go to the theatre and the shops together. Jane made some purchases, but saved the buying of caps until Cassandra, who was due to join her in London later that month, could choose them with her. While Fanny was staying in Hans Place she received a visit from John Pemberton Plumptre, the young man she had been seeing recently, and Henry detected a 'decided attachment' between them.

On 5 April, just after Cassandra and Jane arrived home, Napoleon abdicated and was exiled to the island of Elba. His abdication meant that hostilities between Britain and France were at an end after twenty years. As a result, much to his sisters' delight, Frank left HMS *Elephant* at Spithead to live on shore with his wife and young children.[5] He kept his naval rank and went onto half-pay. Charles remained as commander of HMS *Namur* at the Nore Station.[6] Later that month the Knight family arrived in Hampshire for a two-month stay at Chawton Great House, bringing with them some members of the Bridges family, including Edward's mother-in-law.

On 9 May 1814 *Mansfield Park* was published by Thomas Egerton. An advertisement for the novel appeared in *The Star,*[7] stating that it was written 'by the author of *Sense and Sensibility* and *Pride and Prejudice*'. It was priced at 18*s* for the three-volume set, the same price as *Pride and Prejudice. Mansfield Park* was not reviewed in the press, unlike Jane's first two novels, but this did not prevent it from selling well. Again there was speculation as to the identity of the author among the literati.

Jane wrote down her family and friends' responses to her new novel. Among these opinions she noted that Cassandra thought *Mansfield Park* was 'quite as clever, tho' not so brilliant as *Pride and Prejudice*'. Frank and Mary sent the following carefully considered opinion:

> We certainly do not think it as a **whole,** equal to *P. & P.* – but it has many & great beauties. Fanny is a delightful Character! and Aunt Norris is a great favourite of mine. The Characters are natural & well supported, & many of the Dialogues excellent. – You need not fear the publication being considered as discreditable to the talents of its Author.[8]

Jane's friend Anne Sharp thought the characters were good but, like Cassandra, she preferred *Pride and Prejudice.* Among other opinions was the qualified praise of Lady Anne Romilly, who enquired of the novelist Maria Edgeworth:

> Have you read *Mansfield Park*? It has been pretty generally admired here [London], and I think all novels must be that are true to life which this is, with a good strong vein of principle running thro' the whole. It has not however that elevation of virtue, something beyond nature, that gives the greatest charm to a novel, but still it is real natural every day life, and will amuse an idle hour in spite of its faults.[9]

Jane would have been pleased with the positive comments about the novel being true to life, as this was an effect she worked hard to achieve.

In the summer of 1814 peace celebrations were held all over the country, marking the end of the war with France. Fanny took her grandmother to see the illuminations at Alton. She then travelled with her father to London to join Henry and Cassandra and take part in the celebrations there. The sovereigns and generals of Britain's allies were on a state visit to the capital. Crowds lined the streets to greet them wherever they went. In a letter to Cassandra dated 14 June, Jane told her to 'Take care of yourself, & do not be trampled to death in running after the Emperor [Alexander I of Russia]. The report in Alton yesterday was that they w^{d} certainly travel this road either to, or from Portsmouth.'[10]

Henry was invited to a celebration ball held at White's, the private gentleman's club in Burlington House, Piccadilly, on 21 June. The 2,000 guests included the Prince Regent, the Emperor of Russia and the King of Prussia. 'Henry at Whites!' exclaimed Jane on hearing of this. 'Oh! What a Henry.'[11]

In June, Jane took another break from writing *Emma* to spend two weeks with her godfather, the Reverend Samuel Cooke, and his family in Great Bookham in Surrey. The Cookes were reading *Mansfield Park* during Jane's visit. 'They admire *Mansfield Park* exceedingly,' she told Cassandra. 'Mr Cooke says "it is the most sensible Novel he ever read" – and the manner in which I treat the Clergy, delights them very much.'[12]

Emma, which was set in Surrey, was very much on Jane's mind during her stay. There have been a number of attempts to identify the locality of the fictional town of Highbury, where most of the action in the novel takes place. Leatherhead, Dorking and Esher have all been suggested as the real Highbury. Although Jane used her visit to the neighbourhood of Leatherhead and Box Hill to check geographical and other details for her novel, Highbury is a fictional town. As Jane used qualities and characteristics of various people when creating her fictional characters, it is likely that she took features from a variety of real places when creating her fictional localities. As she stated herself, her desire was 'to create not to reproduce'.

When Jane was writing *Emma* she found time to help and encourage Anna, who was attempting to write a novel of her own.

Anna sent each completed chapter of her novel, which was called *Enthusiasm,* to Jane, who read them to her mother and Cassandra before sending them back with criticism and advice. In a letter written in July Jane wrote:

> I am very much obliged to you for sending your MS. It has entertained me extremely, all of us indeed; I read it aloud to your G.M. – & A^{t}.C. – and we were all very much pleased… A few verbal corrections were all that I felt tempted to make.[13]

Anna continued to send each completed chapter to her aunt. Some of Jane's advice to her provides an interesting insight into her views on the best way to write a novel. It also reveals the high standards she imposed on herself. Jane stressed the importance of accuracy, including topographical accuracy, the drawing of natural and consistent characters, and the creation of an illusion of truth. She advised Anna to write only about types of people and places she was familiar with, to avoid giving 'false representations'. Jane described exactly what she was doing herself as she wrote *Emma:*

> You are now collecting your People delightfully, getting them exactly into such a spot as is the delight of my life; – 3 or 4 Families in a Country Village is the very thing to work on – & I hope you will write a great deal more, & make full use of them while they are so favourably arranged.[14]

In late August, Jane went to London to pay another visit to Henry. This time, unusually, she travelled alone on a crowded public stagecoach. In her letter to Cassandra reporting her safe arrival, Jane wrote:

> Henry himself met me, & as soon as my Trunk & Basket could be routed out from all the other Trunks & Baskets in the World, we were on our way to Hans Place in the Luxury of a nice large cool dirty Hackney Coach.[15]

Henry had recently moved back to Chelsea and was now living at 23, Hans Place, not far from his former home in Sloane Street. His business partner and friend James Tilson and his wife Frances lived three doors away and conversations were often conducted over the back gardens in between.

This was a quiet and restful break for Jane. In a letter dated 2 September to Martha, who was in Bath, Jane wrote:

> I shall have spent my 12 days here very pleasantly, but with not much to tell of them; two or three **very** little Dinner-parties at home, some delightful Drives in the Curricle, & quiet Tea-drinkings with the Tilsons, has been the sum of my doings.[16]

As usual Jane enjoyed looking at the clothes worn by the fashionable ladies in the capital, and told Martha:

> I am amused by the present style of female dress; – the coloured petticoats with braces over the white Spencers [short jackets] & enormous Bonnets upon the full stretch, are quite entertaining. It seems to me a more marked **change** than one has lately seen. – Long sleeves appear universal, even as Dress [formal dress], the Waists short, and as far as I have been able to judge, the Bosom covered.[17]

Before she left London on 3 September, Jane took an afternoon drive out to Streatham to see her old friend Catherine Hill.

On 31 August, while Jane was in London, Charles' wife Fanny gave birth to their fourth daughter, Elizabeth. The baby was delivered on board the *Namur*, a few weeks earlier than expected. Initially all seemed well, but complications arose during Fanny's recovery and she died a few days later. The baby only survived for two weeks. Edward, who had lost his wife in the same way, hurried to Sheerness to support his brother. Although death in or shortly after childbirth was common at that time, this was another severe loss to the family. Three more of Cassandra's and Jane's nieces had now lost their mother.

Charles resigned from his post as commander of HMS *Namur* at the end of September to make arrangements for the care of his three young daughters. The little girls went to live with their maternal grandparents in Keppel Street in Bloomsbury, where their unmarried Aunt Harriet looked after them. A memorial tablet to Fanny and Elizabeth was placed in the Church of St John the Baptist in Kentish Town, near the home of the Palmer family. One month after the death of his wife, Charles was appointed Commander of HMS *Phoenix* in the Mediterranean.[18]

There was further bad news for the Austen family that autumn, when some neighbours in Chawton took out a lawsuit against Edward. Mr and Mrs Hinton of Chawton Lodge and their nephew James Hinton Baverstock, a brewer in Alton, who were heirs-at-law, or heirs by right of blood, of the Knight family, were trying to get possession of Edward's Hampshire properties and estates. If Edward lost this lawsuit it could have resulted in him being ejected from his Chawton estates, and his mother and sisters losing their home. There are a number of references to this worrying affair in Jane's letters to Cassandra. This was to hang over the family for several years.

There was some good news for the family in November when Anna married Ben Lefroy, who had finally settled on a career in the Church. Anna's grandmother and aunts did not attend the ceremony, which was held in Steventon Church, as it was the custom then that only the very closest family members attended weddings. In Georgian and Regency England, weddings were very quiet affairs – it was not until the Victorian period that they became big celebrations. Caroline Austen, who was one of the two bridesmaids, described the occasion as being 'in the extreme of quietness; yet not so as to be in any way censured or remarked upon.'[19] Following a simple wedding breakfast the newlyweds left for Hendon, then a small village on the outskirts of London, where they were to live with Ben's brother. They left early in order to cross Hampstead Heath in daylight, as it was a notorious haunt of highwaymen.

Mrs Austen composed a congratulatory poem for Anna and Ben. Cassandra and Jane were pleased that Anna's future was finally settled. They wrote to Anna regularly and she continued to send Jane the completed chapters of her novel for criticism.

That month a correspondence began between Jane and her niece Fanny, who wanted her advice about John Plumptre. Fanny was in turmoil over her feelings for this young man, who she had been seeing for some time. Jane gave her some wise and sensible advice, taking into account the feelings of both parties. In one letter she wrote:

> Your mistake has been one that thousands of women fall into. He was the **first** young Man who attached himself to you. That was the charm, & most powerful it is.[20]

One of Fanny's worries was that John lacked wit and a sense of humour. Jane replied with one of her most famous comments that 'Wisdom is better than Wit, & in the long run will certainly have the laugh on her side.'[21] Jane strongly advised Fanny not to think of accepting John unless she really liked him. She warned her that 'Anything is to be preferred or endured rather than marrying without Affection'[22] and that 'nothing can be compared to the misery of being bound **without** Love, bound to one, & preferring another.'[23] She was careful to add 'Your own feelings & none but your own, should determine such an important point.'[24] Jane did, however, advise Fanny to make up her mind and not string John along. She also assured her that she was likely to meet someone else, in the next few years, who she could truly love. Fanny eventually decided to discourage John Plumptre.

Fanny asked Jane not to discuss her problem with anyone else, not even Cassandra. She sent one letter to her aunt inside a music manuscript, so that Cassandra would not find out about their correspondence. Neither Jane nor Cassandra would ever have betrayed the confidence, even to each other, of a nephew or niece who had sought their advice.

On 25 November Jane travelled to London, at Henry's request, to talk to Egerton about the possibility of a second edition of *Mansfield Park*. The first edition had already sold out, making Jane the considerable sum of £350. Jane was not hopeful about a second edition because, as she explained in a letter to Fanny, 'People are more ready to borrow & praise, than to buy – which I cannot wonder at; – but tho' I like praise as well as anybody, I like what Edward calls Pewter too.'[25]

During her brief visit Jane went to see her young nieces at Keppel Street. She told Fanny, 'I called in Keppel Street & saw them all, including dear Uncle Charles, who is to come & dine with us quietly today. – Little Harriot sat in my lap – & seemed as gentle & affectionate as ever, & as pretty…'[26] Jane also drove out to Hendon to see Anna and Ben, and managed to fit in a trip to the theatre with Henry.

While in London, Jane met Harriet Moore, one of three ladies in whom Henry had been romantically interested since the death of his wife. Jane told her niece that she liked Harriet, whom she referred to as 'the Hanwell favourite', 'as much as one can at my time of Life after a day's acquaintance'.[27] Both Jane and Cassandra wanted their brother to marry again.

Henry wanted to introduce Jane to a London literary society, and used the fact that the famous author Madame de Staël was a member to persuade her to agree. Jane rejected the idea immediately, as she had no wish to be part of any literary group. Even though she was well aware of the success of her novels and that they were widely regarded as superior to the works of many contemporary writers, Jane did not want to receive any public recognition. In his *Biographical Notice of the Author*, which was published in 1818 with *Northanger Abbey* and *Persuasion*, Henry Austen made the following observations on Jane's wish to avoid fame:

> … so much did she shrink from notoriety, that no accumulation of fame would have induced her, had she lived, to affix her name to any productions of her pen. In the bosom of her own family she talked of them [her novels] freely, thankful for praise, open to remark, and submissive to criticism. But in public she turned away from any allusion to the character of an authoress.[28]

For some unknown reason, Thomas Egerton decided not to go ahead with a second edition of *Mansfield Park*. This may explain why Henry approached the fashionable publisher John Murray, of Albemarle Street in London, when *Emma* was completed. Henry accompanied his sister back to Chawton on 5 December.

Once she was home again Jane went straight back to work on *Emma*. Although she was busy she found time to read and comment on some stories written by her nine-year-old niece Caroline. She sent her the following letter dated 6 December.

> My dear Caroline,
>
> I wish I could finish Stories as fast as you can. – I am much obliged to you for the sight of Olivia, & think you have done for her very well, but the good for nothing Father, who was the real author of all her Faults & Sufferings, should not escape unpunished. – I hope he hung himself, or took the sur-name of Bone or underwent some direful penance or other.
>
> Yours affec^{ly}
>
> J. Austen [29]

After Christmas, Jane had a break from writing when she and Cassandra went to Winchester to stay with their friends Alethea Bigg and Elizabeth Heathcote. A week later they travelled to Steventon Rectory, from where they paid visits to some old friends and neighbours in Steventon and Ashe. When they returned home, Jane resumed writing and the sisters slipped back into their usual daily routine.

In March 1815 Napoleon escaped from the island of Elba and returned to Paris, where he resumed power. Hostilities broke out again between Britain and France and her allies. Charles was in the Mediterranean commanding the *Phoenix* and other ships, which were engaged in pursuing French and Neapolitan ships. He received a special commendation for his part in the blockade of the port of Brindisi.[30]

On 29 March Jane finished writing *Emma*. Not long afterwards, she received a letter from Charles, who was in Palermo, which shows how popular her novels were with the reading public. He wrote:

> Books became the subject of conversation, and I praised *Waverley* highly, when a young man present observed that nothing had come out for years to be compared with *Pride and Prejudice, Sense and Sensibility* & c. As I am sure you

> must be anxious to know the name of a person of so much taste, I should tell you it is Fox, a nephew of the late Charles James Fox. That you may not be too much elated at this morsel of praise, I shall add that he did not appear to like *Mansfield Park* so well as the two first, in which, however, I believe he is singular.[31]

Mary Austen and Caroline stayed at Chawton Cottage for several weeks in the summer of 1815. Many of Caroline's childhood memories of life at the cottage date from this time. Jane may have found the presence of Mary irritating, but having their niece there would have been a great pleasure for both her aunts. There are no letters from Jane to Cassandra until September of this year, as they were both at home together.

On 4 June 1815, Frank, who had already received several honours during his distinguished naval career, was made a Companion of the Order of the Bath.[32] He was staying with his wife and children at Chawton Great House then and was in regular contact with his mother and sisters. The long war with France finally ended with the Battle of Waterloo on 18 June. Napoleon was exiled to St Helena. Following the end of hostilities Charles Austen became engaged in the suppression of piracy in the Greek Archipelago.[33]

In August, Anna and Ben Lefroy left Hendon and stayed at Chawton Cottage briefly before moving into a new house near Alton. Their new home was half of a large farmhouse named 'Wyards'. Anna's grandmother and aunts were glad that she would be living within walking distance of the cottage. Cassandra and Jane now had somewhere new to visit on their afternoon walks.

That month Jane began work on her sixth novel, which she did not name; it was later given the title *Persuasion* by Henry. The manuscript of *Emma* was now in the hands of the publisher John Murray. Jane soon heard that Murray's reader, William Gifford, had 'nothing but good to say'[34] of the novel and had offered to revise it.

On 4 October Henry collected Jane to take her to London for a short stay. He probably wanted Jane to be nearby while he conducted negotiations with the publisher. In a letter to Cassandra dated 17–18 October Jane announced that Murray's acceptance letter had finally arrived.

> Mr Murray's Letter is come; he is a Rogue of course, but a civil one. He offers £450 – but wants the Copyright of *M.P. & S.& S.* included. It will end in my publishing for myself I dare say. – He sends more praise however than I expected. It is an amusing Letter. You shall see it.[35]

In the same letter Jane told her sister that Henry was 'not quite well'. He had come home early from work on 16 October with what he thought was a bilious attack. Jane was not unduly worried at first, but when she added to the letter on 18 October, she wrote:

> Henry's illness is more serious than I expected. He has been in bed since three o'clock on Monday. It is a fever – something bilious, but cheifly Inflammatory. I am not alarmed – but I have determined to send this Letter today by the post, that you may know how things are going on.[36]

Jane told her sister that Mr Haden, an apothecary from Sloane Street, had been summoned.

> Mr H. calls it a general Inflammation.– He took twenty ounces of Blood from Henry last night – & nearly as much more this morn[g] – & expects to have to bleed him again tomorrow, but he assures me that he found him **quite** as much better today as he expected. Henry is an excellent Patient, lies quietly in bed & is ready to swallow anything. He lives upon Medicine, Tea & Barley water. – He has had a great deal of fever but not much pain of any sort – & sleeps pretty well... You must fancy Henry in the back room upstairs – & I am generally there also, working or writing.[37]

Jane assured Cassandra that she would be home as soon as she could be. Over the next two days Henry began to feel better, and by the 20th he was able to dictate a reply to the letter from John Murray about *Emma*. He told the publisher that his offer was 'so very inferior to what we had expected' and pointed out that the sum he offered for the copyright of *Sense & Sensibility, Mansfield Park* and *Emma* was 'not equal to the Money which my Sister has actually cleared by one very moderate Edition of *Mansfield Park* ... & a still smaller one of *Sense & Sensibility*'.[38]

Before a reply was received from John Murray, Henry had a relapse. On 22 October Jane wrote summoning Edward, James and Cassandra to London because she feared that Henry was dying. She was relieved when her brothers and sister arrived, especially Cassandra, whose reassuring presence always calmed her. Jane and Cassandra nursed Henry together over the next week during which his life was in the balance. Mr Haden called an eminent London doctor to assist him. He is thought to have been Dr Matthew Baillie, who had treated Henry in the past, and was one of the physicians who attended the Prince Regent. After the doctor's intervention Henry gradually improved, until a week later the crisis had passed. Edward and James were then able to return home, leaving Cassandra behind to help Jane look after their brother until he recovered.

While this drama was happening in London, Anna gave birth to her first child, Anna Jemima, on 30 October, making her nine-year-old half-sister Caroline an aunt. Jane wrote to Caroline thanking her for sending some stories she had written and explaining why she could not read the stories just then. She added:

> Now that you are become an Aunt, you are a person of some consequence & must excite great Interest whatever You do. I have always maintained the importance of Aunts as much as possible, & I am sure of your doing the same now – Beleive me my dear Sister-Aunt.
>
> Yours affect[ly]
>
> J. Austen[39]

Cassandra would, no doubt, have echoed those sentiments.

Henry's illness led to what James Edward described in his *Memoir* as 'the only mark of distinction ever bestowed'[40] on his aunt. By this time, although Jane's name had never appeared on the title page of any of her novels, it was not difficult to discover that she had written them. The Prince Regent's physician became aware that his patient's nurse was the author of *Pride and Prejudice*. One day he informed Jane that the Prince Regent was a great admirer of her novels and that he kept a set in every one of his residences. The physician told Jane that he had informed the prince that Miss Austen was staying in London and the prince had asked the librarian at Carlton House, his London residence, to call on her. The next day the librarian, the Reverend James Stanier Clarke, paid Jane a visit and invited her, at the prince's request, to visit Carlton House to see the library and other apartments. The invitation was accepted and on 13 November Jane went to Carlton House. During her tour of the prince's residence, Mr Clarke said that he had been charged to say that Jane was at liberty to dedicate any forthcoming novel to the Prince Regent.

Jane did not particularly like the Prince Regent because of the way he had treated his wife Caroline. She was not at first inclined to dedicate any novel to him until she was advised, probably by Henry and Cassandra, to regard the invitation as a command. Jane, therefore, asked her publisher to dedicate *Emma* to the prince. She later used this dedication to urge the printers, who were holding up the publication, 'to greater Dispatch and Punctuality'.[41] Before long the printers' boys were hurrying to and from Hans Place with the proof sheets of her novel.

Edward and Fanny arrived in London on 15 November. After a few days Edward escorted Cassandra home to Chawton, leaving Fanny behind to help Jane. As Henry's health improved Jane and Fanny were able to go out shopping together. In the chilly winter evenings Henry's friends and neighbours called to cheer him up, and sometimes, to stay for dinner. One of his evening visitors was Mr Haden, the young apothecary, who had attended him at the start of his illness. Fanny entertained the visitors by playing a harp she had hired from a shop in New Bond Street and Mr Haden, in particular, enjoyed listening to her play. Fanny recorded in her diary that she found him 'agreeable' and Jane suspected that an attraction was developing between them, a suspicion which, probably because of his lowly social status, alarmed Cassandra when she heard about it. Fanny's visit, and any possibility of a romantic attachment with Mr Haden, ended on 8 December when her father collected her. Jane stayed with Henry until he was fully recovered. She returned home on 16 December, her fortieth birthday, to be reunited with Cassandra after a separation of nearly a month.

At the end of the month *Emma* was published in three volumes, priced at one guinea. The novel was dedicated to the Prince Regent, as requested, but the author's identity was not revealed. A handsomely bound copy of the novel was sent to the Prince Regent at Carlton House. According to Caroline Austen the 'little gleam of Court favor [sic]' which shone upon Jane 'was talked of for a while with some interest, and afforded some amusement'.[42]

Jane sent copies of *Emma* to Maria Edgeworth, one of her favourite novelists, and to the Countess of Morley, who had, at one time, been thought to be the author of *Pride and Prejudice*. Lady Morley wrote back thanking Jane and, having started reading the novel, said she expected that the Woodhouse family 'will not amuse & interest me less than the Bennetts, Bertrams, Norriss & all their admirable predecessors – I can give them no higher praise.'[43] Jane was pleased with Lady Morley's praise. In response she wrote that this encouraged her 'to believe that I have not yet – as almost every Writer of Fancy does sooner or later – overwritten myself'.[44]

Maria Edgeworth's response to the gift of a copy of *Emma* is not known.

13

CHAWTON

1816

It was tragic that Jane's life was to be cruelly cut short just when she and Cassandra were finally settled in a permanent home and she was achieving success and fulfilment as a novelist. The peaceful and happy years at Chawton Cottage were destined not to last much longer. The stress and anxiety of nursing her brother through his serious illness had sapped Jane's strength and left her susceptible to illness herself. She had also worked continuously on her novels since moving to Chawton Cottage in 1809, and had exhausted herself mentally. According to Henry 'the symptoms of a decay, deep and incurable, began to shew themselves at the commencement of 1816.' This was completely unexpected, as Henry explained.

> The natural constitution, the regular habits, the quiet and happy occupations of our authoress, seemed to promise a long succession of amusement to the public, and a gradual increase of reputation to herself.[1]

Jane's earliest symptoms were tiredness and weakness, but she was not too concerned, and carried on as normal. Early in January Jane sent a copy of *Emma* to Anna and a letter saying:

> As I wish very much to see **your** Jemima, I am sure you will like to see **my** Emma, & have therefore great pleasure in sending it for your perusal. Keep it as long as you chuse; it has been read by all here.[2]

Jane had been in London nursing Henry when Anna had given birth to her daughter Anna Jemima, who was known as Jemima. She had not been able to see the baby after arriving home due to the severe winter weather. Again Jane was likening the creation of her novels to having a child. The long process of writing a novel from conception to publication day seemed to Jane, who would never be a mother herself, analogous to having a baby.

It was probably around this time that Jane decided to buy back the manuscript of *Susan* from the publisher Richard Crosby. Henry visited Crosby's office and found him willing to sell the copyright back for the sum he had paid for it. When the deal was completed Henry had the great satisfaction of informing Crosby that the work, which he had considered not worth publishing, was by the author of the popular novels *Sense and Sensibility, Pride and Prejudice* and *Mansfield Park*. Having recovered and revised her manuscript, however, Jane did not attempt to get it published. This may have been because she thought that a novel written many years earlier would appear out of date and not be successful. Jane told Fanny:

> Miss Catherine [Susan] is put upon the Shelve for the present, and I do not know that she will ever come out; – but I have a something ready for Publication, which may perhaps appear about a twelvemonth hence. It is short, about the length of Catherine.[3]

The 'something' was her last novel, *Persuasion*.

In addition to Edward's lawsuit, which was still hanging over the family, two more troubling events occurred around the time Jane began to feel unwell, and added to her anxiety. On 21 February Charles Austen's ship, HMS *Phoenix*, was wrecked in a hurricane off the coast of Turkey. Fortunately no lives were lost, but Charles had to face a court martial. It was found that the fault lay with the local pilots who were guiding the vessel, and Charles was absolved of all blame, but it had been a worrying time for his family.[4]

A few weeks later, Henry was declared bankrupt. Due to the economic problems following the Napoleonic Wars his Alton branch failed, which led to the collapse of Austen, Maunde &

Tilson, and Henry's army agency. His bankruptcy also led to the loss of his position as Receiver General of Oxfordshire, which he had held since 1813. Several family members lost money as a result of Henry's misfortune, including Edward and James Leigh-Perrot. Jane lost thirteen pounds, part of the profits of *Mansfield Park,* which was held in an account in Henry's bank.

Although the family were very anxious about Henry, one positive consequence of his bankruptcy was that he left London and spent more time in Chawton. Cassandra and Jane were both pleased to see more of him. For the next few months Henry moved between Chawton, Steventon and Godmersham. With his usual cheerfulness and optimism, Henry soon bounced back. He decided to take holy orders, which had been his original career plan, and began to revise his knowledge of the Greek Testament with this object in mind. There was no bitterness or rift in the family as a result of Henry's bankruptcy, showing the strength and unity of the family.

The largely positive response to the publication of *Emma* helped to distract Jane from family worries. She received twelve presentation copies of the novel to give away. As she had done with *Mansfield Park,* Jane carefully recorded the opinions of *Emma* expressed by family members and friends. Opinions of the novel were divided. Cassandra liked *Emma* better than *Pride and Prejudice*, but not so much as *Mansfield Park*. Her mother held the opposite opinion – she found it more entertaining than *Mansfield Park,* but not so interesting as *Pride and Prejudice.* Mrs Austen also thought that *Emma* contained no characters to equal Lady Catherine de Bourgh and Mr Collins. Frank 'liked it extremely' and 'on account of its peculiar air of nature throughout' preferred it to *Pride and Prejudice* and *Mansfield Park.*[5] Charles, who received his copy of *Emma* while at sea told Jane, 'I am delighted with her, more so I think than even with my favourite *Pride and Prejudice* and have read it three times in the Passage.'[6] Anna's comments were that she 'rank'd *Emma* as a composition with *S.& S.*, – not so Brilliant as *P.& P.* – nor so equal as *M.P.*'. Anna also preferred Emma to all the other heroines.[7]

Emma was reviewed in a number of magazines and periodicals. Among these reviews was one in the *British Lady's Magazine*, which considered the novel to be inferior to *Pride and Prejudice* and *Mansfield Park*.[8] The reviewer in *The Champion* was more positive, praising Jane's 'easy, unaffected and fluent style' of writing and 'the lively sketches of comfortable home scenes'. This reviewer also described Jane as 'a woman of good sense, knowledge of the world, discriminating perception and acute observation'.[9]

Jane was pleased to hear the opinions of other people such as the novelist Susan Ferrier, who described *Emma* as 'excellent' and noted that 'the characters are all so True to life.'[10] An article by Walter Scott on *Emma* and Jane's previous novels appeared in the *Quarterly Review,* a paper founded and owned by her publisher John Murray. This article praised her skill in 'copying from nature as she really exists in the common walks of life, and presenting to the reader, instead of the splendid scenes of an imaginary world, a correct and striking representation of that which is daily taking place around him.'[11]

Scott's article delighted Jane but she was surprised, and disappointed, that he did not make any reference to *Mansfield Park*. When she returned the copy of the *Quarterly Review* sent to her by John Murray she wrote – 'I cannot but be sorry that so clever a Man as the Reviewer of *Emma,* should consider it as unworthy of being noticed.'[12]

The mainly positive reviews of Jane's latest novel gave a boost to her confidence and Cassandra must also have been pleased, knowing how much hard work had gone into its creation. As always, Cassandra was close at hand to share in her sister's success. Jane was more than happy with the praise and appreciation she received for her novels. She was so modest that she never felt that she deserved more recognition or money for her work.

Another rather amusing distraction for Jane at this time was an exchange of letters between her and the Prince Regent's librarian, the Reverend James Stanier Clarke. Mr Clarke, who was also the prince's chaplain, wrote asking Jane

> ... to delineate in some future Work the Habits of Life and Character and enthusiasm of a Clergyman – who should pass his time between the metropolis & the Country – who should be something like Beatties Minstrel

> Silent when glad, affectionate tho' shy
> And now his look was most demurely sad
> & now he laugh'd aloud yet none knew why –
>
> Neither Goldsmith – nor la Fontaine in his *Tableau de Famille* – have in my mind quite delineated an English Clergyman, at least of the present day – Fond of, & entirely engaged in Literature – no man's Enemy but his own. Pray dear Madam, think of these things.[13]

Mr Clarke, who was rather full of his own importance, must have reminded Jane of her own Mr Collins. He clearly wanted her to write a novel with a hero modelled on himself. When Jane responded to this suggestion she thanked Mr Clarke for his 'very high praise' of her other novels and revealed her fears that *Emma* would not live up to her readers' expectations. She also stated that she would not be capable of 'drawing such a Clergyman' as he had outlined. She told him:

> The comic part of the Character I might be equal to, but not the Good, the Enthusiastic, the Literary. Such a Man's Conversation must at times be on subjects of Science & Philosophy of which I know nothing – or at least be occasionally abundant in quotations & allusions which a Woman, who like me, knows only her own Mother-tongue & has read very little in that, would be totally without the power of giving. – A Classical Education, or at any rate, a very extensive acquaintance with English Literature, Ancient & Modern, appears to me quite Indispensable to the person who w[d] do any justice to your Clergyman – And I think I may boast myself to be, with all possible Vanity, the most unlearned, & uninformed Female who ever dared to be an Authoress.[14]

Although Jane was an excessively modest person she could not seriously have considered this to be a fair description of herself.

Despite Jane's rejection of his proposal, Mr Clarke persisted. His next suggestion was that she should write a novel about a clergyman 'after your fancy', and then he suggested 'a Historical romance illustrative of the History of the august House of Cobourg'. Jane turned down these ideas as well and, in her reply, once again assessed her own ability as a novelist.

> You are very, very kind in your hints as to the sort of Composition which might recommend me at present, & I am fully sensible that an Historical Romance, founded on the House of Saxe Cobourg might be much more to the purpose of Profit or Popularity, than such pictures of domestic Life in Country Villages as I deal in – but I could no more write a Romance than an Epic Poem. – I could not sit seriously down to write a serious Romance under any other motive than to save my Life, & if it were indispensable for me to keep it up & never relax into laughing at myself or other people, I am sure I should be hung before I had finished the first Chapter. – No – I must keep to my own style & go on in my own Way; And though I may never succeed again in that, I am convinced that I should totally fail in any other.[15]

There must have been a few giggles behind their bedroom door when Jane and Cassandra read Mr Clarke's letters together, and Jane composed her polite, but firm, replies.

A letter Jane wrote to Caroline in March shows no sign of her gradually worsening health. It was written in response to an 'agreable little Letter' she had received from her niece and suggests that life at Chawton Cottage was as hectic and enjoyable as ever.

> We have had a great deal of fun lately with Post-chaises stopping at the door; three times within a few days, we had a couple of agreable Visitors turn in unexpectedly – your Uncle Henry & Mr Tilson, Mrs Heathcote & Miss Bigg, your Uncle Henry & Mr Seymour. Take notice, that it was the same Uncle Henry each time.[16]

In April Jane wrote another letter to Caroline in which she talked about a book Caroline had been reading, and went on to say:

> Your Grandmama is not **quite** well, she seldom goes through the 24 hours without some pain in her head, but we hope it is lessening, & that a continuance of such weather as may allow her to be out of doors & hard at work every day will gradually remove it.[17]

Frank's daughter Cassy was staying at Chawton Cottage and, in her letter, Jane enclosed a quilt which Cassy had made for Caroline's wax doll.

It is clear from this letter that Cassandra was carrying a heavy burden at this time. With Martha's help she was running the household, looking after her mother and her niece as well as other family members who stayed or visited. Although Jane seemed to be carrying on as usual, Cassandra was aware that she was struggling with her daily routine, and was worried about her. Being strong and capable, Cassandra stoically kept going, hiding her anxiety and keeping her concerns to herself.

On 2 May Edward and Fanny arrived in Hampshire for a three-week stay. Despite the extra work involved for Cassandra, this visit was good for both her and Jane. Edward and Fanny helped to keep Jane's spirits up and Cassandra was always pleased to see her favourite brother. Jane and her niece amused themselves by using the many suggestions and pieces of advice that Jane had received from different people to put together a *Plan of a Novel According to Hints from Various Quarters*. This humorous burlesque included the suggestions from the Prince Regent's librarian. The plan concluded with a list of the contributors whose hints had been used.

It was probably in the late spring of 1816 that Jane's family began to realise that her complaint was serious. She had been putting on a brave face and seemed to be her usual positive and cheerful self. She had been busy with *Persuasion,* writing letters, receiving visitors and callers, visiting Frank and his family in Alton and maintaining an interest in everyone around her. Underneath, however, her illness had taken hold and its effects were becoming more noticeable.

Jane's daily walks became shorter and she began to use the donkey carriage to get about. She also stopped doing the few household chores that were her responsibility. Caroline noticed when she visited that her aunt needed to rest more. In her *Memoir* Caroline wrote:

> In my later visits to Chawton Cottage, I remember Aunt Jane used often to lie down after dinner – My Grandmother herself was frequently on the sofa – sometimes in the afternoon, sometimes in the evening, at no fixed period of the day, – She had not bad health for her age, and she worked often for hours in the garden, and naturally wanted rest afterwards – There was only one sofa in the room – and Aunt Jane laid upon 3 chairs which she arranged for herself – I think she had a pillow, but it never looked comfortable – She called it **her** sofa, and even when the **other** was unoccupied, **she** never took it – It seemed understood that she preferred the chairs –
>
> I wondered and wondered – for the real sofa was frequently vacant, and **still** she laid in this comfortless manner – I often asked her how she **could** like the chairs best – and I suppose I worried her into telling me the reason of her choice – which was, that if she ever used the sofa, Grandmama would be leaving it for her, and would not lie down, as she did now, whenever she felt inclined.[18]

On 22 May Cassandra took Jane to the spa town of Cheltenham, in the hope that taking the waters would improve her condition. They stopped for a day at Steventon Rectory on the way and left Cassy there to be looked after by Mary. Cheltenham, like Bath, was a bustling health resort. It had increased in popularity after a visit by George III and Queen Charlotte in 1788. Jane and Cassandra stayed there for two weeks but, unfortunately, taking the waters did not lead to an improvement in Jane's health. On their way home they stopped briefly at the home of the Fowles at Kintbury, in Berkshire. The Fowles' daughter Mary Jane told Caroline later that Jane 'went over the old places, and recalled old recollections associated with them, in a very particular manner – looked at them, my cousin thought, as if she never expected to see them again.'[19] Fulwar and Eliza Fowle noticed that Jane looked unwell, although no particular malady was mentioned.

On 9 July Jane wrote a cheerful letter to James Edward, who was home from college. 'We are a small party at present,' she wrote, 'only G.Mama, Mary Jane & myself. – Yalden's Coach cleared off the rest yesterday.' Frank and Cassandra had gone to London on some business of Henry's, and Martha had gone with them as she had 'some business of her own to do'.[20] Jane described watching the endless stream of Winchester College boys passing the cottage on their way home at the end of term.

> We saw a countless number of Postchaises full of Boys pass by yesterday morn[g] – full of future Heroes, Legislators, Fools and Villains.[21]

Jane also told James Edward that she and her niece Mary Jane had tried to get to Farringdon in the donkey carriage but had been forced to turn back due to heavy rain – 'but not soon enough to avoid a Pelter all the way home'.[22] This affectionate letter, written in her usual lively and chatty style, does not mention or show any sign of Jane's illness.

Jane continued to write *Persuasion* whenever she felt well enough. Despite her bodily symptoms Jane's mind remained unaffected by her illness, but it is clear that the physical effort of writing was sometimes difficult. Her handwriting was not always steady and she occasionally resorted to using a pencil, because it was easier to write with than a pen. As with Jane's previous novels, Cassandra was fully aware of the progress of the novel and was the first person to get to know her sister's newly created characters. Cassandra recorded that the first draft was completed on 18 July, nearly a year after Jane began work on it.

After completing the first draft of *Persuasion,* Jane became dissatisfied with the ending. She decided that it was 'tame and flat'.[23] This bothered Jane so much that she went to bed one night worrying about it and feeling depressed. Her mood improved overnight, however, and she was her usual cheerful self the next morning. She then cancelled the final chapter and wrote two new chapters in which Anne Elliot and Frederick Wentworth were reunited in a different, and more satisfactory, way. Cassandra noted that the final version of the novel was completed on 6 August 1816. Jane did not decide on a title at this time, although she discussed several options with Cassandra, including 'The Elliots'. *Persuasion* was the title given to the novel when it was published after Jane's death.

James Edward described *Persuasion* as her 'last contribution to the entertainment of the public'.[24] What Jane and her nephew did not know, when she put her pen down at the end of the final draft of this novel, was that she had secured her future place as one of England's best-loved novelists and that she would, eventually, achieve worldwide fame.

Persuasion, like all Jane's novels, is about the gentry class of rural England in the late Georgian and Regency periods from a woman's perspective. All the novels are focused narrowly on the lives of a few families in a country village. With the possible exception of *Mansfield Park,* they are all light-hearted love stories. Each has its own distinctive atmosphere.

Being lost in her imaginary world, as she wrote her final novel, served as a distraction for Jane when she was feeling unwell. Even after a novel was completed the characters were still alive in Jane's imagination. She told Cassandra what happened to her characters after their stories ended, and later told other members of her family. Kitty, in *Pride and Prejudice,* for example, married a clergyman and her sister Mary married one of her uncle's clerks. She also told Cassandra that, in *Emma*, the word swept away unread by Jane Fairfax was 'pardon' and that Mr Woodhouse died two years after the end of the story, enabling Emma and Mr Knightley to move to Donwell.

While Jane was occupied with *Persuasion* she found the time and energy to read and comment on another story written by Caroline. In a letter to her dated 15 July, Jane wrote:

> I have been very much entertained by your story of Carolina & her aged Father, it made me laugh heartily, & I am particularly glad to find you so much alive upon any topic of such absurdity, as the usual description of a Heroine's father. – You have done it full justice – or if anything be wanting, it is the

> information of the venerable old Man's having married when only Twenty one, & being a father at Twenty two.[25]

In September Cassandra went to Cheltenham again, this time with James' wife Mary, who had also been unwell. James Edward stayed at Chawton Cottage to keep Jane company. Cassandra and Mary stayed at lodgings in Cheltenham High Street. Jane wrote two letters to Cassandra while she was away. The first letter was dated 4 September and was in reply to one from Cassandra, which Jane described as 'a treasure, so full of everything'. Jane updated her sister on family news:

> We go on very well here, [James] Edward is a great pleasure to me; – he drove me to Alton [to visit Frank] yesterday; I went principally to carry news of you & Henry, & made a regular visit, staying there while [James] Edward went on to Wyards with an invitation to dinner.[26]

She also told Cassandra that James Edward, like Anna, was writing a novel.

> ... we have all heard what he has written – it is extremely clever; written with great ease & spirit; – if he can carry it on in the same way, it will be a firstrate work, & in a style, I think, to be popular.[27]

Jane's second letter, dated 8–9 September, contains the usual news of family, friends and neighbours, and household matters, but is not as lively as her letters usually were. In her opening sentence she wrote 'I have borne the arrival of your Letter extremely well; anybody might have thought it was giving me Pleasure.' There is a hint of resentment here that Cassandra was having an agreeable time with Mary in Cheltenham when Jane needed her at home. Later in the letter she wrote:

> When you have once left Cheltenham, I shall grudge every half day wasted on the road. If there were but a Coach from Hungerford to Chawton.[28]

In response to Cassandra's enquiry about her new symptom of back pain Jane wrote:

> Thank you, my Back has given me scarcely any pain for many days. – I have an idea that agitation does it as much harm as fatigue, & that I was ill at the time of your going, from the very circumstance of your going.[29]

Despite Jane's assurance that she was not in much pain, and that she had even managed to walk home from Alton, she refers to a visit she was due to receive from Dr White, an Alton surgeon.

In another indication that all was not well, Jane told Cassandra that she had enjoyed James Edward's company very much, '& yet I was not sorry when Friday came. It had been a busy week, & I wanted a few days quiet, & exemption from the Thought & contrivances which any sort of company gives.'[30] Jane would not normally have looked forward to the end of a visit from her beloved nephew.

Jane's letter shows that she was aware of the heavy burden Cassandra was bearing at that time, as she wrote – 'I often wonder how **you** can find time for what you do, in addition to the care of the House.'[31] This was the last letter Jane ever wrote to her sister as, after Cassandra's return from Cheltenham in late September, they were never separated for any length of time again.

Jane wrote another affectionate and amusing letter to James Edward in December, in which she congratulated him on leaving Winchester College, which meant that she could now address him as Esquire. James Edward was about to go up to Exeter College, Oxford. Jane passed on news of Henry and Charles, who were both staying at Chawton Cottage. Henry had been writing what Jane described as 'very superior sermons' in preparation for his new career and she suggested that they should try to get hold of one or two of them '& put them into our Novels; – it would be a fine help to a volume…'[32]

Referring to the loss of some of the pages of her nephew's novel Jane made an interesting comparison between their two different styles. She wrote

> By the bye, my dear [James] Edward, I am quite concerned for the loss your Mother mentions in her Letter; two Chapters & a half to be missing is monstrous! It is well that I have not been at Steventon lately, & therefore cannot be suspected of purloining them; – two strong twigs & a half towards a Nest of my own, would have been something. – I do not think however that any theft of that sort would be really very useful to me. What should I do with your strong, manly, spirited Sketches, full of Variety & Glow? – How could I possibly join them on to the little bit (two Inches wide) of Ivory on which I work with so fine a Brush, as produces little effect after much labour?[33]

There is one reference in this letter to Jane's health – she told James Edward that she had been forced to decline an invitation to visit Wyards to see Anna's second baby Julia. 'The walk is beyond my strength (though I am otherwise very well),' she wrote '& this is not a Season for Donkey Carriages.'[34]

That month Henry was ordained a deacon in Salisbury Cathedral. When he went to be examined by the Bishop of Winchester before being ordained Henry was expecting to show off his knowledge of the Greek Testament. Much to his disappointment, however, the Bishop merely put his hand on a copy and said 'As for this book Mr Austen, I dare say it is some years since either you or I looked into it.'[35] Following ordination Henry was appointed to the curacy of Chawton, under John Rawstorn Papillon, who had been rector since 1801. Cassandra and Jane were very proud of Henry, who became a diligent and earnest preacher.

14

CHAWTON AND WINCHESTER

1817

At the beginning of the new year, Jane's illness appeared to be in remission. In late January she wrote cheerful and hopeful letters to Caroline and to her old friend Alethea Bigg. They show Jane in a positive frame of mind and continuing to enjoy life among her loving family at Chawton Cottage. In her letter to Caroline she wrote:

> I feel myself getting stronger than I was half a year ago, & can so perfectly well walk to Alton, or back again, without the slightest fatigue that I hope to be able to do both when Summer comes.[1]

James Edward was staying at Chawton Cottage at this time and Jane told his sister what an 'unexpected pleasure' it was when he arrived. It was a great help to Cassandra to have her nephew there because he could keep Jane company and take her out.

Jane told Alethea that she had grown stronger over the winter and that she was not far from being well. She went on:

> I think I understand my own case now so much better than I did, as to be able by care to keep off any serious return of illness. I am more & more convinced that **Bile** is at the bottom of all I have suffered, which makes it easy to know how to treat myself.[2]

Jane also wrote a glowing description of James Edward:

> He grows still, & still improves in appearance, at least in the estimation of his Aunts, who love him better & better, as they see the sweet temper & warm affections of the Boy confirmed in the young Man.[3]

Henry was due to preach his first sermon, possibly on the following Sunday, and Jane told her friend that she would be glad when it was over.

> It will be a nervous hour for our Pew, though we hear that he acquits himself with as much ease & collectedness, as if he had been used to it all his Life.[4]

His sisters were immensely proud of Henry, especially considering the misfortunes he had overcome in the last few years.

Jane felt well enough to start a new novel set in a seaside resort named Sanditon, which was also the name later given to this unfinished novel by her family. Cassandra was pleased to see Jane occupied, but she was also aware that it was sometimes a struggle for her to concentrate on writing. Starting a new novel may have been part of an attempt by Jane to put on a brave face so as not to add to the anxiety of her family. She wrote out a plan for the first volume of the three she hoped to write. Anna visited Chawton Cottage early in the year and Jane talked to her about her new novel.

Jane also wrote an *Advertisement,* which would be published as a preface to *Northanger Abbey*. In this preface she explained why the novel, which was finished in 1803, was not published at that time. She went on to point out to the 'public' that due to the lapse of time since the novel was written some parts of the work had become 'comparatively obsolete' and 'places, manners, books and opinions have undergone considerable changes.' She was referring here to the Gothic novel, full of fear and mystery, which was very popular when she wrote her first novel, originally named *Susan,* which parodied that style.

Around this time Fanny sought Jane's advice again about men and marriage. Fanny's letters amused her aunt greatly. In the opening sentences of a letter dated 20–21 February Jane wrote:

> You are inimitable, irresistable. You are the delight of my Life. Such Letters, such entertaining Letters as you have lately sent! – Such a description of your queer little heart! – Such a lovely display of what Imagination does. – You are worth your weight in Gold, or even in the new Silver Coinage. – I cannot express to you what I have felt in reading your history of yourself, how full of Pity & Concern & Admiration & Amusement I have been.[5]

There was a new man in Fanny's life – James Wildman of Chilham Castle, near Godmersham. Fanny was in turmoil because, despite this new admirer, she had been upset to hear that John Plumptre was engaged to be married. Fanny was worried that she had missed her only opportunity of marriage by rejecting him. Jane assured her that she had never really loved John, and reminded Fanny of her reasons for rejecting him. She also reassured her niece that she would find the right man to marry in due course. Jane went on to tell Fanny that she was 'almost entirely cured' of her illness, which she described as 'rheumatism', and added that 'Aunt Cassandra nursed me so beautifully.'[6]

Caroline also wrote to her aunt with news of her old friends and neighbours in Steventon. Jane's replies, written in January and February, contained family news and comments on the stories that Caroline was still sending her to read. 'I look forward to the 4 new Chapters with pleasure,' she wrote. 'But how can you like Frederick better than Edgar? – You have some eccentric Tastes however I know, as to Heroes and Heroines.'[7]

On 13 March Jane replied to another letter from Fanny. As well as the usual family news and enquiries about Fanny's neighbours in Kent, Jane gave her niece further advice on finding the right husband. Her letter contained her well-known comment about the most serious disadvantage of being a single, financially dependent woman in a patriarchal society.

> Single women have a dreadful propensity for being poor – which is one very strong argument in favour of Matrimony.[8]

Jane assured Fanny that by her description her new admirer, Mr Wildman, could not be in love with her. She added the following wise advice:

> Do not be in a hurry; depend upon it, the right Man will come at last; you will in the course of the next two or three years, meet with somebody more generally unexceptionable than anyone you have yet known, who will love you as warmly as ever He did, & who will so completely attach you, that you will feel you never really loved before.[9]

She also pointed out that by waiting to marry Fanny would delay the 'business of mothering', thus retaining her 'Constitution, spirits, figure and countenance.'[10]

Jane seemed to be feeling better and more optimistic about the future, as she wrote:

> I am got tolerably well again, quite equal to walking about & enjoying the Air; & by sitting down & resting a good while between my Walks, I get exercise enough – I have a scheme however for accomplishing more, as the weather grows springlike. I mean to take to riding the Donkey. It will be more independant & less troublesome than the use of the Carriage, & I shall be able to go about with A[t] Cassandra in her Walks to Alton and Wyards.[11]

In her next letter to Fanny, Jane described another bout of illness that she had just suffered.

> Many thanks for your kind care for my health; I certainly have not been well for many weeks, & about a week ago I was very poorly. I have had a good deal of fever at times & indifferent nights, but am considerably better now, & recovering my Looks a little, which have been bad enough, black & white & every wrong colour. I must not depend upon being ever very

> blooming again. Sickness is a dangerous Indulgence at my time of Life.[12]

She told Fanny that she had been out for her first ride on the donkey the previous day, with Cassandra and James Edward at her side. 'Aun^t^ Cass', she added 'is such an excellent Nurse, so assiduous & unwearied!'[13]

Jane gave a similar report to Caroline two days later.

> I have taken one ride on the Donkey & like it very much – & you most try to get me quiet, mild days, that I may be able to go out pretty constantly. – A great deal of Wind does not suit me, as I have still a tendency to Rheumatism – [In] short I am a poor Honey at present. I will be better when you can come & see us.[14]

It is probable that Jane dismissed her illness as rheumatism to her nieces so as not to worry them unduly. The alarming symptoms she described to Fanny, however, suggest that her illness was probably Addison's disease, a chronic adrenal disorder, or some type of lymphoma.

Cassandra was pleased that Fanny, James Edward and Caroline were all in correspondence with Jane. Their letters gave Jane much pleasure and helped to maintain her interest in life and what was happening to those around her. They were also a distraction for Jane when she was feeling unwell, but replying to them could not have been easy for her.

Jane had another relapse at the end of March. This followed news of the death of James Leigh-Perrot on the 28th at his home in Berkshire, at the age of eighty-two. He had been ill for some time, so the news of his death was not unexpected. Mrs Austen had, not unreasonably, expected to benefit from her brother's will, as he had always been good to her and her family. In his will, however, James Leigh-Perrot left everything to his wife for life. A large sum, subject to his wife's life interest, was left to James Austen, and £1,000 to each of Mrs Austen's children who survived Jane Leigh-Perrot. The Austen family did not, therefore, benefit immediately. Mrs Austen and her daughters seem to have been counting on

Mr Leigh-Perrot's will to help them out. Both Henry and Frank were no longer able to give their mother any financial assistance, so an immediate bequest would have been very welcome.

Mrs Austen soon got over her disappointment. Her expectations had been moderate and she concluded that her brother had always expected to outlive her. Jane, however, was extremely upset by this blow, probably because of her fragile state of health. To make matters worse for Jane, Cassandra had to go to Berkshire to comfort her bereaved aunt. The distressing news about the will, and Cassandra's absence, led to Jane's illness flaring up again.

On 6 April Jane wrote to her brother Charles in reply to an affectionate letter from him. Her letter shows how badly affected she was by the contents of her uncle's will. She explained why she had not replied earlier.

> … I have really been too unwell the last fortnight to write anything that was not absolutely necessary. I have been suffering from a Bilious attack, attended with a good deal of fever. – A few days ago my complaint appeared removed, but I am ashamed to say that the shock of my Uncle's Will brought on a relapse…[15]

Jane had been so ill that she had written to Cassandra asking her to come back from Berkshire immediately after their uncle's funeral. She was now feeling better, she told Charles, either because of her sister's return, a visit from the apothecary or her disorder's 'chusing to go away'.

> I live upstairs however for the present & am coddled. I am the only one of the Legatees who has been so silly, but a weak Body must excuse weak Nerves.[16]

This weakness is evident in Jane's handwriting. She finished her letter with the following postscript.

> Tell dear Harriet [Charles' sister-in-law] that whenever she wants me in her service again, she must send a Hackney

> Chariot all the way for me, for I am not strong enough to travel any other way, & I hope Cassy will take care that it is a green one.[17]

Charles wrote on the back of this letter, which was passed on to his granddaughters, that this was the last letter he received from 'dearest Jane'.

After writing this letter Jane seems to have recovered a little, as Cassandra reported a slight improvement to James and Charles. By this time, though, Jane knew that death was approaching because on 27 April she wrote her will, which reads as follows:

> I Jane Austen of the Parish of Chawton do by this my last Will & Testament give and bequeath to my dearest Sister Cassandra Eliz^th every thing of which I may die possessed, or which may be hereafter due to me, subject to the payment of my Funeral Expences, & to a Legacy of £50 to my Brother Henry, & £50 to M^de Bigeon – which I request may be paid as soon as convenient. And I appoint my said dear Sister the Executrix of this my last Will & Testament.
>
> Jane Austen[18]
> April 27th, 1817

The sum of £50 left to Madame Bigeon, Henry's housekeeper, was to compensate her for money she had lost when his bank failed. The will was not witnessed, probably because Jane did not want to distress her family by letting them know that she was putting her affairs in order.

Caroline first realised how seriously ill her aunt was in March, shortly before she saw her for the last time. Plans were made for Caroline to stay at Chawton Cottage while her parents went to Berkshire to help Jane Leigh-Perrot to sort out her late husband's affairs. Jane was too unwell, however, for Caroline to stay there and she went instead to stay with Anna and Ben Lefroy in Alton. Caroline described her last visit to Jane, which took place in late March or early April, in her *Memoir.*

> The next day we [Caroline and Anna] walked over to Chawton to make enquiries after our Aunt – She was

> keeping her room but said she would see us, and we went up to her – She was in her dressing gown and was sitting quite like an invalide in an arm chair – but she got up, and kindly greeted us – and then pointing to seats which had been arranged for us by the fire, she said, 'There's a chair for the married lady, and a little stool for you, Caroline.' – It is strange, but those trifling words are the last of her's that I can remember – for I retain **no** recollection **at** all of what was said by any one in the conversation that of course ensued –
>
> I was struck by the alteration in herself – She was very pale – her voice was weak and low and there was about her, a general appearance of debility and suffering; but I have been told that she never **had** much actual pain –
>
> She was not equal to the exertion of talking to us, and our visit to the sick room was a very short one – Aunt Cassandra soon taking us away – I do not suppose we stayed a quarter of an hour; and I never saw Aunt Jane again.[19]

Jane suffered another serious relapse soon after, which she described to her friend Anne Sharp in a letter dated 22 May.

> Your kind letter my dearest Anne found me in bed, for inspite of my hopes & promises when I wrote to you I have since been very ill indeed. An attack of my sad complaint seized me within a few days afterwards – the most severe I ever had – & coming upon me after weeks of indisposition, it reduced me very low. I have kept my bed since the 13th April, with only removals to a Sopha – **Now**, I am getting well again, & indeed have been gradually tho' slowly recovering my strength for the last three weeks. I can sit up in my bed & employ myself, as I am proving to you at this present moment, & **really** am equal to being out of bed, but that the posture is thought good for me.[20]

Jane also praised her family, especially Cassandra, for their loving support and kindness.

> How to do justice to the kindness of all my family during this illness, is quite beyond me! – Every dear Brother so affectionate & so anxious! – And as for my Sister! – Words must fail me in any attempt to describe what a Nurse she has been to me. Thank God! she does not seem the worse for it yet, & as there was never any Sitting-up necessary, I am willing to hope she has no after-fatigues to suffer from. I have so many alleviations & comforts to bless the Almighty for...I have not mentioned my dear Mother; she suffered much for me when I was at the worst, but is tolerably well. – Miss Lloyd too has been all kindness. In short, If I live to be an old Woman I must expect to wish I had died now, blessed in the tenderness of such a Family, & before I had survived either them or their affection.[21]

By May the Alton apothecary Mr Curtis was no longer able to help Jane and Dr Giles King Lyford, a surgeon at Winchester Hospital, took over her treatment. In his *Memoir* James Edward described Dr Lyford as 'a man of more than provincial reputation, in whom great London practitioners expressed confidence.'[22] Jane's nephew believed that he 'had, from the first, very little expectation of a permanent cure'.[23] During this month Jane's family decided that she should move to Winchester to be near Dr Lyford, because she had reached the stage when she needed constant medical attention. Her family wanted to ensure that Jane had the best care available.

Jane accepted her family's advice and agreed to go to Winchester. On Saturday 24 May Jane said goodbye to her mother and Martha and left Chawton Cottage, her home for the last eight years, for the last time. She set off with Cassandra to travel the 16 miles to Winchester in James' and Mary's carriage. Henry and William Knight travelled with them on horseback. It was a rainy day and Jane was very concerned about her brother and nephew getting wet.

When they arrived in Winchester, Jane and Cassandra were taken to 8, College Street, which was situated behind the cathedral. These lodgings, in a house belonging to a Mrs David, had been found for them by their friends Elizabeth Heathcote and Alethea Bigg, who lived nearby at 12, The Close. Their friends did all they could to make sure Jane and Cassandra were comfortable in their lodgings and to keep them company. Jane was pleased that the bow window of their small sitting room overlooked the garden of Dr Gabell, the headmaster of Winchester College. The morning after their arrival Charles Knight, a student at the college, visited his aunts and had breakfast with them.

Three days after arriving in Winchester Jane wrote a letter to her nephew James Edward. This was a more hopeful letter than she had written for some time.

> I know no better way my dearest [James] Edward, of thanking you for your most affectionate concern for me during my illness, than by telling you myself as soon as possible that I continue to get better. – I will not boast of my handwriting, neither that, nor my face have yet recovered their proper beauty, but in other respects I am gaining strength very fast. I am now out of bed from 9 in the morn^{g} to 10 at night – Upon the Sopha t'is true – but I eat my meals with Aunt Cass: in a rational way, & can employ myself, & walk from one room to another.

Jane jokingly added,

> Mr Lyford says he will cure me, & if he fails I shall draw up a Memorial & lay it before the Dean & Chapter, & have no doubt of redress from that Pious, Learned & disinterested Body.[24]

She concluded her letter with the following heartfelt tribute to the family members and friends who had eased her suffering.

> God bless you my dear Edward. If ever you are ill, may you be as tenderly nursed as I have been, may the same Blessed alleviations of anxious, simpathising friends be Yours, & may you possess – as I dare say you will – the greatest blessing of

> all, in the consciousness of not being unworthy of their Love – I could not feel this.
>
> Your very affect. Aunt [25]

This was the last letter Jane ever wrote to a member of her family, and it is both fitting and poignant that it contains such a tender tribute to her sister. The hopeful tone of Jane's earlier letters written at Chawton has been replaced by a tone of resignation, if not of acceptance. Her Christian faith had brought her to this state; in a phrase Jane used more than once – 'It has been the appointment of God.'

Jane's last letter, written on 28 or 29 May, was to Frances Tilson, the wife of Henry's former business partner James Tilson. There is a note of hope in this brief letter but, sadly, it was a false hope. Once again she pays tribute to Cassandra.

> My attendant is encouraging, and talks of making me quite well. I live chiefly on the sofa, but am allowed to walk from one room to the other. I have been out once in a sedan-chair, and am to repeat it, and be promoted to a wheel-chair as the weather serves. On this subject I will only say further that my dearest sister, my tender, watchful, indefatigable nurse, has not been made ill by her exertions. As to what I owe to her, and to the anxious affection of all my beloved family on this occasion, I can only cry over it, and pray to God to bless them more and more.[26]

James' wife Mary went to Winchester on 6 June to support her sisters-in-law and to help Cassandra with nursing. Soon after Mary's arrival Jane suddenly took a turn for the worse. Dr Lyford thought the end was near and Jane believed that she was dying. She therefore took her leave of those around her and thanked Mary for being there. She added 'You have always been a kind sister to me, Mary,'[27] suggesting that, despite their strained relationship, Jane had come to recognise and appreciate Mary's strengths. This crisis passed, however, and Jane rallied. Charles, who had been ill himself, arrived just as Jane was emerging from this crisis.

Jane recovered enough to raise hopes that she might be granted a respite from death. Mrs Austen reported to Anna that Jane was sleeping better and feeling more comfortable. Mary returned home, but a few days later she was summoned back to Winchester. This was not because Jane was any worse, but because the nurse who was helping Cassandra had difficulty staying awake when she was on night duty. From then on Jane was nursed by Cassandra, Mary and Jane's maid.

In the last weeks of her life Jane was visited by Henry and James, who was unwell himself with a digestive disorder. They administered Holy Communion to Jane while she was still able to participate in it. Frank did not visit Jane, as his wife had recently given birth to their seventh child, and because Mrs Austen needed one of her sons nearby at this difficult time. Charles was unable to visit again as his daughter Harriet was undergoing treatment for a serious medical condition.

According to James Edward his aunt was 'fully aware of her danger, though not appalled by it'.[28] Jane had a lot of good reasons to carry on living, including her happy family life and the pleasure and fulfilment of using her creative talent, as well as the success she had achieved through writing. According to her family, she would gladly have lived longer but, due to her strong Christian faith, she was able to prepare for death and enjoy peace of mind in her last days.

Henry recorded that Jane put up with the 'all the varying pain, irksomeness & tedium' of dying 'with more than resignation – with a truly elastic cheerfulness. She retained her faculties, her memory, her fancy, her temper and her affections, warm, clear and unimpaired to the last.'[29] This made it easier for Cassandra and Mary to nurse her. Cassandra's Christian faith and strength of character also helped her to keep going. In the letters she sent to her mother and Martha, Cassandra tried hard to be positive and hopeful.

Some time in June, James wrote to his son at Oxford telling him that there was no longer any hope that Jane would recover. 'Mr Lyford,' he wrote, 'has candidly told us that her case is desperate' and all they could pray for was 'an easy departure from this to a better world'.[30]

On 15 July, three days before she died, Jane dictated a humorous poem, showing that her mind and her sense of fun remained intact. July 15 was St Swithin's Day and, according to legend, if it rains on that day it will continue to rain for forty days. St Swithin was a ninth-century Bishop of Winchester. A race meeting was always held on this day on a plain outside Winchester and, in her poem, Jane playfully admonished the crowds who gathered there. She imagined the saint cursing them and threatening that future race meetings would always be wet. The final stanzas read –

> These races and revels and dissolute measures
> With which you're debasing a neighbouring Plain
> Let them stand – You shall meet with your curse in your pleasures
> Set off for your course, I'll pursue with **my** rain.
>
> Ye cannot but know my command o'er July
> Henceforward I'll triumph in shewing my powers
> Shift your race as you will, it shall never be dry
> The curse about Venta [the Roman name for Winchester] is July in showers.[31]

The events leading up to Jane's death were described by Cassandra in a letter to Fanny dated Sunday 20 July.

> My dearest Fanny – doubly dear to me now for her dear sake whom we have lost.
>
> She did love you most sincerely, & never shall I forget the proofs of love you gave her during her illness in writing those kind, amusing letters at a time when I know your feelings would have dictated so different a style. Take the only reward I can give you in my assurance that your benevolent purpose *was* answered, you *did* contribute to her enjoyment. Even your last letter afforded pleasure, I merely cut the seal & gave it to her; she opened it & read it herself, afterwards she gave it me to read, & then talked to me a little & not unchearfully of its contents, but there was then a languor about her which prevented her taking the

same interest in any thing, she had been used to do. Since Tuesday evening, when her complaint return'd, there was a visible change, she slept more & much more comfortably; indeed, during the last eight & forty hours she was more asleep than awake. Her looks altered & she fell away, but I perceived no material diminution of strength & tho' I was then hopeless of a recovery I had no suspicion how rapidly my loss was approaching. – I *have* lost a treasure, such a Sister, such a friend as never can have been surpassed, – She was the sun of my life, the gilder of every pleasure, the soother of every sorrow, I had not a thought concealed from her, & it is as if I had lost a part of myself. I loved her only too well, not better than she deserved, but I am conscious that my affection for her made me sometimes unjust to & negligent of others, & I can acknowledge, more than as a general principle, the justice of the hand which has struck this blow. You know me too well to be at all afraid that I should suffer materially from my feelings; I am perfectly conscious of the extent of my irreparable loss, but I am not at all overpowered & very little indisposed, nothing but what a short time, with rest and change of air, will remove. I thank God that I was enabled to attend her to the last, & amongst my many causes of self-reproach I have not to add any wilfull neglect of her comfort. She felt herself to be dying about half an hour before she became tranquil & apparently unconscious. During that half hour was her struggle, poor Soul! she said she could not tell us what she suffered, tho' she complained of little fixed pain. When I asked her if there was anything she wanted, her answer was she wanted nothing but death, & some of her words were: 'God grant me patience, Pray for me, oh, Pray for me!' Her voice was affected but as long as she spoke she was intelligible. I hope I do not break your heart my dearest Fanny by these particulars, I mean to afford you gratification whilst I am relieving my own feelings. I could not write so to anybody else, indeed you are the only person I have written to at all excepting your Grandmama, it was to her not your Uncle Charles I wrote on Friday. – Immediately after dinner on Thursday I went into the Town to do an errand which your dear Aunt was anxious about. I returnd about a quarter before six & found her recovering from faintness and oppression, she got so well as to be able to give me a minute account of her seizure & when the clock struck 6 she was talking quietly to me. I cannot say how soon afterwards she was seized again with the same faintness, which was followed by the sufferings she could not describe; but Mr. Lyford had been sent for, had applied something to give her ease & she was in a state of quiet insensibility by seven o'clock at the latest. From that time till half-past four when she ceased to breathe, she scarcely moved a limb, so that we have every reason to think, with gratitude to the Almighty, that her sufferings were over. A slight motion of the head with every breath remaind till almost the last. I sat close to her with a pillow in my lap to assist in supporting her head, which was almost off the bed, for six hours, – fatigue made me then resign my place to Mrs J. A. for two hours & a half when I took it again & in about one hour more she breathed her last. I was able to close her eyes myself & it was a great gratification to me to render her these last services. There was nothing convulsed or which gave the idea of pain in her look, on the contrary, but for the continual motion of the head, she gave me the idea of a beautiful statue, & even now in her coffin, there is such a sweet serene air over her countenance as is quite pleasant to contemplate. This day my dearest Fanny you have had the melancholy intelligence & I know you suffer severely, but I likewise know that you will apply to the fountain-head for consolation & that our merciful God is never deaf to such prayers as you will offer.

The last sad ceremony is to take place on Thursday morning, her dear remains are to be deposited in the Cathedral – it is a satisfaction to me to think that they are to lie in a Building she admired so much – her precious soul I presume to hope reposes in a far superior Mansion. May mine one day be reunited to it. – Your dear Papa, your Uncles Henry &

Frank & [James] Edwd Austen instead of his Father will attend, I hope they will none of them suffer lastingly from their pious exertions. – The ceremony must be over before ten o'clock, as the Cathedral service begins at that hour, so that we shall be at home early in the day, for there will be nothing to keep us here afterwards. – Your Uncle James came to us yesterday & is gone home to-day – Uncle H. goes to Chawton tomorrow morning, he has given every necessary direction here & I think his company there will do good. He returns to us again on Tuesday evening. I did not think to have written a long letter when I began, but I have found the employment draw me on & I hope I shall have been giving you more pleasure than pain.

Remember me kindly to Mrs J. Bridges (I am so glad she is with you now & give my best love to Lizzy & all the others. I am my dearest Fanny

Most affect^{ly} yrs
Cass. Elizth Austen

I have said nothing about those at Chawton because I am sure you hear from your Papa.[32]

The arrangements for Jane to be buried in Winchester Cathedral were probably made through clerical connections of James and Henry. It was not customary for women to attend funerals in the early nineteenth century, so Cassandra and Mary had to watch the funeral procession, accompanied by three of Jane's brothers and her nephew, from the front window of 8, College Street.

Jane was buried in the north aisle of the cathedral where her burial place is marked by a black marble slab. The inscription on her gravestone reads

In Memory of
JANE AUSTEN
youngest daughter of the late
Revd. GEORGE AUSTEN
formerly Rector of Steventon in this County
she departed this Life on the 18th July 1817

aged 41, after a long illness supported with
the patience and hopes of a Christian.

The benevolence of her heart,
the sweetness of her temper, and
the extraordinary endowments of her mind
obtained the regard of all who knew her, and
the warmest love of her intimate connections.
Their grief is in proportion to their affection,
they know their loss to be irreparable,
but in their deepest affliction they are consoled
by a firm though humble hope that her charity,
devotion, faith and purity, have rendered
her soul acceptable in the sight of her
REDEEMER [33]

Although the inscription refers to the 'extraordinary endowments' of Jane's mind, no mention is made of the fact that she was an author. This was because when the inscription was written Jane's name had not been linked to her published novels.

Cassandra wrote the following letter to Fanny, dated 29 July, after she returned home.

> My dearest Fanny,
>
> I have just read your letter for the third time & thank you most sincerely for every kind expression to myself & still more warmly for your praises of her who I believe was better known to you than to any human being besides myself. Nothing of the sort could have been more gratifying to me than the manner in which you write of her & if the dear Angel is conscious of what passes here & is not above all earthly feelings, she may perhaps receive pleasure in being so mourned. Had *she* been the survivor I can fancy her speaking of *you* in almost the same terms – there are certainly many points of strong resemblance in your characters – in your intimate acquaintance with each other & your mutual strong affection you were counterparts.

Thursday was not so dreadful a day to me as you imagined, there was so much necessary to be done that there was not time for additional misery. Everything was conducted with the greatest tranquillity, & but that I was determined I would see the last & therefore was upon the listen, I should not have known when they left the House. I watched the little mournful procession the length of the Street & when it turned from my sight & I had lost her for ever – even then I was not overpowered, nor so much agitated as I am now in writing of it. – Never was human being more sincerely mourned by those who attended her remains than was this dear creature. May the sorrow with which she is parted from on earth be a prognostic of the joy with which she is hailed in Heaven! – I continue very tolerably well, much better than any one could have supposed possible, because I certainly have had considerable fatigue of body as well as anguish of mind for months back, but I really am well, & I hope I am properly grateful to the Almighty for having been so supported. Your Grandmama too is much better than when I came home. – I did not think your dear Papa appeared unwell & I understand that he seemed much more comfortable after his return from Winchester than he had done before. I need not tell you that he was a great comfort to me – indeed I can never say enough of the kindness I have received from him & from every other friend. – I get out of doors a good deal & am able to employ myself. Of course those employments suit me best which leave me most at leisure to think of her I have lost & I do think of her in every variety of circumstance. In our happy hours of confidential intercourse, in the chearful family party, which she so ornamented, in her sick room, on her death bed & as (I hope) an inhabitant of Heaven. Oh, if I may one day be reunited to her there! – I know the time must come when my mind will be less engrossed by her idea, but I do not like to think of it. If I think of her less as on Earth, God grant that I may never cease to reflect on her as inhabiting Heaven & never cease my humble endeavours (when it shall please God) to join her there.

In looking at a few of the precious papers which are now my property I have found some Memorandums, amongst which she desires that one of her gold chains may be given to her God-daughter Louisa & a lock of her hair be set for you. You can need no assurance my dearest Fanny that every request of your beloved Aunt will be sacred with me. Be so good as to say whether you prefer a brooch or ring. God bless you, my dearest Fanny.

Believe me most affectionat[ly] yours,
Cass Elizth Austen

Miss Knight, Godmersham Park
Canterbury.[34]

The tender emotion in these letters disproves her family's statement that Cassandra had a colder nature than Jane. Cassandra possessed as much emotion and feeling as her sister, but it was deeply hidden. The feelings she had held in check, for the sake of those around her, during the last months of Jane's life came to the surface in these letters. She had stayed strong through the long period in which she nursed and supported Jane, through the hours spent at her deathbed and while she watched her funeral procession recede down College Street. It was only when she sat down to describe Jane's final hours to their niece Fanny that she broke down.

Cassandra also wrote to Jane's friend Anne Sharp, enclosing a lock of Jane's hair, a pair of clasps and a small bodkin belonging to her. She told Anne that she was 'quite well in health', that her mother was 'very tolerably well' and that she was 'much more tranquil than with your ardent feelings you could suppose possible'. In conclusion Cassandra wrote:

What I have lost, no one but myself can know, you are not ignorant of her merits, but who can judge how I estimated them? – God's will be done, I have been able to say so all along, I thank God that I have.[35]

Despite all the people around her Cassandra must have felt very alone.

Anna offered to be with her grandmother in the days after Jane died. Mrs Austen wrote to thank her, but declined the offer:

> I am certainly in a good deal of affliction, but trust God will support me – I was not prepared for the Blow, for tho' it in a manner hung over us I had reason to think it at a distance, & was not quite without hope that she might in part recover ... I had a Letter from Cassandra this morning, she is in great affliction, but bears it like a Christian.[36]

In her *Memoir* of Jane, Caroline reflected on the feelings of the Austen brothers following her death.

> I need scarcely say she was dearly loved by her family – Her Brothers were very proud of her – Her literary fame, at the close of her life, was only just spreading – but they were proud of her talents, which **they** even then estimated highly – proud of her home virtues, of her cheerful spirit – of her pleasant looks – and **each** loved afterwards to **fancy** a resemblance in some daughter of his own, to the dear 'Aunt Jane', whose perfect equal they **yet** never expected to see.[37]

15

CHAWTON

1817–1828

Cassandra and Mary left Winchester the day after Jane's funeral and returned to their homes. Despite her deep and lasting sorrow Cassandra had to stay strong for her mother, who needed her to care for her and to run the household. The rest of Jane's grieving family also needed Cassandra to be strong. Although Jane was never far from her thoughts, Cassandra buried her feelings by getting on with life and thinking of the needs of those around her. She was always aware of her duty to her family, and the needy villagers she and Jane had visited together. These villagers, sadly, no longer included Miss Benn, who had died the previous year.

Cassandra's Christian faith gave her the strength to carry on. She accepted the loss of Jane as being the will of God, and was sustained by the firm belief that she would one day be reunited with her in a better life. The support of Martha, her brothers and many nephews and nieces also helped Cassandra to adjust to life without her sister.

One of the first things Cassandra did after her sister's death was to have a lock of Jane's hair set in pearls and made into a ring, which she wore for the rest of her life. A lock of hair was set in a brooch for Fanny. It is believed that locks were also given to other members of the family. Martha received the topaz cross which Charles had given to Jane many years before. Cassandra also copied out Jane's poem about the Winchester Races, her epitaph and an obituary placed in a Winchester newspaper by Henry to send to Charles.[1]

Shortly after Jane's death, James and his son both wrote poems lamenting their loss. The final stanza of her brother's long eulogy, which was written in James' usual stilted and formal style, included the lines,

But to her family alone
Her real, genuine worth was known.

He concluded by expressing his hopes for Jane's immortality.

When by the Body unconfined
All Sense, Intelligence & Mind
By Seraphs borne through realms of light
(While Angels gladden at the sight)
The Aetherial Spirit wings its way
To regions of Eternal day.[2]

Jane's will was proved on 10 September 1817. As the signing of the will was unwitnessed, Harriet Palmer and her father John Palmer, of Keppel Street in London, swore that the signature was Jane's. After the funeral expenses, legal fees and other costs, Cassandra inherited just over £561 – a considerable portion of the £630 Jane had earned during her lifetime from writing. Among the personal effects, which Cassandra also inherited, were the manuscripts of Jane's unpublished and unfinished novels.

On 15 November Edward and his three eldest children arrived at Chawton Cottage to stay for a few weeks. They immediately noticed the sad atmosphere in the cottage and how different it felt without Jane. The inhabitants and Henry, who was staying there, were no doubt glad of the company of Edward and his children. Cassandra and Henry walked to Alton with them to visit Frank, Mary and their family. Everyone tried to carry on as normal, but life could never be the same without Jane.

Soon after Jane's death Henry, as her literary executor, began to prepare her two unpublished novels for the press. To the first novel Jane wrote, which she had originally named *Susan* and then *Miss Catherine*, he gave the title of *Northanger Abbey*. To her final novel, which Jane had not had time to revise, he gave the title of

Persuasion. These were published together, as a four-volume set, by John Murray at the end of 1817. As with Jane's other works, her name did not appear on the title page, but Henry included a *Biographical Notice of the Author*, in which he identified her as the author of all six of her novels.

This *Notice*, which contained the first information to be published about Jane's life, is more like an epitaph to his lost sister. It is written in a solemn, elegiac style, using flowery language, and portrays her, unrealistically, as a perfect human being. Jane, who once stated that she hated 'pictures of perfection', would not have been happy with this idealised portrait of herself.

Northanger Abbey and *Persuasion* received only two reviews. The more complimentary of these was published in *The Edinburgh Magazine and Literary Miscellany* in May 1818. The reviewer suggested that her novels deserved 'a higher claim to public estimation than perhaps they have yet attained' and predicted that in time 'the delightful writer of the works now before us will be one of the most popular of English novelists.'[3] It would be many years before the prediction of this reviewer became true. Meanwhile, the first edition of Jane's two posthumous novels sold out within the first year, but thereafter sales dropped considerably.

There was relief in the Austen family when, in 1818, Edward finally settled the lawsuit that had threatened the loss of his Hampshire estates and property, including Chawton Great House and Chawton Cottage. The matter was concluded by Edward paying the large sum of £15,000 to the other party. Mrs Austen, Cassandra and Martha no longer had to fear losing their home.

In the two years since Jane died, her brother James' health declined markedly until he was eventually bedridden. At the end of 1819 it became clear that his death was approaching and James died on 13 December, at the age of fifty-four, with his family at his bedside. He was buried in a corner of the churchyard of St Nicholas Church, Steventon, where he had been rector for the past eighteen years. A memorial tablet inscribed with a tribute written by his son was erected in the chancel of the church.

Anna and her husband were now living at Compton, near Guildford in Surrey, where Ben had been appointed to a curacy the previous year. It was now more difficult to visit their family at Chawton Cottage, which was nearly 20 miles away. Anna had given up writing novels; this was partly because she had little spare time as the mother of three young children, but also because writing reminded her too painfully of her great loss. Anna's daughter remembered watching her mother burn the manuscript of *Who is the Heroine?* because of the sad memories associated with it.

In 1820 Henry succeeded his brother as rector of Steventon until his nephew William, for whom the living was intended, was old enough to be ordained. Henry also married again. His new wife was Eleanor Jackson, a niece of the Reverend John Papillon, rector of Chawton. Mary, James Edward and Caroline had to leave Steventon Rectory when Henry took over the living. They moved into rented accommodation in the Newbury area of Berkshire. James Edward was awarded his degree by Oxford University that year and went on to prepare for ordination.

Mrs Austen wrote to Mary soon after she moved from Steventon, in reply to a letter from her. After reporting on her state of health, Mrs Austen gave a brief update on her family.

> I am much better than I have been, & have been out of doors several days, but I have by no means recovered my flesh, my strength or my looks. My two companions are well, & so are the family at the Great House, & a fine large family it is – 28 in number, Mr Knight, his 4 daughters, & two eldest sons & Miss Bridges – the governess, and 19 servants. I do not suppose they will stay late in July, so hope you will not put off coming to Chawton to a later time than you mention.[4]

She told Mary that Edward and Cassandra had recently spent two nights at Steventon Rectory and had met Henry's new wife, 'who seems much pleased with her habitations and environs'. Mary may not have been too pleased to hear about her successor at Steventon Rectory.

That year Charles Austen was appointed to a position in the coastguard service in Cornwall. This involved patrolling a stretch of coastline on horseback looking out for smuggling vessels. In August Charles married Harriet Palmer, the older sister of his first wife Frances. Harriet had cared for Charles' three young daughters since their mother died in 1814. There was some displeasure at Charles' choice of a second wife, whom Mrs Austen had once described as 'not agreeable', although she had conceded that she was 'very good and very useful'.

Anna also disliked Harriet, although she could not explain why.[5] There may have been some misgivings in the family because marriage to a deceased wife's sister, although not illegal, was not approved of by the Church. Charles and Harriet went on to have four children together.

As Jane had predicted, her niece Fanny did find a man she loved enough to marry. He was Sir Edward Knatchbull, 9th baronet of Mersham Hatch, near Ashford in Kent, a widower with six children. Fanny and Edward, who became engaged in 1820, had known each other for several years. Two weeks after their engagement was announced, Edward, who was M.P. for Kent, paid a visit to Chawton to meet Fanny's grandmother and aunt. He liked Cassandra and told Fanny that 'she has quite won my heart.'[6] The couple married in October and Fanny soon began what Jane had termed the 'business of mothering'. It is sad that Jane, who would no doubt have approved of the match, did not live to see her beloved niece happily married. After Fanny's marriage her sister Marianne took over as mistress of Godmersham, and supported her father, who never married again, with his work in the local community. Marianne remained single and, like Cassandra and Jane, became a much-loved maiden aunt.

Two years later Edward's son William, who had accompanied his aunts in the pouring rain to Winchester in 1817, was ordained. He took over the living of Steventon, which Henry had been looking after for him. Henry and Eleanor moved to Surrey, where he became curate of Farnham, a job that he combined with teaching at Farnham Grammar School.

In March 1822 Mrs Austen wrote another letter to her daughter-in-law Mary. This reveals that she was becoming increasingly frail and, presumably, even more dependent on Cassandra and Martha. It also mentions a welcome improvement in her financial circumstances.

> Our little party are much as usual, I grow weaker and more infirm every day, but I am able to walk about the house, or creep about the garden. I never go beyond it – and do a great deal of patch-work. Yes, the lawyers have at last settled that I am to have half of my late Brother [Thomas Leigh]'s property, but we are not yet in possession of the money … this acquisition of wealth comes to me just at the right time.[7]

Although life went on in the same quiet and uneventful way at Chawton Cottage, Jane was still sorely missed. James Edward recorded in his *Memoir* the feelings of his cousin Henry, Frank's son, whenever he went there after Jane's death.

> A nephew of hers used to observe that his visits to Chawton, after the death of his aunt Jane, were always a disappointment to him. From old associations he could not help expecting to be particularly happy in that house; and never till he got there could he realise to himself how all its peculiar charm was gone. It was not only that the chief light in the house was quenched, but that the loss of it had cast a shade over the spirits of the survivors.[8]

Anna also recalled her sense of loss.

> It comes back to me now how strangely I missed her; it had become so much a habit with me to put by things in my mind with a reference to her and to say to myself, 'I shall keep this for Aunt Jane.'[9]

James Edward noticed that Cassandra 'lived much on the memory of her lost sister'.[10] She kept Jane's memory alive by talking about her frequently to her nephews and nieces, who learned from her to admire Jane. She also discussed Jane's novels with them and told them what Jane had imagined happening to her characters after the novels ended. Cassandra kept copies of all the positive reviews and articles praising Jane's novels, and neatly wrote out three prayers written by her, under the heading 'Prayers composed by my ever dear sister Jane.'

In July 1823 the Austen family suffered another bereavement, when Frank's wife Mary died giving birth to their eleventh child, who survived her by only a few months. Frank's eldest daughter Mary-Jane took over the role of running her father's household and caring for her younger siblings – just as her cousin Fanny had done in 1808. Unlike Fanny, however, Mary-Jane could not call on her Aunt Cassandra to help her.

Around this time Anna and Ben Lefroy moved back to Hampshire, when he succeeded his brother as rector of Ashe. Although Mrs Austen and Cassandra were pleased to have them living nearby again, it was not easy for Anna to visit Chawton as she was now the mother of five children. It was also difficult for Cassandra to leave her mother to walk to Ashe.

In 1824 Steventon Rectory was demolished. It must have been painful for Cassandra to see her childhood home pulled down, with all its happy memories of Jane. All that remained was the water-pump, which used to stand outside the kitchen door. No trace was left of the house, the terraced garden or the outbuildings. The only surviving pictures of the childhood home of Cassandra, Jane and their brothers are sketches of its front and rear views by Anna, a talented amateur artist. Anna also wrote down her memories of the interior of the building, before she forgot them. A new rectory was built for William Knight and his wife Caroline on the hill opposite the site of the old one.

James Edward was ordained that year and became curate of a Church in the village of Newtown, near Newbury, in Berkshire. His mother and sister Caroline moved to Newtown to live with him. Around the same time, Henry Austen was appointed perpetual curate of Bentley, near Alton, a position he held until he retired fifteen years later.

Charles Austen returned to sea in 1826, as commander of the frigate *Aurora*, which was based in Jamaica. He was mainly engaged in the suppression of the slave trade. He later became flag captain of the *Winchester*, on the North American and West Indian station. It would be some years before his sister saw him again.

There was a new resident in Chawton Great House that year, when young Edward Knight moved in as caretaker for his father. Edward, a graduate of Oxford University, had recently completed a Grand Tour of Europe. There was soon a new generation of the Knight family living within a short walk of Chawton Cottage.

Mrs Austen was becoming more and more frail, and was in almost constant pain from rheumatism. She endured the pain stoically and cheerfully. James Edward remembered one occasion when he visited his grandmother and she said 'Ah, My dear, you find me just where you left me – on the sofa. I sometimes think that God Almighty must have forgotten me, but I dare say He will come for me in His own good time.'[11]

Mrs Austen died in January 1827, at the age of eighty-seven. She was buried in the churchyard of St Nicholas Church, Chawton. On her mother's death Cassandra assumed the honorary title of Mrs, as was customary for older unmarried women.

On hearing the news of Mrs Austen's death Philadelphia Walter, now Philadelphia Whittaker, wrote a letter of condolence to Cassandra. The following long letter, written by Cassandra in reply, gives an interesting insight into her life at this time and her feelings on the death of her mother.

Feby. 14th [1827]

My Dear Cousin,

I am very much obliged to you for your kind affectionate, feeling letter, which proves you to be unaltered in heart & mind, however old you may be grown in person. I am at present on a visit to my Brother Frank, & had left Chawton before your letter arrived there, which will partly account for your not receiving an earlier reply to it. All that you say on the subject of my recent loss is very just; my grief must be entirely selfish, for my dear Mother's sufferings for a long time back had been such as to make a continuance of existence any thing rather than a blessing & the whole tenor of her past too long life encourages us to hope that she is removed from a state of severe endurance to one of exquisite enjoyment. For the last year and half my Mother had been confined almost entirely to her Bed, which to a person of her active habits must of itself have been a great evil, & in addition to this, not a day passed without her suffering severe & increasing pain, which was latterly so acute & so unremitting, that I assure you my most earnest prayer to the Almighty was that she might be released. My dear Mother was 87 last September, a great age for a person who had been ailing for the greatest part of her life! Her constitution was certainly a wonderful one & so were the powers of her mind likewise, for her faculties remained unimpaired to the last & even her cheerfulness continued till a very late period of her existence.

My brother Henry was our frequent visitor during the last few weeks & Mr Knight had left us only just before Christmas & if my Mother had felt the slightest wish of seeing them, they would any of them have come at the shortest notice & as it was they all came to me as soon as everything was over. All at least who are in England, for my youngest Brother Charles is so unfortunate as to have the command of a frigate in the West Indies. Nothing can exceed the kindness which I have rec'd from each of them in every instance in which they have an opportunity of shewing it, & I am fully aware that I have still a great many blessings to be grateful for. Thanks to my Brother Knight, I shall still be able to occupy the same comfortable cottage at Chawton which has been our home for seventeen years past & where I shall be very glad to receive you and Mr Whitaker should any thing bring you within reasonable distance of me. If it please God to continue to me the same tolerable health that I have hitherto been blessed with, I shall probably for some time to come be less at home than I have been of late years. Several kind friends are so good as to wish me to visit them & you see I have begun already. I have not been in Kent for almost eight years & I look forward with great pleasure to the prospect of going there in the course of the summer, but I am afraid there is little chance of my being in your part of the county. I am very much obliged to you for your kind invitation, which I assure you I should have great pleasure in accepting, should circumstances make it practicable. I am glad to hear that your health is tolerably good & that you are settled in a home which you find comfortable. I am sorry that Mr W. should have been deprived of any of the goods of this world to which he was entitled, but I am fully convinced that beyond a competence suited to our habits, increase of wealth is not increase of happiness. My letter is full of blunders, which require an apology & I am sure you will admit the one I am about to make. I am at present writing in a room in which half a dozen nephews & nieces are repeating their different lessons of Geog., Arith. & c. & tho' I must approve of the manner in which they & their Father employ their mornings I cannot but acknowledge that a school room is not the most favourable field for letter-writing, at least to such a crazy head as mine. The family circles of my bros. are now too large for me to enter into a particular description of them, I can only say in general that they are well & prosperous. My Brother Knight has now two Sons and two Daurs. married, all of whom have children, so the family does not at present seem likely to come to an end.

I am sincerely glad to hear a good account of your numerous connections for whom, tho' most of them are personally unknown to me, I shall ever feel an interest.

With kind regards to Mr. W. believe me my dear Cousin.

Yrs affectly Cass. Elizth. Austen

My address in future will be Mrs C. E. Austen[12]

The following year Cassandra became the sole occupant of Chawton Cottage, apart from one or two servants, when Martha became Frank's second wife, at the age of sixty-three, and moved to Portsmouth. Many years earlier Cassandra and Jane had hoped that their close friend would marry Frank, and now it had finally happened.

Cassandra's life continued to revolve around her family and the villagers she helped. There were several great-nephews and nieces living not far away at Steventon Rectory, who often called on her. That year young Edward Knight inherited Chawton Great House on his marriage to Mary Knatchbull, his sister Fanny's step-daughter. Before long a new generation of Knights was born there.

Among the villagers who knew Cassandra at this period of her life was a farmworker named John White. Many years later, when Jane had become a household name, he dictated the following memories of her to his daughter.

> Miss Cassandra Austen lived at the corner house by the Pond. She took a great interest in young girls, and taught them reading, the catechism and sewing. I remember a nice dog, his name was 'Link', that she had. He always went with her manservant, William Littleworth, to Chawton House for milk, and carried it home in his mouth.[13]

Although Cassandra was now alone at Chawton Cottage, she finally had the freedom to visit her relatives who lived further away, instead of having to wait for them to visit her. She was able to make frequent trips to Portsmouth to stay with Frank and Martha. Cassandra enjoyed talking to them about Jane and reading her novels aloud with them. She was so familiar with the stories that she was able to recite long portions of the texts. On one occasion Cassandra took the manuscripts of the unfinished works *The Watsons* and *Sanditon*. She read them to Frank's daughters and one of them, Catherine, later wrote an ending to *The Watsons*, based on Jane's plan for the novel as revealed to her by Cassandra. *The Younger Sister*, Catherine's story, was published in 1850, after Cassandra's death.

There was another wedding in the family in 1828, when James Edward married Emma Smith, a niece of Mrs William Chute of The Vyne. James Edward and Emma went on to have ten children, all of whom were born while he was curate of Newtown.

It was around this time that Cassandra told Caroline about Jane's seaside romance, at the beginning of the century, with the unnamed man who subsequently died. Cassandra, who did not speak about this to anyone else, was reminded of it by the death of one of James Edward's friends.

16

CHAWTON

1828–1845

A letter written by Cassandra in January 1832 to her cousin Philadelphia Whitaker reveals that she remained in 'tolerably good health' and received frequent visits from family members. She told Philadelphia that she also paid return visits, including a recent five-month stay at Godmersham and two weeks with her nephew William and his family at Steventon Rectory. Of her brothers she reported that Edward now had twenty-two grandchildren, Henry was an 'excellent parish priest', Frank had been promoted to Rear-Admiral, and Charles was 'the fond father' of three daughters and two sons.[1]

Later that year Cassandra went on an expedition to the Wye Valley with Charles, two of his daughters and Frank's daughter Cassy. While on holiday, Cassandra met the Reverend Samuel Blackall, who had been an admirer of Jane's more than thirty years before. Cassandra noted that the once good-looking young man was now 'stout & red-faced'[2] and middle-aged.

Early the next year Cassandra wrote another letter to her cousin, while staying with Charles and his family in their home near Portsmouth. This letter gives an insight into the stoical and philosophical attitude to life, underpinned by her Christian faith, which Cassandra tried to practise, an attitude shared by Philadelphia.

> ...but you & I have lived long enough not to expect perfection in this imperfect world & to be thankful for the blessings

> we are allowed to enjoy, without embittering them with vain wishes for what is unattainable. You have all your life practised this Christian philosophy, & if I have not always imitated, I have always admired you for it.[3]

Cassandra assured Philadelphia that though she lived on her own, she never needed to be more alone than she wanted. 'My possessions in great-nephews and nieces,' she wrote, 'are so extensive that I have done keeping an exact account of them.' When not with her family, Cassandra told her cousin, she enjoyed knitting and needlework, and working in her garden, which she described as 'a constant object of interest.'[4]

In 1833 Jane's six novels were published by the London publisher Richard Bentley, in his series of one-volume 'Standard Novels'. The previous year he had bought the copyright of all Jane's novels, except *Pride and Prejudice*, from Cassandra and Henry for £250. He then bought the copyright of *Pride and Prejudice* from the executors of Thomas Egerton, to whom Jane had sold it. Bentley's edition of the novels included a *Memoir of Miss Austen* by Henry, which was a revised and extended version of his *Biographical Notice* of 1817. Bentley also included an *Editorial Paragraph,* in which he claimed that Jane was 'the founder of a school of novelists', who had broken free from the influence of her contemporary writers and 'with combined boldness and modesty struck into a path of her own, of which she remains to this day, the undisputed mistress.' He described Jane as 'emphatically the novelist of home.'[5]

By this time there were a number of enthusiastic admirers of Jane's novels, both in England and America. Jane's reputation had been helped by another review of her work by Walter Scott, who wrote –

> Read again, and for the third time at least, Miss Austen's very finely written novel of Pride and Prejudice. That young lady had a talent for describing the involvements and feelings and characters of ordinary life which is to me the most wondrous I have ever met with. The Big Bow-wow strain I can do myself

> like any now going; but the exquisite touch, which renders ordinary common place things and characters interesting, from the truth of the description and the sentiment, is denied to me. What a pity such a gifted creature died so early.[6]

While her sister's literary reputation was beginning to grow, life carried on for Cassandra and her family. In 1836 her aunt, Jane Leigh-Perrot, died at the age of ninety-two. Under the terms of her late husband's will, Cassandra and her surviving brothers now inherited £1,000 each. James Edward inherited Scarlets, the Leigh-Perrot's estate in Berkshire, and added the name of Leigh to his own, which was a condition of his inheritance. After coming into his inheritance James Edward was able to pay his mother and sister a generous allowance, which enabled them to rent a comfortable home in Speen, in Berkshire.

The careers of Cassandra's sailor brothers continued to flourish in the 1830s. Frank, who was still based in Portsmouth, became a Knight Commander of the Order of the Bath in 1837, and was promoted to the rank of Vice-Admiral the following year.[7] Charles, meanwhile, was involved in the Anglo-French campaign against Egypt in 1838. He was later made a Companion of the Order of the Bath for his part in the bombardment of St Jean d'Acre in the Mediterranean.[8]

In the late 1830s Anna Lefroy and her daughter Fanny visited Cassandra. Fanny wrote the following brief account of the visit and of Chawton Cottage.

> The small house and pretty garden must have been full of memories of them [Mrs Austen and Jane]. She read the same books [that they had read] and kept in the little dining-room the same old piano on which her dear sister had played, and though gentle and cheerful and fond of her nephews and nieces … I am sure never thought any one of them to be compared in beauty and sweetness and goodness to her beloved Jane.[9]

Fanny also remembered being 'greatly struck and impressed by the way in which she spoke of her sister, there was such an accent of **living** love in her voice.'[10]

Despite increasing age Cassandra enjoyed reasonable health and, right to the end of her life, she continued to travel some distance from home to stay with relatives. Cassandra was reminded of her mortality, however, when in 1843 both Martha and Mary, her sisters-in-law and old friends, died within months of each other.

In May of this year Cassandra wrote her will and, at the same time, looked through her letters. She destroyed all the letters she had written to Jane and, according to her niece Caroline, 'burnt the greater part'[11] of Jane's letters to her. She cut portions out of some of the letters she saved. Cassandra had always been a very private person and there was information in Jane's letters to her that she did not want anyone else to see. Some letters, which were destroyed or censored, had also contained material, such as criticisms of people and unkind or cruel remarks, which Cassandra did not want future generations of her family to read. A few such comments, however, escaped this censorship. The following examples from early letters give an idea of the sort of comments Cassandra removed.

> Mrs Hall of Sherbourn was brought to bed yesterday of a dead child, some weeks before she expected, oweing to a fright – I suppose she happened unawares to look at her husband.[12]
>
> I was as civil to them [the Misses Debary] as their bad breath would allow me.[13]

In censoring Jane's letters Cassandra was not, as has sometimes been suggested, trying to protect her sister's reputation with future readers. At that time Cassandra had no idea that Jane would one day become such an important writer that people would want to read her letters. She simply did not want any family members who read the letters to know that her beloved sister was sometimes critical and unkind.

Having sorted through her letters Cassandra bundled up a few of those left, with other papers, and set them aside to be left to the people who would value them most. The remainder of Jane's letters, manuscripts and personal effects were distributed according to the will and a testamentary letter listing Jane's expressed wishes.

Cassandra was occasionally seen at family events in the early 1840s. One such occasion was a family christening, where James Edward's daughter Mary-Augusta recalled seeing her. She described her as 'a pale dark-eyed old lady, with a high-arched nose and a kind smile, dressed in a long cloak and a large drawn bonnet, both made of black satin.'[14] Edward Knatchbull, Fanny's son, also remembered meeting Cassandra around the same time and described her as a 'very sensible, charming and agreeable person'.[15]

In 1845 Frank was appointed Commander of the *Vindictive* on the North American and West Indian Station. In March Cassandra went to Portsmouth to say goodbye to her brother and the daughters who were going abroad with him. While she was there, Cassandra suffered a sudden stroke. Frank summoned Henry, Charles and Caroline to be with her, as he could not put off his departure. They all hastened to Portsmouth and Caroline later recalled what happened next.

> In March, on the 17th, being much alarmed by bad reports of Aunt Cassandra, I went off to Portsdown Lodge [Frank's home] – where she was lying in the last stage of weakness. She had gone there as well as usual to take leave of her brother and his family – for Sir Francis was on the point of sailing in the *Vindictive*, to take his command on the West India Station. All the inmates had cleared out and were on board the vessel at Portsmouth when I got there. It was impossible for Uncle to delay his departure. He came over to see his sister once – that was all he could do – I found Uncle Henry left in charge. My Uncle Charles joined us ere long. On the morning of Saturday 22nd Aunt Cassandra passed away at 20 minutes before 4. Her illness had begun with some sort of seizure in the head – and she had never rallied much; though her mind was not at all affected even up to the last.[16]

Cassandra died still firmly believing that she would be reunited with her beloved sister and Tom Fowle, the fiancé she had lost so many years before. Her body was returned home and her coffin was placed in the dining room at Chawton Cottage, near Jane's piano. There were many more mourners at Cassandra's funeral than had been at Jane's, nearly twenty-eight years earlier. Cassandra was buried beside her mother in the churchyard of St Nicholas Church in Chawton. James Edward wrote the following letter describing her funeral to his sister Anna, who was unable to attend.

> My dear Anna,
> I have been attending Aunt Cassandra's funeral... I went on Thursday & found in the cottage my Uncles Henry & Charles with Mr Charles Jackson [curate of Bentley], who to my utter astonishment was invited to join in the procession & was come for that purpose, there being no more reason for his presence on the occasion than for that of Bentley Church itself. I dined with this party in the drawing-room, (the coffin being placed in the dining-room) & slept at the Parsonage – Uncle Henry struck me as very agreeable & not very old; Uncle Charles was kind, grave & thoughtful. Next morning the ceremony took place & was all done between the hours of 10 & 11. Charles Knight officiated. The followers were my two Uncles together, then Edw[d] Knight & myself, then William Knight & Mr Charles Jackson; the servants followed; a very few villagers were in attendance. The day was fine, but the wind exceedingly boisterous, blowing the pall almost off the coffin, & quite sweeping away all sound of Charles' voice between the gate & church-door. It also struck me as remarkably emblematic of her age & condition that the wind whisked about us so many withered beech leaves, that the coffin was thickly strewed with them before the service closed. I went up to the great house afterwards for a few minutes & then drove home. My Uncles went up to London the same day, Charles to remain for a few days on executor's business & then to return to Chawton. Henry intending to proceed to Leamington by that night's mail train.
>
> I am very pleased with the contents of my Aunt's will & especially with the part that concerns you. I think she was right in leaving the same sum to her elder brother's family which she bequeathed to the others, & that she has selected the right person in leaving it to you. She has by memorandum left the beautiful miniature of Mr Leigh-Perrot, set in pearls,

to Emma, (James Edward's wife) & a ms. of Aunt Jane's containing two of her favourite stories to me, & some little matters to Caroline.

Caroline stayed with us till this morning, & then moved into her own house.

Ever aff^{tly} yours
J.E. Austen-Leigh[17]

For some unknown reason, Cassandra's favourite brother Edward did not attend her funeral. Not long after Edward converted Chawton Cottage into homes for his estate workers.

Cassandra's will was proved shortly after her death. The bulk of Jane's letters, apart from those marked for specific people, were left to Fanny, in a package labelled 'For Lady Knatchbull'. Charles' eldest daughter Cassy was left twelve letters of particular interest to her, the ring containing a lock of Jane's hair and her sister Fanny received the topaz cross and gold chain, which her father had given to Cassandra in 1801. Frank's daughters are believed to have received some letters. Anna was left the contents of a small drawer in her aunt's bureau, which contained the cancelled chapter of *Persuasion* and the fragment *Sanditon*. The remaining nieces were all left small keepsakes. A gold watch and chain, which had belonged to Jane, were left to Henry. The three volumes of Jane's *Juvenilia* went to Charles, Frank and James Edward, and the manuscript of the unpublished short story *Lady Susan* to Fanny. Caroline received the manuscript of *The Watsons* and Jane's writing desk. Various other items, including Cassandra's watercolour paintings of Jane, were kept by Cassy Austen, who was her aunt's personal effects administrator. Cassandra's money was distributed among the different branches of her family.

Cassandra did not live to witness the growth in her sister's fame. Jane's novels were reprinted several times during the thirty years after Bentley's edition was published. Despite the recognition of her genius by Bentley and a few others, including the author Mary Russell Mitford and the historian Lord Macaulay, her fame increased only gradually. In the words of her nephew:

> Seldom has any literary reputation been of such slow growth as that of Jane Austen... To the multitude her works appeared tame and commonplace, poor in colouring, and sadly deficient in incident and interest. It is true that we were sometimes cheered by hearing that a different verdict had been pronounced by more competent judges; we were told how some great statesmen or distinguished poet held these works in high estimation; we had the satisfaction of believing that they were most admired by the best judges... But though such golden opinions were now and then gathered in, yet the wide field of public taste yielded no adequate return either in praise or profit. Her reward was not to be the quick return of the cornfield, but the slow growth of the tree which is to endure to another generation.[18]

In the early Victorian period Jane's novels were not as popular as the passionate works of Charlotte Brontë or the social novels of Elizabeth Gaskell and Charles Dickens. Her works were regarded by many as superficial and she herself was considered rather prim, cold and prudish. In time, however, Jane's reputation grew. According to her brother Henry the 'merit' of her eventually being recognised as a great writer belonged 'less to reviewers than to general readers'.[19]

17

THE 1860s AND BEYOND

In the 1860s Jane's novels became increasingly popular with the reading public. As her fame and reputation grew her readers wanted to know more about her life and character. People began to flock to her grave in Winchester Cathedral, which led to a puzzled verger enquiring, 'Is there anything particular about that lady? So many people want to know where she was buried.'

With interest in Jane increasing so fast her nephew James Edward, who was now vicar of Bray, in Berkshire, decided that the time was right to record family memories of her. All of Jane's surviving siblings had now died except Frank, who was nearing the end of his very long life, and James Edward thought that it was important that the memories of those still alive should be preserved. In the words of Caroline Austen:

> The generation who knew her is passing away – but those who are succeeding us must feel an interest in the personal character of their Great Aunt, who has made the family name in some small degree, illustrious.[1]

Another reason for James Edward's decision to write a biography of Jane was his fear that, with the increasing interest in her, someone from outside the family with less knowledge of her might attempt to write one. He therefore started to gather material.

In addition to his own memories of Jane and the letters she had written to him, he also had his sisters' recollections.

Anna recorded her memories in a letter written in December 1864. Caroline, although she was only twelve years old when her aunt died, was able to write down some very detailed memories from the last years of Jane's life. Caroline also remembered much that her mother had told her about Jane, and she possessed her mother's pocket books containing her contemporaneous record of events.

Cassy, Charles Austen's eldest daughter, offered her cousin the use of the letters she had inherited from Cassandra and the two watercolour sketches of Jane by her sister. Frank's daughter Catherine was helpful in responding to enquiries. James Edward asked Fanny Knatchbull to contribute her memories to the biography and requested sight of the letters in her possession. Fanny, who held an important position in Victorian society as the wife of a politician, had developed a rather snobbish attitude towards her humble Austen forebears and chose not to be involved. Fanny also claimed that she did not know where she had put her letters.

In the course of his research James Edward visited the site of Steventon Rectory and reported what he found to Anna.

> All traces of former things are even more obliterated than I had expected. Even the terrace has been levelled, & its site is to be distinguished only by the finer turf on that place.[2]

Once he began work on his biography it took James Edward less than six months to complete it. *A Memoir of Jane Austen and Other Family Recollections* was published in December 1869. As well as being a straightforward biography the *Memoir* traced Jane's development as a novelist, the history of the publication of the novels and outlined the growth of her fame and reputation. It contained four illustrations, including a portrait of Jane. This was an improved version of one of the watercolour pictures painted by Cassandra. As this was not thought to be a good likeness of Jane, James Edward had it made prettier by an artist.

The *Memoir* portrayed Jane as a kind, much-loved daughter, sister, aunt and friend as well as a talented writer. It also made many references to Cassandra and the close bond between the Austen sisters. There were a few shortcomings to the *Memoir,* such as the author's tendency to digress, often at great length, and the inaccurate depiction of Jane's life as sheltered and uneventful. It also presented an unrealistic, somewhat idealised picture of Jane. Nevertheless, the *Memoir* was well received by the reading public and the Austen family, and the material it contains has been used by every subsequent biographer of Jane Austen. Even Cassandra, who was anxious that future generations of the family should not find out that Jane sometimes made critical and unkind comments in her letters, could not have objected to it.

James Edward was delighted and surprised to receive letters of praise for his biography from strangers in England and America. According to his daughter:

> Until that period he had not realised to how large a number of readers, and in what a high degree, the Aunt to whom he as a boy and a young man had been so warmly attached, had also become a living, though an unseen, friend.[3]

Among the complimentary letters received by James Edward was one from the Reverend Fulwar William Fowle, to whom a copy of the *Memoir* had been sent. He wrote:

> I have read it with the greatest interest… Your 'dear Aunt Jane' I can testify to as being the attractive animated delightful person her biographer has represented her.[4]

The success of the *Memoir* led to further editions of Jane's novels, including colour-illustrated and collector's editions. It also led to a spate of new articles and reviews of the novels as well as a demand for more information about Jane's life and works. To satisfy this demand a second edition of the *Memoir* was published in 1871, which included additional material, such as the cancelled chapter of *Persuasion* and the unpublished *Lady Susan*.

The profits from the *Memoir* were spent on a brass memorial tablet to Jane, which was placed near her grave in 1872. By this time, no one needed to ask if there was 'anything particular' about the lady buried in the north aisle of Winchester Cathedral. The inscription on the tablet reads:

> JANE AUSTEN known to many by her writings, endeared to her family by the varied charms of her Character and ennobled by her Christian faith and piety, was born at Steventon in the County of Hants Dec xvi mdcclxxv and buried in this Cathedral July xxiv mdcccxvii. 'She openeth her mouth with wisdom and in her tongue is the law of kindness.'
> Provs. Xxii v. xxvi

In 1884 Lord Brabourne, Fanny Knatchbull's son, published a large number of letters that he had inherited from the Austen and Knight family, including those which his late mother had been unable to find when her nephew wanted to use them in his *Memoir.* This two-volume edition of Jane's letters was accompanied by a biographical essay and a commentary on the novels.

The appetite for Jane's works and the interest in her life continued into the twentieth century. In 1900 a memorial window to Jane, paid for by public subscription, was placed above the brass tablet in Winchester Cathedral. It bears an inscription in Latin, which translates as *Remember in the Lord, Jane Austen who died July 18 AD 1817*. To satisfy the continuing interest in Jane, who was now recognised as having made the novel as important a literary form as drama and poetry, two more family biographies were written.

In 1913 William and Richard Arthur Austen-Leigh, Jane's great-nephew and great-great-nephew, published *Jane Austen, Her Life and Letters, A Family Record,* and in 1920 Mary-Augusta Austen-Leigh, her great-niece, published *Personal Aspects of Jane Austen.* These biographies, like her nephew's *Memoir,* make many references to Cassandra and the central role she played in Jane's life.

In 1936 a bronze memorial plaque to Jane was placed in Steventon Church by her great-niece, Emma Austen-Leigh, who added four books to the list of those written about Jane by later generations of her family.[5] In 1947 Chawton Cottage, where the Austen sisters had enjoyed too few happy years before being separated by death, became a museum dedicated to Jane.

Jane's reputation reached cult status in the twentieth century. Her works were translated into numerous languages and achieved a worldwide readership. Her fame and popularity show no sign of abating in the twenty-first century. Jane would have been astonished to know that the novels, which were originally written to amuse and entertain herself and her family, have achieved such recognition.

She would have been the first to acknowledge the vital role played in her achievement by her beloved sister Cassandra, whose love, support and belief in her helped to bring it about.

NOTES

1 Steventon, 1773–1775

1. Tucker, George Holbert, *A History of Jane Austen's Family* (Sutton Publishing, 1998), 68
2. Ibid, 28
3. Ibid, 64
4. Austen-Leigh, J.E. *A Memoir of Jane Austen and Other Family Recollections* (Oxford University Press, 2002) p.13
5. Tucker, 29
6. Ibid, 40
7. Ibid, 37
8. Ibid, 38
9. Le Faye, Deirdre, *Jane Austen's 'Outlandish Cousin'* (The British Library, 2002) 12
10. Tucker, 40
11. Austen-Leigh, J.E., 23
12. Ibid, 26
13. Austen-Leigh, William and Richard Arthur and Le Faye, Deirdre, *Jane Austen, A Family Record* (The British Library, 1989), 16
14. Austen-Leigh, J.E., 39
15. Ibid, 14
16. Hill, Constance, *Jane Austen, Her Homes and Her Friends* (John Lane, The Bodley Head, 1923), 29–30
17. Ibid, 14–15
18. Austen-Leigh, W. and R.A. and Le Faye, 14
19. Hill, 18
20. Austen-Leigh, W. and R.A. and Le Faye, 14

21. Tucker, 41
22. Austen-Leigh, W. and R.A. and Le Faye, 32
23. Austen-Leigh, William and Richard Arthur, *Jane Austen, Her life and Letters, A Family Record* (Memphis; General Books, 2010), 14
24. Austen-Leigh, Richard Arthur, *Austen Papers, 1704–1856* (Spottiswoode and Ballantyne, 1942), 22–4
25. Austen-Leigh, W. and R.A., 15
26. Ibid, 15
27. Tucker, 31
28. Austen-Leigh W. and R.A., and Le Faye, 23
29. Austen-Leigh, W. and R.A., 15
30. Ibid, 15
31. Ibid, 15
32. Ibid, 16
33. Austen-Leigh, W. and R.A. and Le Faye, 25
34. Austen-Leigh, J.E., 157
35. Austen-Leigh, W. and R.A. and Le Faye, 38

2 *Steventon, Oxford, Southampton and Reading, 1776–1786*

1. Austen-Leigh, J.E., 160
2. Ibid, 18
3. Ibid, 160
4. Austen-Leigh, W. and R.A. and Le Faye, 46
5. Ibid, 46
6. Ibid, 52–3
7. Tucker, 99–100
8. Ibid, 100
9. Ibid, 70–1
10. Ibid, 120 and Austen-Leigh, W. and R.A. and Le Faye, 40–1
11. Austen-Leigh, J.E., 36
12. Ibid, 36
13. Ibid, 36
14. Le Faye, *Jane Austen's Letters* (Oxford University Press, 1995), 176
15. Ibid, 176
16. Austen-Leigh, J.E., 36
17. Ibid, 39
18. Ibid, 19
19. Austen-Leigh, W. and R.A. and Le Faye, 43
20. Ibid, 43
21. Austen-Leigh, J.E., 14
22. Tucker, 33

23. Austen-Leigh, W. and R.A. and Le Faye, 44
24. Ibid, 42
25. Le Faye, Deirdre, *'Outlandish Cousin'*, 47
26. Austen-Leigh, W. and R.A. and Le Faye, 34
27. Le Faye, *'Outlandish Cousin'*, 52–3
28. Tucker, 119
29. Austen-Leigh, Mary Augusta, *Personal Aspects of Jane Austen* (Memphis: General Books, 2009), 9
30. Austen-Leigh, W. and R.A. and Le Faye, 46
31. Ibid, 46
32. Ibid, 46
33. Austen-Leigh, J.E., 160
34. Tucker, 151–3 and Austen-Leigh, W. and R.A. and Le Faye, 47–9
35. Tucker, 153
36. Austen-Leigh, W. and R.A. and Le Faye, 48
37. Le Faye, *Letters*, 5
38. Sherwood, Mary Martha and Henry, *The Life and Times of Mrs Sherwood* (Wells Gardner, Dorton and Co., 1910) 86
39. Ibid, 87
40. Ibid, 87
41. Austen-Leigh, W. and R.A. and Le Faye, 53
42. Tucker, 120–1
43. Austen-Leigh, W. and R.A, and Le Faye, 53–4
44. Ibid, 54

3 Steventon, 1787–1789

1. Austen-Leigh, J.E., 137
2. Ibid, 137
3. Ibid, 141
4. Johnson, R.Brimley, *Jane Austen, Her Life, Her Family and Her Critics* (J.M.Dent and Son, 1930), 76
5. Ibid, 76
6. Jenkins, Elizabeth, *Jane Austen* (Cardinal, 1973), 22
7. Austen-Leigh, J.E., 70–1
8. Austen-Leigh, M.A., 32
9. Austen-Leigh, W. and R.A. and Le Faye, 91
10 .Ibid, 47
11. Austen-Leigh, J.E., 139
12. Ibid, 140–1
13. Hill, 30
14. Austen-Leigh, J.E., 42

15. Ibid, 24
16. Austen-Leigh, W. and R.A. and Le Faye, 58
17. Ibid, 58
18. Ibid, 59
19. Ibid, 59
20. Austen-Leigh, M.A., 54
21. Austen-Leigh, W. and R.A. and Le Faye, 41
22. Ibid, 60
23. Ibid, 61
24. Le Faye, *'Outlandish Cousin'*, 88
25. Austen-Leigh, W. and R.A. and Le Faye, 56
26. Ibid, 56
27. Tucker, 166
28. Hubback, J.H. and Edith C., *Jane Austen's Sailor Brothers* (The Bodley Head, 1905), 16–20
29. Austen-Leigh, W. and R.A. and Le Faye, p.64
30. Ibid, 64
31. Austen-Leigh, J.E., 40

4 *Steventon, 1790–1793*

1. Austen-Leigh, W. and R.A. and Le Faye, 67
2. Ibid, 66
3. Knatchbull-Hugessen, Edward Hugessen, Lord Brabourne, *Letters of Jane Austen* (Cambridge University Press, 2009) volume 2, 357–8
4. Austen-Leigh, W. and R.A. and Le Faye, 68
5. Austen-Leigh, W. and R.A., 32
6. Ibid, 32
7. Austen-Leigh, W. and R.A. and Le Faye, 66
8. Austen-Leigh, J.E., 79
9. Austen-Leigh, W. and R.A., 40
10. Austen-Leigh, W. and R.A. and Le Faye, 70–1
11. Le Faye, *Jane Austen's 'Outlandish Cousin'*, 116
12. Ibid, 108
13. Austen-Leigh, W. and R.A., 42
14. Ibid, 43
15. Austen-Leigh, W. and R.A. and Le Faye, 72
16. Austen-Leigh, J.E., 19
17. Austen-Leigh, W. and R.A. and Le Faye, 77
18. Le Faye, *Jane Austen's Letters*, 294
19. Austen-Leigh, W. and R.A. and Le Faye, 77

20. Ibid, 77
21. Ibid, 77
22. Ibid, 78
23. Austen-Leigh, J.E. 17
24. Austen-Leigh, W. and R.A. and Le Faye, 79
25. Austen-Leigh, J.E., 32
26. Ibid, 42–3
27. Ibid, 40
28. Le Faye, *Letters,* 26

5 Steventon, 1794 – 1797

1. Austen-Leigh, W. and R.A., 26–7
2. Austen-Leigh, W. and R.A. and Le Faye, 81
3. Austen-Leigh, J.E., 158
4. Le Faye, *Letters,* 57
5. Ibid, 10
6. Austen-Leigh, W. and R.A. and Le Faye, 79–80
7. Austen-Leigh, W. and R.A., 38
8. Ibid, 38
9. Ibid, 38
10. Austen-Leigh, W. and R.A. and Le Faye, 83
11. Le Faye, *Letters*, 312
12. Austen-Leigh, J.E., 118
13. Austen-Leigh, W. and R.A. and Le Faye, 84
14. Ibid, 84
15. Austen-Leigh, W. and R.A., 40
16. Austen-Leigh, J.E., 141
17. Le Faye, *Letters*, 31
18. *Austen Papers*, 330 and Tucker, 156
19. Austen-Leigh, W. and R.A., 45
20. Amy, Helen, *The Jane Austen Marriage Manual* (Amberley Publishing, 2017), 15
21. Le Faye, *Letters*, 1
22. Ibid, 2
23. Ibid, 3
24. Ibid, 4
25. Austen-Leigh, J.E., 133–4
26. Tucker, 170
27. Ibid, 181
28. Austen-Leigh, W. and R.A. and Le Faye, 90

29. Le Faye, *Letters*, 5
30. Ibid, 12
31. Ibid, 8
32. Ibid, 6
33. Ibid, 7
34. Austen-Leigh, W. and R.A. and Le Faye, 91
35. *Austen Papers*, 228
36. Ibid, 157
37. Austen-Leigh, W. and R.A. and Le Faye, 92–3

6 Steventon, 1797–1799

1. *Austen Papers*, 159
2. Tucker, 157
3. Ibid, 158
4. Austen-Leigh, W. and R.A. and Le Faye, 93
5. Austen-Leigh, W. and R.A., 52
6. Austen-Leigh, J.E., 185
7. Austen-Leigh, W. and R.A. and Le Faye, 95
8. Le Faye, '*Outlandish Cousin*', 151
9. Le Faye, *Letters*, 127
10. Ibid, 28
11. Ibid, 15
12. Ibid, 20
13. Ibid, 16
14. Ibid, 20
15. Ibid, 20
16. Ibid, 21
17. Ibid, 32
18. Tucker, 181
19. Le Faye, *Letters*, 29
20. Austen-Leigh, W. and R.A. and Le Faye, 97
21. Le Faye, *Letters*, 19
22. Ibid, 25–6
23. Ibid, 33
24. Ibid, 35
25. Ibid, 33
26. Ibid, 40–1
27. Ibid, 42–3
28. Ibid, 45
29. Ibid, 47

30. Austen-Leigh, W. and R.A. and Le Faye, 106–10 and Austen-Leigh, W. and R.A., 70–1
31. Le Faye, *Letters*, 54
32. Ibid, 64
33. Ibid, 65
34. Austen-Leigh, W. and R.A., 82

7 Steventon and Bath, 1800–1802

1. Austen-Leigh, J.E., 24
2. Le Faye, *Letters*, 68
3. Ibid, 77
4. Austen-Leigh, W. and R.A. and Le Faye, 115
5. Le Faye, *Letters*, 73
6. Ibid, 71–2
7. Ibid, 79
8. Ibid, 78–9
9. Ibid, 80
10. Ibid, 81
11. Ibid, 82
12. Ibid, 87
13. Ibid, 84–5
14. Ibid, 85–6
15. Ibid, 91
16. Ibid, 91
17. Ibid, 88
18. Austen-Leigh, W. and R.A. and Le Faye, 119
19. Hill, 104–5
20. Austen-Leigh, J.E., 29
21. Ibid, 188
22. Austen-Leigh, W. and R.A. and Le Faye, 120
23. Ibid, 120
24. Le Faye, *Letters*, 267
25. Austen-Leigh, W. and R.A. and Le Faye, 121
26. Austen-Leigh, J.E., 29
27. Austen-Leigh, W. and R.A. and Le Faye, 122

8 Bath, 1803–1806

1. Austen-Leigh, W. and R.A., 91
2. Ibid, 92
3. Austen-Leigh, W. and R.A. and Le Faye, 128

4. Tucker, 182
5. Ibid, 172
6. Ibid, 172
7. Ibid, 172
8. Austen-Leigh, W. and R.A. and Le Faye, 125
9. Austen-Leigh, W. and R.A., 92
10. Austen-Leigh, M.A., 29–30
11. Le Faye, *Letters*, 93
12. Ibid, 94
13. Austen-Leigh, W. and R.A. and Le Faye, 129
14. Ibid, 152
15. Le Faye, *Letters*, 95–6
16. Ibid, 97–8
17. Austen-Leigh, W. and R.A., 95
18. Ibid, 96
19. Austen-Leigh, W. and R.A. and Le Faye, 130
20. Le Faye, *Letters*, 101
21. Ibid, 99
22. Ibid, 105
23. Ibid, 68
24. *Fanny Knight's Diary*, U95/F24/2
25. Le Faye, *Letters*, 110
26. *Fanny Knight's Diary*, U95/F24/2
27. Tucker, 172
28. Ibid, 172–3
29. Ibid, 173–4
30. Austen-Leigh, W. and R.A. and Le Faye, 136
31. Le Faye, *Letters*, 138

9 *Southampton, 1806–1809*

1. *Austen Papers*, 244–7
2. Ibid, 244–7
3. Le Faye, *Letters*, 119
4. Ibid, 119
5. Ibid, 119
6. Ibid, 123
7. Ibid, 119–20
8. Ibid, 114
9. Ibid, 114
10. Ibid 121
11. Austen-Leigh, W. and R.A. and Le Faye, 101

12. Tucker, 174
13. Ibid, 184
14. Ibid, 184
15. Austen-Leigh, W. and R.A. and Le Faye, 144
16. Ibid, 145
17. *Fanny Knight's Diary*, U951/F24/5
18. Austen-Leigh, W. and R.A. and Le Faye, 147
19. Ibid, 246
20. Le Faye, *Letters*, 125
21. Ibid, 127
22. Ibid, 136
23. Austen-Leigh, J.E., 16
24. Austen-Leigh, W. and R.A. and Le Faye, 149
25. Le Faye, *Letters*, 144
26. *Fanny Knight's Diary*, U951/F24/5
27. Le Faye, *Letters*, 146
28. Ibid, 147
29. Ibid, 149
30. Ibid, 150
31. Ibid, 149
32. Ibid, 154
33. Ibid, 158
34. Ibid, 151
35. Ibid, 163
36. Austen-Leigh, W. and R.A. and Le Faye, 151
37. Le Faye, *Letters*, 156
38. Ibid, 157
39. Ibid, 161
40. Ibid, 174–5
41. Ibid, 175

10 Chawton, 1809–1812

1. Austen-Leigh, Caroline, *My Aunt Jane Austen, A Memoir* (Jane Austen Memorial Trust, 1991), 4
2. Ibid, 4
3. Austen-Leigh, W. and R.A. and Le Faye, 161
4. Le Faye, *Letters*, 175–7
5. Ibid, 156
6. Austen, Caroline, 8
7. Ibid, 6
8. Le Faye, *Letters*, 191

9. Austen, Caroline, 5
10. Ibid, 11
11. Austen-Leigh, J.E., 140
12. Austen-Leigh, W. and R.A. and Le Faye, 102
13. Fanny Knight's Diary, U951/F24/5
14. Austen-Leigh, W. and R.A. and Le Faye, 162
15. Le Faye, *Letters*, 179
16. Ibid, 179
17. Ibid, 180
18. Ibid, 179–80
19. Ibid, 180
20. Ibid, 182
21. Ibid, 186
22. Ibid, 183
23. Tucker, 176
24. Le Faye, *Letters*, 182
25. Ibid, 184
26. Ibid, 187–8
27. Ibid, 190
28. Ibid, 191–2
29. Ibid, 194
30. Ibid, 187
31. Ibid, 191
32. Ibid, 192
33. Ibid, 193
34. Ibid, 191
35. Ibid, 192
36. Ibid, 194
37. Austen-Leigh, J.E., 194
38. Tucker, 185
39. Ibid, 186
40. Austen-Leigh, W. and R.A. and Le Faye, 167
41. Ibid, 167–8
42. Ibid, 168
43. Austen-Leigh, W. and R.A., 123

11 Chawton, 1812–1813

1. Austen-Leigh, J.E., 158
2. Austen, Caroline, 5
3. Austen-Leigh, J.E., 70

4. Austen-Leigh, W. and R.A. and Le Faye, 75
5. Austen, Caroline, 5
6. Austen-Leigh, J.E., 19
7. Ibid, 79
8. Ibid, 160
9. Austen, Caroline, 11
10. Austen-Leigh, J.E., 160
11. Ibid, 198
12. Austen, Caroline, 5–6
13. Ibid, 5
14. Austen-Leigh, J.E., 10
15. Ibid, 158
16. Ibid, 159
17. Ibid, 159
18. *Fanny Knight's Diary,* U951/F24/5
19. Austen-Leigh, 140
20. Le Faye, *Letters*, 197
21. Ibid, 196
22. Ibid, 201
23. Ibid, 201
24. Austen-Leigh, J.E., 191
25. Austen-Leigh W. and R.A. and Le Faye, 174–5
26. Ibid, 175
27. Ibid, 175
28. Ibid, 175
29. Le Faye, *Letters*, 205
30. Austen-Leigh, W. and R.A. and Le Faye, 93
31. Ibid, 178
32. Le Faye, *Letters*, 209
33. Ibid, 211
34. Ibid, 212
35. Ibid, 213–4
36. Fanny Knight's Diary, U951/F24/5
37. Austen-Leigh, W. and R.A. and Le Faye, 181
38. Ibid, 180
39. Le Faye, *Letters*, 215–6
40. Ibid, 217
41. Ibid, 231–2
42. Ibid, 217–8
43. Ibid, 218

44. Ibid, 220
45. Ibid, 220
46. Ibid, 221
47. Ibid, 221
48. Ibid, 224
49. Ibid, 223
50. Ibid, 230
51. Ibid, 226
52. Ibid, 253
53. Ibid, 245
54. Ibid, 237
55. Ibid, 239
56. Hill, 202

12 *Chawton, 1814–1815*

1. Le Faye, *Letters*, 255
2. Ibid, 255
3. Ibid, 255
4. Ibid, 255–6
5. Tucker, 177
6. Ibid, 186
7. Austen-Leigh, W. and R.A. and Le Faye, 189
8. Ibid, 189
9. Ibid, 190
10. Le Faye, *Letters*, 263
11. Ibid, 264
12. Ibid, 263
13. Ibid, 267
14. Ibid, 275
15. Ibid, 270
16. Ibid, 273
17. Ibid, 273
18. Austen-Leigh, W. and R.A. and Le Faye, 194
19. Ibid, 195
20. Le Faye, *Letters*, 279
21. Ibid, 280
22. Ibid, 280
23. Ibid, 286
24. Ibid, 285
25. Ibid, 287
26. Ibid, 287

27. Ibid, 287
28. Austen-Leigh, J.E., 140
29. Le Faye, *Letters*, 288
30. Tucker, 187
31. Austen-Leigh, W. and R.A. and Le Faye, 199–200
32. Tucker, 177
33. Ibid, 187
34. Austen-Leigh, W. and R.A. and Le Faye, 201
35. Le Faye, *Letters*, 291
36. Ibid, 292
37. Ibid, 292
38. Ibid, 293–4
39. Ibid, 294
40. Austen-Leigh, J.E., 91
41. Le Faye, *Letters*, 297
42. Austen, Caroline, 13
43. Le Faye, *Letters*, 308
44. Ibid, 309

13 Chawton, 1816

1. Austen-Leigh, J.E., 138
2. Le Faye, *Letters*, 310
3. Ibid, 333
4. Tucker, 187
5. Austen-Leigh, W. and R.A. and Le Faye, 207
6. Ibid, 207
7. Ibid, 208
8. Ibid, 209
9. Ibid, 209
10. Ibid, 208
11. Ibid, 209
12. Le Faye, *Letters*, 313
13. Ibid, 296–7
14. Ibid, 306
15. Ibid, 312
16. Ibid, 311
17. Ibid, 314
18. Austen, Caroline, 13
19. Austen-Leigh, W. and R.A. and Le Faye, 213
20. Le Faye, *Letters*, 316
21. Ibid, 316

22. Ibid, 316
23. Austen-Leigh, J.E., 125
24. Ibid, 125
25. Le Faye, *Letters*, 317
26. Ibid, 318
27. Ibid, 319
28. Ibid, 320
29. Ibid, 320
30. Ibid, 321
31. Ibid, 321
32. Ibid, 323
33. Ibid, 323
34. Ibid, 323
35. Tucker, 146

14 *Chawton and Winchester, 1817*

1. Le Faye, *Letters*, 326
2. Ibid, 326–7
3. Ibid, 327
4. Ibid, 327
5. Ibid, 328
6. Ibid, 329
7. Ibid, 331
8. Ibid, 332
9. Ibid, 332
10. Ibid, 332
11. Ibid, 333
12. Ibid, 335
13. Ibid, 337
14. Ibid, 338
15. Ibid, 338
16. Ibid, 338
17. Ibid, 339
18. Ibid, 339
19. Austen, Caroline, 14–15
20. Le Faye, *Letters*, 340
21. Ibid, 340–1
22. Austen-Leigh, J.E., 128
23. Ibid, 128
24. Le Faye, *Letters*, 342
25. Ibid, 342

26. Ibid, 343
27. Austen-Leigh, W. and R.A., 203
28. Austen-Leigh, J.E., 130
29. Ibid, 147
30. Austen-Leigh, W. and R.A. and Le Faye, 225
31. Honan, Park, *Jane Austen, Her Life* (Fawcett Columbine, 1989), 401
32. Le Faye, *Letters*, 343–6
33. Amy, Helen, 168
34. Le Faye, *Letters*, 346–8
35. Ibid, 346
36. Austen-Leigh, W. and R.A. and Le Faye, 230
37. Austen, Caroline, 17

15 Chawton, 1817–1828

1. Austen-Leigh, W. and R.A. and Le Faye, 232
2. Ibid, 232
3. Ibid, 234–5
4. *Austen Papers*, 266
5. Austen-Leigh, W. and R.A. and Le Faye, 237–8
6. Wilson, Margaret, *Almost Another Sister* (Kent Arts and Libraries, 1990), 41
7. *Austen Papers*, 268
8. Austen-Leigh, J.E., 73
9. Ibid, 159
10. Ibid, 131
11. Ibid, 15
12. *Austen Papers*, 274–6
13. Austen, Caroline, 20

16 Chawton, 1828–1845

1. *Austen Papers*, 284
2. Austen-Leigh, W. and R.A. and Le Faye, 241
3. *Austen Papers*, 287–8
4. Ibid, 287–8
5. Austen-Leigh, J.E., 154
6. Amy, 179
7. Tucker, 178
8. Ibid, 189
9. Hill, 258
10. Austen-Leigh, W. and R.A. and Le Faye, 241
11. Austen, Caroline, 10

12. Le Faye, *Letters*, 17
13. Ibid, 61
14. Austen-Leigh, W. and R.A., 207
15. Brabourne, 29
16. Lane, Maggie, *Jane Austen's Family* (Robert Hale, 1984), 229–30
17. *Austen Papers*, 294
18. Austen-Leigh, J.E., 104–5
19. Ibid, 151

17 The 1860s and Beyond

1. Austen, Caroline, 2
2. Austen-Leigh, J.E., 189
3. Austen-Leigh, M.A., 24
4. Austen-Leigh, J.E., 194
5. These books are –

   Jane Austen and Steventon (Spottiswoode, Ballantyne and Co., 1937)
   Jane Austen and Bath (Spottiswoode, Ballantyne and Co., 1939)
   Jane Austen and Lyme Regis (Spottiswoode, Ballantyne and Co., 1944)
   Jane Austen and Southampton (Spottiswoode, Ballantyne and Co., 1949)

BIBLIOGRAPHY

Unpublished Sources

Knatchbull, Lady (Fanny Knight), *Diaries, 1804 – 72;* Kent County Archives (U951 F24/2 and F24/5)

Published Sources

Amy, Helen, *Jane Austen* (Amberley Publishing, 2013)

Austen, Caroline, *My Aunt Jane Austen, A Memoir* (Jane Austen Memorial Trust, 1991)

Austen-Leigh, J.E., *A Memoir of Jane Austen and Other Family Recollections* (Oxford University Press, 2002)

Austen-Leigh, Mary Augusta, *Personal Aspects of Jane Austen* (Memphis General Books, 2009)

Austen-Leigh, Richard Arthur, *Austen Papers, 1704–1856* (Spottiswoode and Ballantyne, 1942)

Austen-Leigh, William and Richard Arthur, and Le Faye, Deirdre, *Jane Austen, A Family Record* (The British Library, 1989)

Austen-Leigh, William and Richard Arthur, *Jane Austen, Her Life and Letters, A Family Record* (Memphis General Books, 2010)

Hill, Constance, *Jane Austen, Her Homes and Her Friends* (John Lane, The Bodley Head, 1923)

Honan, Park, *Jane Austen, Her Life* (Fawcett Columbine, 1989)

Hubback, J.H. and Edith C., *Jane Austen's Sailor Brothers* (The Bodley Head, 1905)

Jenkins, Elizabeth, *Jane Austen* (Cardinal, 1973)

Johnson, R. Brimley, *Jane Austen, Her Life, Her Family and Her Critics* (J.M.Dent and Son, 1930)

Knatchbull-Hugessen, Edward Hugessen, Lord Brabourne, ed. *Letters of Jane Austen* (Cambridge University Press, 2009)

Lane, Maggie, *Jane Austen's Family* (Robert Hale, 1984)

Le Faye, Deirdre, *Jane Austen's Letters* (Oxford University Press, 1995)

Le Faye, Deirdre, *Jane Austen's Outlandish Cousin* (The British Library, 2002)

Sherwood, Mary Martha and Henry, *The Life and Times of Mrs Sherwood* (Wells Gardner, Dorton and Company, 1910)

Tucker, George Hulbert, *A History of Jane Austen's Family* (Sutton Publishing, 1998)

Wilson, Margaret, *Almost Another Sister* (Kent Arts and Libraries, 1990)

INDEX